Children with Physical Handicaps

A Guide for Parents and Carers

RENEE MYERS

The Crowood Press

First published in 1988 by
The Crowood Press
Ramsbury, Marlborough
Wiltshire SN8 2HE

1600221

© Renee Myers 1988

British Library Cataloguing in Publication Data

Myers, Renee
  Children with physical handicaps: a guide for parents
  and carers.
  1. Physically handicapped children. Care
  I. Title
  362.4

  ISBN 1 85223 074 6

Typeset by Graphic Image, Cosham.
Printed in Great Britain by Billing & Sons Ltd, Worcester.

Contents

I dedicate this book to some very special children. In particular, to Joanne, Charles and Neil.

Acknowledgements

It is customary for an author to thank all the people who helped in the writing of a book, but I must first thank all those parents who shared their experiences with me, who cared so much for their children and from whom I learned about special needs.

There are many professionals, doctors, therapists, nurses, social workers and counsellors whom I have had the good fortune to count as colleagues, and to work with for many years. I take this opportunity to express my deep appreciation to them. Also to Tony, who encouraged me to write as I speak.

There are two people in particular whom I have always found to be unstinting with their time in helping handicapped children. They are Alison Blakey of the Wolfson Centre and Eric Booth of the Development Trust for the Young Disabled.

My thanks to the pupils of Northfield School for their interest in handicapped children and the many letters they wrote to me on the subject. I know that they are growing up with the right attitudes.

I owe my affectionate gratitude to Lorraine Langan, who painstakingly typed and retyped many drafts with unfailing patience and skill, giving up her weekends so generously, with never a grumble.

Last, but certainly not least, I thank my husband and our family for permitting endless discussion, for their constructive criticism and generally for being there.

(The references to families and children are based on an amalgam of personalities and I have not necessarily referred to particular characters.)

Foreword

'I am Afraid your Child is Handicapped . . .'

Words like these herald a situation which affects all members of the family for years. Parents want to know what these conditions are which affect their child so seriously. Why did it happen to them, and what can they do about it?

Professional discussions and advice may not be sufficient to meet all their needs, and an opportunity to consult a suitable book quietly in the comfort of their own home can be very helpful and is often much appreciated. This book has been written for just that purpose. It is written for parents by a concerned and astute person who has many years' experience of working with professionals to improve the care and treatment of handicapped children. By combining clear realism with care and compassion Renée Myers illustrates the value of the expression that through our understanding of the problems comes true sympathy and effective help.

She has written for parents and many will greatly appreciate her efforts. I feel I can commend this book to all readers – to parents of handicapped children who will find much to help them in many ways – and to others, both lay and professional who will come to understand the problems and needs of individuals less fortunate than themselves.

Kenneth S. Holt, M.D., F.R.C.P., D.C.H.
Professor of Developmental Paediatrics

Prologue

London, 1973: Victoria Station

Sunlight filtered through dusty glass. The warm rays fell upon our little group as we stood on the platform. Newspaper reporters had been and gone, and the Paris train awaited its passengers.

No one could have been more excited than Paul. This European trip had taken many weeks of planning and even now Paul's family had considerable reservations about the wisdom of such a journey. Hitch-hiking around Europe held more fears for them than it did for the young man.

We rechecked his luggage. Passport, tickets and money were in the roomy pockets of his hooded jacket. He had newspapers and books, and had provided himself with sandwiches and a flask of coffee.

The guard blew his whistle. Paul's mother asked once more, 'Is there anything else you need?'

He replied with a grin, 'All I need mum, is my wheelchair!'

INTRODUCTION

1 Living a Full Life

The Challenge of Handicap

The advent of a handicapped child presents families with problems and with challenges. Throughout the child's life the challenges continue. The desire to have a life of interest and quality, to be part of the community and to fulfil yearnings all present problems just as they do for able-bodied people.

Meeting Families in Need

This book introduces readers to some physically disabled children and how they and their families have faced these challenges. My studies and experience over the past thirty years have been with a wide range of disabilities. The families involved have needed advice and help and I, in turn, learned much from them. One felt humility in the face of their courage, wonder at the strength of their determination, moved to tears at their pain and to laughter at their comic experiences. They preserved a sense of humour, rarely grumbled, and faced reality, getting on with what they had to do. We met in schools, hospitals, clinics, and at equipment exhibitions. I called on families at their home – sometimes they called on me.

Some Useful Experience

As a member of the National Hospital Nursing Reserve I worked in children's wards. My training with Citizens Advice Bureaux prepared me to deal with a wide variety of family problems. Working on the Handicapped Children's Equipment Research Unit one became familiar with items designed, or specially adapted, to make life easier or more fun for children with special needs. Serving on the Social Security Appeal Tribunal I know of the hardships poor families suffer, particularly where there is a handicapped child. This background enables me to advise in a practical way those families who do not have the know-how to get what they need and are entitled to.

What Does 'Special Needs' Mean?

These days being handicapped no longer means being isolated as it once did. Most people have no idea how chilling that is or what it means to have a severe disability. The term implies inability, that one is unable to do things in the usual way. Often an alternative way has to be found of doing a particular job. The terms 'disablement' and 'handicap' are relative to the constraints they impose. The provision of certain items may remove the handicap, as with hearing equipment for the deaf, computers for communication, typewriters when handwriting is not possible and wheelchairs for those whose ability to walk is impaired.

Life in a wheelchair must certainly be different. But it need not be any less rewarding or fulfilling. There are many examples of people who have sustained serious disability and go on to achieve success in their careers far exceeding all previous ambition.

What Causes Handicap?

Handicaps may be caused by a number of circumstances. For example, through viral infections or damage before, during or after birth, or accidents. Quite unknowingly a parent may be the carrier of a gene likely to cause a problem. For instance, it is estimated that one in twenty-three white people carry the gene responsible for cystic fibrosis. The chance that two people who carry that gene will meet and produce a handicapped child is not all that remote.

What causes alterations in genes is a matter of deep interest and ongoing research. When a serious disability in children is the outcome then the wisdom of genetic counselling for that family becomes apparent.

Families must be able to understand clearly the chances of recurrence of the disability. They need to be aware of the risks that exist of reproducing the defect, and it may be considered necessary to inform the extended family as well. Genetic defects may be present in other members without having caused any harm. Confirmation of the presence elsewhere of defective genes assists doctors to identify the problem and could be helpful in preventing the birth of additional affected children in the family.

Problems for Baby

Giving birth can be a difficult process for the mother. Being born can be just as difficult for the child. Problems are comparatively rare – some ten per cent of babies having unusual symptoms at birth. Apart from the genetic factor, trouble may be caused by the position of the child in the womb, the absence of certain proteins or vitamins, a lack or over-provision of oxygen – any of these may produce damage of a temporary or permanent nature.

Viral Infection

Viral infections such as rubella can severely malform a child before birth. Meningitis is capable of causing damage during childhood and any infections should be watched for unusual symptoms.

Handicap Through Accident

Accidents of all kinds account for quite a proportion of

disabilities. Very young children must be watched carefully or they get into mischief that could injure them. Toddlers fall out of windows, play with fire and pull saucepans of steaming liquid over themselves. Given the chance, youngsters experiment with sharp knives and swallow poisonous substances.

Hospital casualty departments are all too familiar with the consequences of these mishaps. For some there will be brief periods in hospital before they are restored to their former good health. For others permanent damage may ensue and life changes for everyone in the family.

Traffic Accidents

Children starting school are at risk from traffic and do *not* appreciate potential dangers. Older children need ongoing training so that they are aware of their vulnerability on busy or deceptively quiet roads.

The Risks of Sport

No one would wish to deny children the many benefits to be gained from sport. Yet there are dangers through carelessness and high spirits. The result can be physical or mental handicap for someone.

Water holds fascination for children and they should be taught to swim at an early age and to regard the element of water, both indoor and outdoor, with due respect. Despite regular warnings, accidents occur each year and casualty figures remain disturbingly high.

Parents Bear the Brunt

Whether a child is born with damage or suffers it accidentally, the family faces a new and unexpected burden. The duty of achieving the maximum potential in life for

16

such children falls mainly upon the parents. It is they who face a daily challenge to satisfy routine demands as well as to accomplish progress, but they should *not* bear the burden alone. Legislation by a caring government must ensure that this duty is shared fairly.

Parents do Know

The value of parents' intuitive feelings about their children has not always been recognised. Instinctive suspicions are often found to be justified, although the idea that parents may know best is not an easy one for many medical professionals to accept. Today, more than ever before, parents are drawn into consultation about their children. Views and opinions are sought and taken into account when training and treatment are considered. Their observations are regarded with respect.

Parents Learn New Skills

Family participation is of inestimable value. Who but the parents sees the children day in, day out, through the years? They willingly undertake training and education so that they can give effective remedial treatment. They perform additional tasks in already busy days with enthusiasm, determination and love. Their constant hope is that their child should progress to maximum independence achieving a fulfilling role in life. The realisation of that hope is ample reward.

Back in the Community

There is much talk today about the return of the handicapped from residential homes and hospitals to the community. The care of the majority of physically handicapped children has traditionally been in the community, usually within their own families. When parents can undertake this task, stress is reduced for all concerned, despite the burden of work. But if the disabled are to be properly integrated into the community, whether with their families or in small family-type units, sufficient support services and respite care must be made available.

The Cost of Special Needs

The cost, in every sense of the word, is great. It is recognised that additional financial expenditure is necessary when there are special problems. Whether this is for equipment, clothing, bedding or the many other requirements, the outlay is considerable.

Emotionally, the effect upon brothers, sisters and the extended family has to be considered. Ideally the family devotes love and care to the physically handicapped child. Frailties and special needs arouse compassion, but they may also arouse resentment and anger. Often, the child's feelings of love and gratitude may intermingle with periods of rebellious behaviour. Ordinary families have their share of moods, and it is normal that they should. Equally, the family with problems of disability should recognise, without guilt, that bad feelings may develop under special conditions. Bringing up children is both wearing and rewarding. When there are extraordinary problems, deeper despair and greater elation may be experienced. Compassionate counselling is vital to steer families through difficult periods.

Change Over the Years

The last two decades have brought about many improvements. Facilities, equipment and expertise are better and made available to make the carer's job an easier one.

The provision of respite care is a welcome relief to parents. There are families who have given unremitting attention to a child for years without a single day's break, but now holidays can be provided which cater for such children while parents take much-needed time off.

Residential homes and hospitals reserve space so that when emergency situations like illness or accidents occur, children are adequately cared for. Long-term stay in home-like conditions is desirable and this provision is available but regrettably in short supply.

Counselling Helps

It used to be rare for families to receive any kind of counselling. No one was there to make parents aware of the details and facts concerning the disability with which they were faced. There was no comforting reassurance from those with knowledge of dealing with others in similar situations.

Nowadays, general counselling is given by personnel who are trained to listen and to provide sympathetic support. Personal problems may then be resolved before they reach major proportions, often avoiding family breakups.

General medical practitioners are rarely experienced in disability, nor has counselling been part of their curriculum. They may never encounter certain handicapping conditions among their patients.

Hospital consultants are by definition expert in their own field. But individual disabilities are only part of the story. There is a host of problems to be considered when advice is offered. The medical adviser who takes into account the person as a whole and not just the specific problem is a rare bird. It has to be recognised that counselling requires special skills.

Disability Groups

Families already experienced in handicap can provide valuable advice and today groups exist which are concerned with a specific defect, and their knowledge and experience are accessible to everyone who needs them.

19

Such associations bolster and supplement professional expertise and provide information in a more relaxed and informal way. This can help prevent strain in relationships. Dealing with disability and its accompanying problems without awareness of all the implications makes it a constant uphill and often frightening climb.

The Value of Positive Thinking

The presence of a disabled child in the family generates a strength of mind and purpose that may never otherwise surface. Long-term consequences include a variety of problems, and much patience and understanding are needed. But with positive attitudes the challenge of the special child can be met and the result is deeply rewarding and a source of enrichment to the family.

Changing Attitudes

Attitudes have certainly altered in thirty years. Each decade has brought noticeable change, and children who are unlike others are not hidden away as they once were. Such behaviour would be unthinkable, even shocking now.

We have to recognise and appreciate how valuable every person can be; to accept that each of us is entitled to a dignified manner of living and a place in society.

Outdoor Mobility

Outings in the fresh air should be encouraged and able-bodied sisters and brothers can be very supportive in assisting the member of the family with special needs to get around.

It is helpful if independent mobility can be provided by means of an outdoor electric wheelchair. Unfortunately, only indoor and not outdoor electric chairs are provided by the DHSS for children, and families must often have recourse to charities in order to obtain a suitable outdoor electric chair. These are expensive but fund raising can usually take care of needs.

Ways of raising funds are discussed under the voluntary services and charities sector later in this book. The joy of the child who regains his independence by zooming off in an electric wheelchair is wonderful to see.

Obstacles to Daily Living

Leisure time and holidays need careful planning. Pavements, gates and doors provide barriers for the wheelchair-bound child, and buses and trains are no longer suitable transport. Chairs don't easily go on beaches or even across uneven terrain in parks and commons unless they are specifically designed to do so.

Cinemas and theatres, if they admit wheelchairs at all, must limit the numbers because they could block gangways and increase risk during fire. Restaurants must be advised in advance when disabled visitors are coming so that provision of space for the chair can be made. Forethought is necessary prior to *all* outings.

A friendly taxi driver who is accustomed to the problems that go with transporting wheelchairs and disabled children, can make all the difference to a family who do not have transport of their own.

The public is becoming more aware of the need to treat children and adults with special needs as equal citizens with the same rights as anyone else to access and enjoyment of all public amenities. Things are improving all the time, although *not* quickly enough.

A Sensitive and Practical Approach to Problems

The sensitivity of the young needs sympathetic handling and everyone in the family, friends at school and in the community should be aware of the emotional suffering for a child who recognises personal declining ability.

Teenage problems are part of growing up, whether one is handicapped or not. Talking things over is comforting and expert counselling can often help to avoid problems which could otherwise assume undue proportions.

Improving Standards

The improvement in health and the good functioning which comes from care and rehabilitative treatment are the norm today instead of the exception. Good standards of health and happiness are now within reach for many physically handicapped children – undreamed of years ago.

Try a Wheelchair

There is room for further improvement. Those of us who are able-bodied should try going out in a wheelchair for an afternoon. It would be a real eye-opener! Imagine if people thought that since you don't walk you don't talk. Or think. Or hear.

One woman who took her eighteen-year-old wheelchair-bound son shopping always left him at the counter to make his own purchases, otherwise the assistant would not address him or even look at him. But only his ability to walk was impaired.

Early Assessment Vital

Today's early assessment programmes mean that many childhood defects are dealt with promptly and full-blown disabilities that might have resulted are avoided. If the unavoidable disabilities are recognised earlier and receive prompt remedial treatment it means lesser handicap.

Equal Opportunity

Every human being is entitled to achieve the maximum potential of health, happiness and ambition. Whatever dreams we may dream, contentment comes with facing reality and making the best of what we have. We all function differently – some just adequately, others most ably. Our differences in ability are only judged when people know us.

The physically handicapped must *not* be discriminated against. They should have the same opportunities to prove themselves that others have. Their qualities and their values will not then be in question.

Preventing Handicap

The prevention of handicap in the future is the aim and desire of everyone, but despite all precautions there will be children who are born with defects and children who will be damaged through illness and accidents.

For these children and their families a high quality of life is possible and there are many successful and happy individuals to testify to it. If the attitude within the family is a positive one of acceptance and encouragement then the child has a good chance of doing well.

2　Family Genes

Life Begins

The life of a baby begins following conception when the ovum from the mother and the spermatozoa from the father join to make a new unit. This unit contains all the genes which determine the sex, personality, intelligence and appearance of the child which will be produced by the end of the pregnancy.

Chromosomes

Every baby's unique make-up is set in the form of twenty-three pairs of chromosomes which are contained within each of our cells. This huge complex of biological elements is too small to be seen other than under very powerful microscopes.

One half of each of these twenty-three pairs comes from the mother and the other half from the father. Each pair determines different characteristics. For example, one of the pairs is responsible for the sex of the baby. Some disorders are known to be sex-linked which means that the sex-identifying chromosome link is defective.

Genes

When we speak of individual chromosomes and their genetic content we are talking of infinitesimally small threadlike structures. Genes are the important units of heredity which make the proteins needed by our bodies. It over-simplifies matters to say that they contain the instructions or blueprints for a human being. But in effect, this is true – genes dictate every detail of our make-up.

Recessive Genes

Recessive means held back and such genes may be in the background of our systems but carried forward for generations, inactive until they meet with a corresponding gene in another person. Two people, each carrying the same kind of recessive gene, may together produce a child with whatever characteristic that gene dictates.

It may be responsible for blue eyes appearing in the new member of a brown-eyed family but recognisable in a grandparent, cousin or aunt. Some character traits may not be visible, like a love of music, a talent for painting, high intelligence or a tendency to be impatient.

Dominant Genes

These are in a sense the more powerful genes and are responsible for characteristics directly inherited from a parent. Brown eyes are said to be dominant over other colours so that a pair of genes comprising one brown and one blue eye will produce a brown-eyed baby.

When we say, 'She is the spitting image of her father,' we are recognising that a girl has inherited dominant genes directly from the father. Whereas the comment that a boy takes after his maternal grandfather is to say that he has inherited a recessive gene carried by his mother which she inherited from her father.

Twins

When a fertilised cell splits into two and each half goes on to produce a baby, those children will be identical. If the controlling genes contain an abnormal element each child will be equally affected.

If the mother has produced two ova, each of which unites with different spermatozoa then two unalike children grow. And if in one there were abnormal genes then one child becomes affected whilst the other does not.

A Set Pattern

The genetic pattern is thus already set when the unit of life starts to grow. During the next weeks the cell divides into four and again into eight – each portion identical. But we are made up of so many different parts. So how do these identical cells divide and follow the blueprints to become the billions of types needed to make a single human being?

It is a vast jigsaw puzzle. Each scientific genetic discovery provides insight into the process of growth and development. What we do know is that the creation of different cells, which will become the various organs and systems, takes place during the first three months. At the end of that period all is ready for development and growth.

Genetic background is something which we cannot as yet consciously influence in people. When it does become possible it may prove to be a mixed blessing. The possibility of re-patterning genes so that disabling factors in a fertilised ova can be eliminated or corrected is a wonderful notion. But what other powers will such knowledge unleash?

Malformed Genes

It is only imperfectly understood why and how the pattern changes to produce handicap. Why does a chemical fail to be produced so that there is destruction of muscle instead of the building and growth necessary to healthy development? Why is a child born unable to achieve growth? Or in whom there are fluids different from the norm, which retard lung function?

Researchers attempt to trace the source of these and other problems and discover why they happen. Then – it is hoped – cures will be found, not only for children as yet unborn but also for those presently suffering from genetic disorders.

Preventing Genetic Disability

Any disorder of a genetic nature is regarded as potentially

preventable in the future. Until the reasons for disability are identified and cures found, only one way remains to prevent genetically-caused handicap. This is by pre-natal diagnosis, perhaps amniocentesis, and then termination of pregnancy.

Tests for some parents will reveal that either or both of them carry defective genes of a known variety and the decision will have to be made as to whether they should risk bearing handicapped children.

Many natural abortions happen in the early weeks of pregnancy and it is known that a high proportion of these occur where there is an imperfect foetus.

Amniocentesis

This is a test of the cells of the foetus which have been discarded into the surrounding amniotic fluid. A sample of this fluid is withdrawn and tests are made to determine whether there is reasonably conclusive evidence that the child is going to be abnormal. A number of disabilities are now detectable.

Genetic Counselling

It is of paramount importance that anyone suffering from an inherited disability, or from a family where a member has been born with a disability, should be given specialist counselling.

Genetic advisory centres have been set up by the government around the country and anyone in need can request advice or be referred by their GP or consultant.

It is vital too for professional advisers to ensure that information given to families, either to the parents or related carriers, is understood. People must realise that prevention is in their hands. A positive result following genetic testing makes worrying, even heart-breaking news. But at least people then know what they may be in for. And follow-up research has revealed that numbers of births of severely handicapped children have been prevented.

There are increasing numbers of requests for tests during pregnancy where there is already a handicapped child in the family, so that repetition of the defect can be avoided. Most parents agree to terminate, but there are some who elect to have their babies even when they are told results are positive and that their children will be handicapped. It is a difficult decision to have to make.

Are Defects Avoidable?

It is not so long ago that inherited defects were regarded as acts of God or even as retribution for the misdemeanours of the parents or their ancestors. 'Bad blood' was the comment and what misery that must have caused.

It is still not sufficiently understood what causes inherited and congenital defects, but it is thought that some of them may be avoidable – and in a very simple way. If we pay closer attention to keeping healthy, some genetic abnormalities will not occur.

Healthier Living, Healthier Offspring

In 1967, a quote from the Office of Health Economics said, 'One of the most remarkable things about nutrition is that in the area between chronic deficiency and optimum health more is known about animals than about man.' Geoffrey Chamberlain, Professor of Obstetrics and Gynaecology at St George's Medical Hospital, teaches that pre-pregnancy care is vital. Antenatal is too late, beginning when abnormalities are already present.

In Leeds, Professor Smithells found that by giving carefully monitored vitamin supplements to women who had had one spina bifida child the risk of an additional affected child was considerably reduced. Elsewhere there is support for the belief that multi-vitamin and iron supplements to diets for both parents during the three months prior to conception will reduce the chance of producing a seriously malformed baby.

Pre-Conceptual Care

The recent report about a British pressure group named FORESIGHT or The Association for the Promotion of Pre-Conceptual Care included some fascinating information. The philosophy is that six months prior to conception partners should receive physical check-ups. These include blood tests, blood pressure tests and a check on mineral levels in the body.

Advice is given on balanced nutrition and avoidance of stress. It is recommended that smoking and alchohol be given up and no drugs be taken or immunisation given. Parents who joined the programme following unhappy experiences of handicapped, aborted or stillborn babies, went on to produce uniformly fine children. We may be looking to a future where handicaps in children are very much reduced, although it is unlikely that all genetic defects will ever be totally avoided.

Abnormal Births – A Class Problem?

Some eight per cent of all children born now are said to have a genetic problem; of these only a fraction will have a seriously disabling or life-threatening condition. Studies confirm that a higher proportion of malformations will occur among poorer classes.

Environment, housing, diet, education and unemployment are all factors which play an important part in the health of individuals. An awareness on the part of the mother that healthy diet is essential to the health of her family is vital.

INHERITED DISABILITIES

3 Muscular Dystrophy

Muscular dystrophy describes a number of diseases in which progressive degeneration of muscle occurs. The main characteristic is the destruction of muscle fibre. Although these muscles attempt to regenerate, they fail to do so quickly enough and, slowly over the years, the destroyed material is replaced by fibrous tissue and fat.

Different forms of dystrophy result in patterns of muscle weakness which may repeat within families. Childhood muscular dystrophies vary greatly in types and intensity, causing almost total disability in some children whilst others will go right through life scarcely aware that they have an adverse condition.

Spinal Muscular Atrophy

Spinal muscular atrophy affects children of either sex and can bring about such rapid impairment in babies and young children that it is almost always fatal. Numbers of children do survive, however, and sadly there are cases of families having more than one affected child.

The disease does not necessarily show until the baby is over a year old, by which time the mother may have become pregnant again. With this condition there is a one in four chance that the new baby will suffer in the same way. The only possible prevention of this disability at present is termination of pregnancy once the presence of the defective gene is confirmed.

Genetic Advisory Centres

Counselling in these situations is offered by experienced personnel at genetic advisory centres which have been set up by the Government. Every surgery and hospital can provide information about local centres and either GPs or consultants make referrals to them. Trained counsellors are aware of the most recent research and development and will explain what can happen, and why.

It is important that people get clear and unambiguous information. Many parents have failed to grasp the implications of what has been told to them. Frequently they say, 'We didn't realise all that it meant.'

Duchenne Muscular Dystrophy

This is the most frequent and severe type of muscular dystrophy. Duchenne draws no distinction of class, colour or creed but as it is a genetic defect of the sex-linked 'X' component among chromosomes it affects boys only. It can be inherited by females so that sisters and other female relatives may be carriers of the defective gene, and could pass it on to their sons.

It is thought to be an ancient disability and a wall picture found in Egypt depicts a young Pharaoh who shows all the characteristic signs of the affliction. It is a tragic and distressing condition, but despite this there are families with one, two and even three boys with duchenne who enjoy a valuable quality of life.

Relationships are warm and compassionate and the emphasis is on day-to-day living in the best way possible. A father once told me, 'We can't add years to his life, but we can add life to his years.' Positive attitudes allow many ambitions to be realised.

The condition is invariably progressive and, sadly, eventually fatal. In addition to the muscular impairment there may be some limitation of intellect.

Research into duchenne muscular dystrophy has long since identified the sex-linked X-chromosome containing the gene which is responsible for the disorder. The identification of this element caused some elation and, recently, further important progress was received with even more excitement.

Breakthrough in Research

In 1986 Dr Louis Kunkel published a paper which was the result of years of collaborative research in England, Canada and the United States. It has meant an increased understanding of how the defective gene causes duchenne muscular dystrophy. Dr Kunkel, finding that a fragment of gene is missing in duchenne muscular dystrophy sufferers, reasoned that this absent segment must be responsible for the protein which is essential for normal muscle cell development.

He then found the intermediary factor between a gene and its protein. Knowing how the gene is organised points the way forward and will enable researchers to concentrate on this area. With these genetic secrets unravelled, the hope is that a way can be found to enable production of the protein to take place so that muscle cells can grow and be replaced normally.

Testing During Pregnancy

Tests during pregnancy enable doctors to determine with a high degree of certainty whether the foetus will be affected or not. The decision to end the pregnancy may prove a very difficult one to make, but those who understand the traumas which lie ahead of the severely disabled child as well as the family will usually take the advice offered, feeling that it is wiser to do so.

Tests for Babies

Babies of four to six weeks can have blood tests which will reveal whether they have inherited the disorder. This early knowledge allows families to arrange for pre-natal testing in future pregnancies so as to avoid an additional child with the disability.

The prevention of handicap in this way is regarded as an

interim step. The hope is that further development in research will produce corrective treatment that will allow those children born with genetic impairment to grow up normally. Teams of scientists all over the world are working on these problems and every year brings closer the key to a cure.

Early Diagnosis is Important

The disease is comparatively rare and family doctors see too few cases to be sufficiently familiar to identify it. The symptoms in the early stages might be regarded as unimportant and doctors do not want to worry parents needlessly, but where there is any doubt expert opinion should be sought. Remedial work begun at the earliest possible opportunity can stave off the worst effects for considerable periods. Consultation about the most beneficial treatment is best achieved by a team which includes parents, medical advisers, physiotherapists and occupational therapists.

Symptoms of Duchenne Muscular Dystrophy

Boys affected are normal at birth and in early infancy. They may be somewhat delayed in learning to walk. Between the ages of two to four years, after the child has begun to run around, difficulties begin. The boys have frequent falls, walking becomes less steady and they can no longer run as fast as they used to.

As muscles get weaker, it becomes harder to climb steps and stairs and to get up after a fall. There is a characteristic change in the legs as fat replaces muscle, although in fact the legs may then look sturdier than before. These symptoms will lead the doctor to suspect duchenne muscular dystrophy, and available tests will confirm the diagnosis if the disease is present.

By the age of eight or nine there is a tendency for the boy

to walk on tiptoe, arching the spine backwards to maintain balance. Increasing weakness means that the next stage is inevitable; as the boys become unable to walk, they require wheelchairs.

Further changes follow as their arms weaken and contractures of the ankles, knees and hips distort the feet. Finding a comfortable position in bed is not easy and parents become accustomed to getting up frequently at night to change the child's position. Finally, the muscles of the face and hands are affected and breathing becomes laboured. The strain on the heart is great – often too great.

Whose fault is it?

There is no way that blame can be attributed to anyone, least of all to the child or the mother, and yet there will be feelings of guilt and a sense of failure for them to overcome. Both child and parents will need counselling, and confidence will develop as they all learn about helpful techniques.

Treatment

Physiotherapy is very important and quite simple exercises performed regularly and frequently will result in the child staying on his feet for the maximum possible time. Exercising arms and legs helps to keep residual undamaged muscle healthy, but care must be taken that children do not get over tired.

Prolonged rest is to be avoided if possible because there may then be permanent loss of muscle strength. Walking is a good exercise and should be undertaken two or three times a day. Younger children do not partake of formal exercise so it is better to play the kind of games that involve running and walking. Contractures cannot be prevented indefinitely, but stretching limbs regularly can delay their onset and the resulting poor posture.

A physiotherapist will recommend the kind of exercises that are most useful. Any treatment which enables boys with duchenne to remain mobile longer is obviously helpful to morale, although consideration must be given as to whether it is better for the boys to give up precarious mobility in favour of the safety of a wheelchair.

But in all situations a positive attitude has to be encouraged and there are many activities which can be undertaken, always with professional advice.

Therapists

Physiotherapists are trained to know how muscles can best be used and will work out a programme designed to suit individual children. Occupational therapists are ingenious at devising ways and means to accomplish tasks. The child who has grown accustomed to doing things in a certain way will one day find that he can no longer manage to do them.

But there will be encouragement to learn alternative ways and independence can be considerably prolonged. Regular professional monitoring is desirable. The child who has had an early diagnosis of duchenne muscular dystrophy, and whose physical condition is maintained at the best level attainable, will prolong his independence and maintain mobility longer.

Aids to Mobility

When walking becomes too difficult callipers can be provided and fitted under trousers. They will support the failing legs, acting as an external set of muscles. Callipers today are light in weight and simple and easy to use – a young child can put them on and take them off without difficulty.

Custom-made seating helps to maintain posture and expert opinions should be sought when considering aquiring a wheelchair. Too often chairs are prescribed or recommended and chosen without sufficient regard for individual problems or an awareness of what is available.

Every severely disabled child who cannot walk should have a wheelchair on loan at first so that the family can test run for suitability to the home and surroundings, as well as for the comfort of the user. The staff at school or clinic should also have the opportunity to consider whether a particular chair is the right one. It is also most important that once the chair is delivered it should carry an information pack, with instruction in the use of that particular model, a named contact if something goes wrong and a copy of the DHSS booklet *Help for Handicapped People*.

Nothing can be more frustrating to the child who has had a taste of the freedom and independence that a wheelchair brings only to have that freedom removed because the chair proves to be unsuitable or unreliable.

Increasing Independence

It may be possible to ease some of the physical difficulties like getting upstairs by building on ground floor accommodation, to include bedroom, bathroom and toilet and preferably, if it can be managed, with access to the garden or outdoor space. Local authorities can make some provision for this but, unfortunately, it is help which varies according to area and is often limited.

When there are constraints on finance, parents may have to take out a mortgage or seek funding in the voluntary sector. Whatever can be done by the community to preserve the health, dignity and self-esteem of the whole family should be done. A great debt is owed to them for the care they give to their children and all possible assistance should be given as a matter of right.

Assessment Centres

The specialist assessment centres set up across the country

by the Government provide expert guidance when there are serious problems of physical disability with children. Referrals can be made by doctors or consultants to whichever centre is most conveniently placed, and offers the most appropriate advice.

An excellent example is the Wolfson Centre in Mecklenburgh Square in London. Children referred can be accommodated with their parents for the time necessary to determine the problem and the best ways of dealing with it. Paediatricians, educational psychologists, occupational, speech and physiotherapists and social workers use their individual expertise and wide knowledge of equipment to give the best possible advice about what can be done to help the children.

A range of wheelchairs and computers are provided for trials. A designer of wheelchairs is available to advise families and will design equipment to compensate for individual problems. Parents find this kind of comprehensive and caring service both comforting and practical.

Other Families' Experience

Families with handicapped children need every bit of encouragement they can get. Perhaps the best support comes from people who have been through the same experience. No one else could possibly know what it is like.

Margery is an example of a mother who has gone through it all and is always ready with helpful advice for families with duchenne muscular dystrophy. At the time she found out that her sons were affected by it there was no such encouragement or counselling available in her area.

A Family with Duchenne Muscular Dystrophy

Margery and Bill had two children of seven and five, a girl and a boy, when their twin boys were born. Peter and Derek

40

were identical, handsome and lively. She had her work cut out looking after four children, and the marriage was not going well. The couple quarrelled a great deal and, eventually, Bill walked out leaving Margery to cope on her own.

At about this time, when the boys were three, she noticed that one of them walked oddly – with a waddle like a penguin. She thought it was a game, even when the other twin began to walk the same way. Margery took the boys to the family doctor. His examinations revealed nothing untoward, but he asked her to return for a check-up in three months. It was thought that, perhaps, the boys had a virus.

Soon, however, they had difficulty in getting up stairs and they returned to the doctor. Margery thought they had rheumatism. The GP referred Margery to the hospital where she saw a consultant paediatrician. She recounted the interview.

'When I took the boys up to hospital the consultant gave them a check over. He compared them to each other and said we might try some physiotherapy and I could learn about it. He thought the boys might have had a problem in the womb, lying with their limbs awkwardly placed. When we came home I felt happier and confident about the consultant.'

Margery met a pleasant man who got on well with her children and they married within three months. He wanted a child of his own and she was pregnant when the doctor telephoned to ask her to come to see him. She recalled how gentle and kind he was.

'He told me that they had now found out what was wrong with my boys. He said that it was duchenne muscular dystrophy. I didn't even know what that was. Whoever heard of muscular dystrophy? I said, "What's that?" When he told me the boys would get worse and that I must be brave, I could not take it in. At home I held my little boys close and they hugged me back. "What's wrong, mummy?" they asked. I told them "Nothing, nothing at all".'

Margery's fourth son was born and it was a year before they learned that he also had duchenne muscular dystrophy, that Margery was a carrier, and that her eldest child – a daughter – was a carrier too.

The Mother is the Carrier

The traumatic discovery by a woman that she is responsible for defects in her children is devastating. The shock made this mother despair and only the needs of her family enabled her to find the strength to carry on and look after them. In these circumstances the mother suffers in the knowledge that she has imparted the abnormal gene to her child. And the child frets because he is falling behind others of his age-group.

The help which was so sorely needed was thin on the ground. These parents struggled on for years before adequate counselling and support services eased their situation. Only when they joined a muscular dystrophy group and shared the experiences of other families did they receive the right encouragement and practical help.

The twins and their half-brother had the most disabling form of muscular dystrophy. They were each nine years old when they became wheelchair-bound. By then they had to leave their school friends and join a special school equipped to cope with their disability.

Earlier Diagnosis Today

It is unlikely today that there would be a failure to recognise the symptoms of the twins. Early diagnosis is most helpful since remedial treatment can commence and thus delay the progress of the disease. Margery's male children each had a fifty per cent chance of inheriting the disability, and today blood tests are available which offer the choice of termination if they prove positive. She might then have gone on to have a healthy child.

The twins died within a few months of each other in their seventeenth year. Their younger brother is fifteen and despite his severe handicap enjoys his life. He has many friends and is interested in music. His elder half-sister, Laura, recently had a healthy baby girl who is also, like her mother and grandmother, a carrier of the defective gene. Theirs is a serene family despite the tragic circumstances.

The Muscular Dystrophy Group

The Muscular Dystrophy Group of Great Britain and Northern Ireland was formed in 1962 by a group of parents who had been told that their sons were hopelessly stricken by duchenne muscular dystrophy. Encouraged by their neuro-surgeon they decided to raise money for research and today there are 440 groups all over the country.

Locally, people are permitted to retain twenty per cent of funds raised for use by children with the disability. The remaining eighty per cent must go to research and this money has proved to be well spent, giving most encouraging results. One day it is hoped that the long awaited cure of this cruel disability will be discovered.

4 Cystic Fibrosis

Cystic fibrosis, commonly known as CF, is regarded as the most prevalent genetic disorder in Britain today, almost one in twenty among us having the gene responsible whilst remaining quite unaffected by it. It will not occur in children unless both partners have the same abnormality. The odds are that one in four of their children will inherit the disease, two children will be healthy carriers and one child will be quite unaffected. The cystic fibrosis sufferer who marries someone who is not a carrier has a fifty per cent chance of producing a child with the problem. The likelihood that a carrier will marry someone carrying the same defective gene is quite small, most babies after all are born without defect. In fact, the disability occurs in about one in every two thousand births, although surveys suggest that many mild CF children are undiagnosed.

CF itself can produce serious illness, although the outlook has improved considerably and recent discoveries offer the hope that it will be a thing of the past within a generation. It is expected that an accurate test will be developed to identify people who are clear of the abnormal gene even though someone in the family is affected. Hopefully, antenatal diagnosis will also be more accurate, and new approaches to research will uncover the way the gene works to cause the disability – pointing the way to a cure.

The Effects

In good health, we have chest secretions which are clear and thin and which coat and cleanse the lungs, helping to eliminate germs and anything which irritates our breathing. Our bronchial tubes take in air and any foreign substance is expelled in mucus as we cough to be rid of it.

CF causes a change in secretions. Mucus becomes thick and sticky, tending to block the airways and limiting the amount of oxygen that can be drawn in. Children develop persistent coughs, attempting to keep these passages clear. Any infections are resistant to medication and are liable to develop into serious conditions like pneumonia. This disorder fluctuates so much that parents need to be constantly on the look-out for unexpected changes. A child may be enjoying good health and joining in all activities at home and at school one day and the next an infection sets in that causes the greatest anxiety.

The disease varies in its effect both in degree and site of damage from one person to another, each being affected differently. Obstructions through the thickened secretions may occur in the pancreatic gland which cannot then function properly and produce the juices necessary to digest food. Good digestion enables the body to use fats and starch efficiently, and without this process children cannot thrive and attain their potential size and weight.

Intestinal obstruction in the newly born is an immediate indication of cystic fibrosis possibly requiring an operation to clear the intestines – although the underlying cause cannot of course be removed.

Some children may suffer with sinus problems and the appearance of nasal polypi will alert the GP to the possibility that CF is the cause. Diagnosis is confirmed by laboratory tests showing high levels of sodium and chloride in sweat, and mothers talk of the salty taste on children as they kiss them.

Any child with a chronic illness is liable to have emotional and social problems. It is not easy to strike the right balance in caring for children whilst allowing them freedom to develop and live as naturally as possible. The frequent infections can prove very frustrating to someone whose routine is interrupted in this way. Not unexpectedly the child can feel disappointed and thwarted. Shows of bad temper and depression may surface.

Treatment

To the children who suffer CF, physiotherapy becomes the governing factor in their lives. It is of the utmost importance and is begun immediately the diagnosis is confirmed, even on little babies, helping to free the lungs and keep them healthy. Older children are taught breathing routines and parents learn to vibrate the chest wall so that obstructive plugs can be dislodged. Trampolines are useful, encouraging children to do the exercises which enable them to live and breathe more freely.

Daily medicines permit the digestion of food and antibiotics are given regularly to control lung infections whilst inhalations are helpful in easing the condition. Nebulisers are provided on loan by some hospitals and these are useful in administering medicines. It is essential to keep air passages open to make breathing easier and drugs to thin the heavy mucus may be needed. A preparation called pancreatin can be given which is helpful because it assists the replacement of the missing pancreatic juices. Therapy has to be prescribed individually since each child will have different requirements.

Support for Parents

Parents need the support and encouragement of their family doctor and of the local hospital team. The regime of regular medicine and at least twice-daily therapy can soon become both monotonous and arduous. The daily grind of care added to the constant threat of danger can be intensely wearing.

At School

The student with CF is first of all an individual, not a disability, and is possibly bright, interested in sports and capable of doing well. Teachers need to undesrtand the problems children may have in order to be helpful. Medicine times come around in school time too, but these medicines are not habit-forming, neither do they alter behaviour. It is best to ignore coughing bouts and advise other children to do the same. Coughing is necessary and there is no possible contagion from CF itself. Students with CF may be absent more frequently, particularly in bad weather when colds deepen into chest infections.

CF is known to be one of the diseases which can be misdiagnosed as chronic bronchitis or malnutrition. Teachers should be aware of symptoms which could collectively point to cystic fibrosis and discuss any suspect cases with the parents or school doctor.

The Future

The outlook for these children has improved dramatically and their lifetime is constantly being extended by new drug discoveries. Some fifteen years ago seventy-five per cent of children with CF did not live beyond the age of fifteen. Now eighty per cent reach adulthood enjoying a good quality of life. Obviously, it is very important for brothers and sisters to know whether or not they are carriers, and a successful outcome to the search for an accurate test will be a tremendous breakthrough.

A Family's Experience

It was a long shot that brought together two people from different countries who each had the defective recessive cystic fibrosis gene. Their story follows and although some details are altered to preserve anonymity the basic facts are essentially true. They are a family of great courage who have not permitted tragedy to embitter them and whose demeanour has earned for them the admiration and love of many friends.

Marina was at university in England studying languages when she attracted the interest of a visiting professor. The quiet dark-eyed girl captivated Paul and he determined to marry her. Her Greek-born parents were impressed by the status of their daughter's suitor and although they had hoped that she would marry into a Greek family, their daughter's happiness overcame their misgivings and the couple were wed with everyone's blessing.

Two children were born within two years of each other, both of them boys. Marina's days were busy with her family and the charity functions run in their village kept her occupied in her spare time.

Clive, their eldest son, was seven years old when he picked up a cold that quickly turned to flu. He ran a very high temperature and Marina rang their GP for advice. He was concerned about the child's condition, finding the boy flushed and restless and there were signs of infection in his chest so he prescribed an antibiotic. The next day the temperature remained high following a sleepless night and, when the doctor returned, the child's heavy eyes and listlessness worried him. It was decided to get some tests done at the hospital and Marina was told that they were just being cautious and suspected nothing seriously wrong.

The boy was kept in for forty-eight hours and his mother was allowed to stay with him. He improved during this time and Marina felt that all was well. Later in the evening Paul was called to the hospital, and the consultant sat with the parents in the waiting-room. Marina recalled the interview and her feelings of disbelief as they heard the news that shattered their world.

'We were told that Clive had cystic fibrosis. That he was a strong little boy and would be all right. But that he would need daily physiotherapy and medicine for the rest of his life; that he would need careful looking after. And that they – the hospital – would be there when we needed them. I didn't look at Paul. He put his arm around me. As the news sank in I felt one icy sweat after another break out in waves. "Where could he have caught such a thing?" I asked.

48

'The consultant leaned back in his chair and shook his head. "It isn't caught. It happens that you and Paul both have the same recessive gene. And you two have a one in four chance of producing a child with cystic fibrosis."

'I thought, "My baby, Michael, is he all right?" The doctor knew what I was thinking. "We will have Michael in for tests but more than likely he is fine. And in a few days you'll have Clive back home and back at school."

'In the next few weeks everything seemed so normal. But nothing was the same again. I cried a lot. I couldn't break the news to our parents. Our little one, Michael, had his tests and they were negative. Thankfully, we concentrated on Clive and his physiotherapy. We bought a trampoline and an exercise bike and I learned the right way to give treatment. Twice a day Clive submitted to twenty minutes of drill and massage. He had to take a lot of medicines and I noted that certain foods did not agree with him. He was good about everything, wanting to be well. Michael was now five years old and wanting to join in the exercises, bouncing on the trampoline and stretching his little legs on the bike. The children treated it all as fun and got on well, never a sign of jealousy between them.

'In the next two years, Clive went into hospital four times. We watched him carefully each time he caught a chill and the moment a chest infection was suspected his antibiotics were increased, and he went into hospital if there were any further problems. We came to know the ward so well. Michael grew used to Clive's absences and all the special treatment he received. At times I gave him the physiotherapy too, just so that it didn't seem that I was favouring his elder brother.

'We took the boys on a Greek holiday and they had a wonderful time meeting their cousins, and each finding a friend in his own age-group. We talked of having a third child, but I was so afraid of having another with cystic fibrosis that I told Paul I wanted to be sterilised. When we got back home he reluctantly agreed. I didn't tell my parents. Since they were not to know the reason they would never have understood. The operation was quickly over –

so simple. I felt strange, somehow less of a person. It was so final. I would never have more children. I cried on my own and wished that I had someone to talk to.

'It was in the autumn one day when Michael came running to me. He was damp with exertion and as I kissed his forehead I tasted salt. My heart turned over. Clive's sweat was salty. It was a symptom of cystic fibrosis. Why did I feel panicky? Michael's tests had been clear. I kept my voice steady as I answered the children's questions on the way home. I resisted the urge to speak to Paul or to the doctor. One small sweat and I felt alarm bells ringing. But the certainty was growing in me that Michael was not all right.'

Eventually, further tests for Michael showed that he too had the defect. This was indeed a hard blow for these parents. They had come to know all about cystic fibrosis. They read everything, every reference that they could find, and knew all about the research that was undertaken. Marina had become acquainted with the mother of a girl with the disease. They had met at the hospital and had visited a small group of cystic fibrosis parents who gathered regularly in a neighbouring town, where they shared experiences and exchanged advice. All of the parents agreed that these meetings were comforting.

The knowledge of their second child's illness deepened the couple's concern for each other. Paul's tenderness and care for his wife showed in every action. She knew how much he suffered and kept as cheerful as possible, and felt that she must never allow bitterness to sour her. Their doctor was deeply sympathetic and his caring attitude strengthened them.

Events moved rapidly for the younger child. His periods of illness were increasing and everyone recognised that something was wrong. Michael grew frail and, although his interest in life remained keen, his strength decreased. There came a day when Marina was told by the specialist that there was involvement of other organs and that the outlook was poor. When Marina pressed for an explanation of what that meant, she heard that Michael might go on for another year. He could continue at school, there would be periods of well-being – but there was little hope beyond that.

'I knew what it was like to die a little each day. How wrong it was that I should be so healthy and my beloved child so ill. In the quiet evenings I would go into the garden and put my face against the rough bark of a tree and pray for a miracle. I ached for Paul. Often when I looked at him as we sat together his eyes were damp with tears. We were so sad for each other.'

Support and Advice Essential

This family was fortunate in the close support they had from their parents and from their doctor and friends. Their troubles brought them closer together. It was unfortunate that even though coming from different countries they should both have the same abnormal gene. Married to other people, probably without the gene, they would not have passed on the disease, or known of any danger. Neither of them showed any sign of a health problem and indeed were perfectly fit.

The nature of cystic fibrosis demands strict adherence to daily treatment. There must be constant watchfulness for infection, and an attitude of sensible and realistic acceptance by both parents and children is necessary for the best results. Over-protective attitudes on the part of the parents are natural but should be resisted, for they result in greater dependence unless the child has a strong personality and is able to overcome them.

In the case of Marina and Paul the temptation to mollycoddle Clive became overpowering after the death of Michael at the age of eight. But Clive was interested in sport and was encouraged by his doctors to lead an active life. He was fourteen when the school took a trip abroad and he insisted that he be allowed to go along with them. This separation had the effect of cutting the parental tie, and

Marina and Paul began to relax and to take holidays and enjoy life again.

Clive is eighteen and preparing to go to university. He is cautious, especially when there is any infection about, but enjoys academic success, excels at tennis and looks forward to his future. Marina is interested in teaching languages and is hoping to get a post in a nearby school.

Current Research

Four groups engaged in research in Copenhagen, Toronto, Salt Lake City and London found that the gene is on chromosome number seven. They have located the position by 'cloning' a small area of the chromosome and identifying genes which are always inherited with the disease.

Professor Bob Williamson, of St Mary's Hospital Medical School, said 'We are nearing the end of a twenty-year quest to find the gene and to be able to do the carrier tests. There are over two million carriers of this "genetic time bomb" in Britain alone. It is only when we have the gene that a community test for carriers can be devised and a prevention campaign started. But even more important is that knowing which gene is affected, and how, will enable new forms of treatment for the young people with CF.'

Stop-Press

The gene is discovered and tests of the extended family of a cystic fibrosis child can now detect not only the carriers, but can tell with almost one hundred per cent certainty whether or not babies have the defective gene.

5   Sickle Cell and Thalassaemia

What is Sickle Cell?

This is the name of a group of inherited disorders of haemoglobin, which is the important constituent in red blood that carries oxygen. Blood cells pick up oxygen in the lungs and carry it round the body.

When blood cells with sickle haemoglobin release oxygen they can alter shape, becoming curved. The trouble starts when these misshapen cells get stuck at narrow blood vessels, stopping the flow of blood, causing damage and intense pain.

Who Gets It?

The kinds of SC disease which are most common are found in families who come from Africa, the West Indies, the Middle East, the eastern Mediterranean and Asia. The gene has developed in people from hot climates because it does offer protection from an exceedingly dangerous form of malaria. Nature's attempts to immunise us to dangers in our environment are generally welcome; for example, dark skins develop because they are a better protection against the sun than fair skins and beneath them we are all the same. But in this particular case, the cure – sickle cell – proves to be as bad as or worse than the malaria.

No form of SC disease is contagious, nor is it any kind of leukaemia, cancer, or white blood cells eating up the red ones. Neither is it due to a shortage of iron. These are common suppositions and it is reassuring to families to have doubts removed.

Sickle Cell Trait

The trait occurs when one parent passes on the usual haemoglobin and the other passes on sickle haemoglobin. People with SC trait have no awareness of it, nor do they suffer any damage, since less than one per cent of their red cells are sickled in comparison with thirty to sixty per cent in those who have sickle cell disease.

A rare complication of SC trait is sickling in the kidneys which results in blood in the urine, but does not cause illness. The worst of having the trait is that one is a carrier and parents who are each carriers can pass on a more serious disability. So for their children it is quite a different matter. Each child has a one in four chance of developing a potentially serious illness.

Sickle Cell Anaemia

This is the most serious form of sickle cell disease and can result in severe physical disability, sometimes leading to the permanent use of a wheelchair. There are forms of treatment which can help the child or adult, but at present there is no cure.

Symptoms, which are rare before the age of three to six months, manifest themselves as attacks of pain to various parts of the body as the cells curve and cause blockages. There are children who get frequent very painful attacks, requiring admission into hospital on each occasion. For others there may only be an occasional crisis and the anaemia does not greatly disrupt family life.

Painless Attacks

Sickle cell disease often starts in a mild form. Two forms of crisis can occur, one is quite without pain and may begin with an infection, lassitude and a general pallor. It is difficult to diagnose because sickle cell disease imitates many others and is known as a masquerader.

Painful Attacks

These dreaded crises happen when there is a reduction of oxygen in the blood. Attacks of severe pain are caused which are similar to those felt in rheumatic fever. They can occur following exertion, during some anaesthetics or at extreme altitudes. Children must avoid excessive exertion and drink plenty of fluids.

Variety of Symptoms

The nature of the disease means that affected children are always anaemic, which accounts for the feelings of exhaustion and general lethargy. It is difficult for parents to avoid over-protection of youngsters who are prone to minor infections which can flare up into serious conditions, and there is a temptation to keep children in at the least excuse.

There are a number of associated symptoms since this is a multi-system disorder. Children may get painful inflammation of the hands and feet, developing stiff and painful joints or ulcers on the lower legs. Puberty may be delayed. The inconvenient and distressing effects of the condition can be very depressing.

Patience and understanding must be shown, both at home and at school, to young patients who suffer in this way. All of the adults in contact with such children, parents, medical personnel and teachers should make the opportunity to discuss with each other the effects on the child and how they should best be treated.

Education

Whilst sickle cell anaemia has no effect on the intelligence, it can cause difficulty in concentration. Attacks of pain or the typical lethargy caused by anaemia are distracting and can disturb study. Regular visits to the GP and hospital are necessary to monitor both the effects of the disease as well as the medication. It is a pity to miss schooling, but if it is inevitable then children who get behind with their work may need additional help to catch up. Home and hospital tuition may be necessary.

Experienced medical advisers can help to reduce the frequency and severity of crises and their complications by keeping the patient under regular observation and providing preventive advice and treatment. The condition may be worse in damp weather and it is advised that these children should never be allowed to get chilled after physical exercise or swimming.

Whilst the child should be encouraged to join in all sports and activities possible, attention must be paid to their well-being and in particular they should be fully immunised against infectious illnesses. It may be thought wise that they take vitamins and antibiotics, always under the supervision of their GP.

Coping with Problems

It is never easy to come to terms with disability or chronic illness. Knowledgeable professionals who are on hand to give practical and sympathetic counselling can help families to cope with news of their children's handicap. They can provide patients with the treatment which will enable them to bear with the inconvenience and the painful effects of the condition.

It is best by far to try to live as normal a life as possible, ensuring proper nutrition and maintaining general health. Genetic counselling should be given so that the danger of repeating the disability in any additional children is clearly understood.

The progress of the disease and degrees of impairment to health vary greatly, but affected children are generally able to attend normal schools and continue usual activities when they are well. For some, however, the effect of sickle cell anaemia is very damaging and results in severe disablement, when mobility is so impaired that a wheelchair may be needed.

Anaesthesia

Before any operation routine screening will take place, whether in hospital or dental clinics, whenever anaesthesia is proposed. Special blood tests can reveal whether there is sickle cell trait or sickle cell disease. The blood test can be arranged by GPs, or at a local Sickle Cell Centre. Following the blood test the parents are told whether they or their child are sickle positive.

It is obviously important that they do understand whether this means sickle cell trait or sickle cell anaemia so that they can anticipate problems ahead and appreciate the genetic implications for their other children and relatives, as well as for any future children.

Sickle Cell Sisters

Jasmine is the eldest of four sisters. She is fifteen and has sickle cell disease, spending some three to four weeks each year in hospital where she receives treatment and medication to relieve her attacks of excruciating pain.

Once these attacks are over she is able to return to school and enjoy normal life. Her sisters have sickle cell trait and suffer no ill effects whatsoever. Provided that they do not marry someone with the trait or disease, their children should have no problems. Jasmine, however, may have children with the disability. Both parents are fit and well and provide a loving and secure background for their daughters.

Thalassaemia

This condition is mostly seen in children of Mediterranean parentage, but it has been known to occur in other races.

Family studies may be necessary to confirm the diagnosis. It is similar to sickle cell in that abnormally-shaped cells are produced which are deficient in haemoglobin.

There are two forms, thalassaemia major being an extremely severe one and causing anaemia which requires regular blood transfusions. People with thalassaemia inherit it from both parents who are each healthy carriers of the trait. Genetic counselling is provided when the condition is confirmed. There is no cure for either condition.

Counselling

Advice for these conditions is given in weekly children's and adults' medical out-patients clinics in a few areas, as well as in hospitals and at home by specially trained counsellors. They offer advice to families and will visit schools, give talks, lectures and discussions, using videos, slides and films. They aim to make the general public and health professionals more aware of these particular diseases.

There are likely to be numbers of cases which are undiagnosed and it is estimated that there could be as many as 5,000 in the UK. Approximately one in ten people of Afro-Carribean origin have the sickle cell trait. Adults may request blood tests on a walk-in basis at the Sickle Cell Centre in Willesden, North-West London, for themselves or their children. Otherwise tests may be arranged through the family GP.

What the Children Say

Children have written of their painful crises.

The doctors who know about sickle cell, they are good, they understand, you feel safe. They keep you company and explain about the pain to the nurses. Then the nurses don't look at you as though you're acting.   Girl aged 11

The pains began and got worse. Then worse and worse until I hardly knew who I was, just a rag of excruciating pain writhing about like an upturned caterpillar.   Boy aged 14

My first experience when I went in with a crisis was after some junior doctor examined me in casualty. He told my mother I was pregnant and another said I had migraine. God knows how they thought this; doctors in casualty do not like you to tell them your condition.   Girl aged 13

I may feel hot and take clothes off. Then I may feel cold and can't get warm with all the blankets. I had never known such pain. Injections made it less but my head felt so funny. You can see all the doctors and nurses are worried about addiction.   Girl aged 15

6   Brittle Bones
(Osteogenesis Imperfecta)

This is an inherited condition recognisable by a typically delicate appearance and often confirmed by a high incidence of fractured limbs. The fragile state of the bones makes them liable to bend and break, and these fractures are a feature of sufferers – occurring throughout infancy and the early years. Later the condition often improves and bones become stronger.

The name brittle bones has come to be the commonly accepted term for *osteogenesis imperfecta* and it one which aptly describes the condition. There is a wide range of fragile bone disorders and these are classified according to the severity of disablement under four main types. It is most important that parents of a brittle bone child should get an accurate diagnosis so that they can anticipate the problems that their child will face in the future. They will want to establish what risk there is that additional children may inherit the disease. Exact diagnosis is imperative for another reason – treatment is based on the type of brittle bones that the family has.

Although the condition is inherited neither parent may be visibly affected, although one or both parents may show some sign of the trait, possibly in a form too insignificant to have been recorded. A careful study will be made of the known family history to determine the risk of having additional children with this defect.

Where examination of relatives is possible, and these minimal disorders are revealed, there can then be recognition of the way in which the genes are being inherited in a family. There is a fifty per cent risk that parents who have brittle bone disease themselves will have children with the same disorder. However, the chance of a second affected child in a family where the condition is previously unknown is extremely low. The degree of effect varies and cannot be predicted with certainty.

Sporadic Brittle Bones

Where there is a single case of *osteogenesis imperfecta* occurring in a family with no previous history it is known as a sporadic case and is caused by a chance alteration in a gene. In such cases both parents may unknowingly be carriers without any sign of the trait and, at present, it is not possible to distinguish or predict who they are.

The frequency with which such children occur in populations throughout the world is one in fifteen thousand; many of the more seriously affected do not survive so that the condition is present in something like one in 25,000.

General Effects of Brittle Bones

The most careful handling of young children is necessary and even so some fractures occur in simple ways, as they turn in bed, are picked up or reach to retrieve a toy. These children have a fragile appearance with doll-like faces, triangular in shape, and with clear thin skins and lovely eyes emphasised by a very bluish tone of the white of the eye. The characteristic appearance remains as the child grows older, even though the condition itself improves.

Limbs are usually quite short and the back is not straight causing the appearance to be dwarf-like. There is no known cure as yet, but surgery is possible for some children and does alleviate the condition. Bones which have fractured and mended badly can be rebroken, set straight and rodded. Metal rods are inserted alongside the bones and spine providing sufficient strength to enable a child to walk without fear of fracture.

Prior to the operation the limit that is imposed on these children by such fears takes all the fun out of playing or moving at all.

Stretching the Spine

The spine can be stretched by means reminiscent of

medieval torture but accepted by children who anticipate an improvement in their condition as a result of their treatment. A metal crown is secured to the head and the child is stretched as if on a rack. Still, they joke and chat to visitors, tolerating the discomfort with little complaint.

Medical and teaching staff have a wonderful attitude to their young charges and they are as caring about the emotional welfare of their patients as they are about their physical treatment, going to some lengths to enable them to study and to watch television from their prone positions. Most of these children are of normal intelligence, bright and lively and living up to their somewhat cheeky appearance.

Those who remain of diminutive stature and unable to walk at all, or to walk far, have been helped by the development of electric wheelchairs which can be elevated as well as propelled along in the usual way.

Medical Treatment

Medical treatment has been tried and can be helpful in decreasing fracture frequency in some patients, but there must be careful monitoring for side-effects. Curvature of the spine is largely avoided today by early assessment and treatment and many of the handicaps which used to result have been abolished or considerably lessened.

Therapy

Any exercise which strengthens muscle is encouraged and swimming recommended. Sports which involve possible bone fractures have to be avoided, but individual advice must be considered. Many children with brittle bones will grow up into people well able to earn a living, to drive a car, manage a household and family.

Affected women have a fifty per cent risk of having a brittle bone baby and should have pre-natal diagnosis. This may determine the degree of severity of the disease for the baby early enough for the parents to consider termination if the child is severely affected and might either die early or be very disabled.

Genetic research has produced such important advances in recent years that all affected families should take the opportunity to discuss with professionals the known facts. There is always the hope that in the future some treatment will become possible which will correct the defect in the unborn and new-born baby.

Education Important

Having brittle bones is a serious disadvantage and disability, but there is the potential to lead a full and happy life. Children should not be allowed to miss months of learning because they have to spend long periods in hospital and arrangements are generally made to continue education. It is difficult not to worry about delicate children, but it is far better to encourage any child to care for itself and to work within limits – brittle bone children are no exception to this rule.

The type of school the child will attend depends upon the degree of disability. The decision regarding this must be made by everyone interested, that is the family, doctors, therapists and handicapped children's services. Attendance at ordinary schools is best, and there should be access for wheelchairs so that non-mobile OI children are not segregated.

Adolescent Needs

The young OI teenager needs to develop socially and to mix with the non-handicapped. Brittle bone sufferers should be able to discuss their chances of developing relationships of a satisfying nature.

Society now accepts that sexual contacts are not to be

denied simply because one is handicapped. Experience of growing up must encompass all those emotions, tender, sweet, satisfying or hurtful, which any teenager will enjoy or endure.

Adolescent Responsibility

There may be fear that a relaxation of parental control will lead to irresponsible activities, but fully informed and aware adolescents must be allowed to make judgements for themselves. Sex education is important and youngsters should be made clearly aware not only of their responsibilities but that their potential for loving and being loved, their needs for normal relationships, are entirely natural. They are people first and not so very different from anyone else.

Some of the most warm and meaningful relationships develop between handicapped and non-handicapped people, and go on to become lifetime partnerships.

Brittle Bone Confused with Non-Accidental Injury

One of the hazards for parents of undiagnosed brittle bone children is that they may stand accused of causing their children's fractures. It is bewildering for caring families whose children fracture so easily to find themselves the objects of suspicion, and this causes much distress.

Some children have been removed from their families on suspicion of having been deliberately injured. The emotional damage suffered by children and parents under these circumstances is not easily repaired and professionals must be very sure before they take drastic steps.

The Brittle Bone Society of Great Britain, recognising this problem, urges a greater spread of publicity about the condition so that people everywhere, including professional medical workers, may recognise *osteogenesis imperfecta* (OI) when they see it.

Milder cases are not so readily identified, but frequent fractures in delicate children call for tests to establish whether there is a reason other than abuse.

I know a bright little girl with OI whose mother, suffering from the same disease, is bringing her up alone. For many years the young woman longed for a child but had never thought it wise or even possible that she might achieve this ambition. Her pregnancy was not planned and was not in circumstances she would have chosen, but once over the realisation that she was to have a child she found herself in the care of a supportive and sympathetic obstetrician.

This mother, although quite severely affected by OI, was able to walk on crutches and even after seven months of pregnancy had few of the problems which her medical advisers had anticipated. Ultrasound scans showed no damage and everyone was confident that the infant might be free of brittle bones. In the final weeks a single X-ray revealed the news that the baby had a fractured leg.

That mother is quite independent and determined that her daughter's education will be a broad one and her life will be constrained as little as possible.

At a Barnardo's home for handicapped children I met a charming blond child of seven. Unable to walk, she pushed her doll's pram from her wheelchair which she manoeuvred with great dexterity. She was so full of vivacity and fun, enjoying her visitors and telling me about her school work and her dolls.

Today she is a diminutive teenager, interested in clothes and make-up and handicraft. She has a wide circle of friends and is interested in a range of activities. Brittle bones may be her problem but her sunny nature will always ensure that she enjoys her life.

In 1978 a good deal of publicity was accorded to brittle bone children, and in that year Thames Television granted the Brittle Bone Society their 'Magpie Appeal'. This resulted in considerable funding and many hundreds of children benefited, receiving comforts in their homes and mobility aids, including special wheelchairs.

Independent mobility is taken for granted by the able-bodied but for youngsters who cannot walk, the possession of an electric wheelchair can mean a complete change of life, allowing further education, shopping trips, walks in the streets with their friends and rambles in the woods. Privacy becomes a meaningful word and horizons expand.

7 Friedrich's Ataxia

This is a comparatively rare condition with some 2,000 sufferers among our population, although there are likely to be mild cases which have not been diagnosed. The problem is inherited in a similar way to cystic fibrosis when both parents carry the recessive faulty gene. Their children have a one in four chance of inheriting the problem and it is rare in today's small families to find two children with Friedrich's Ataxia.

The onset of the disease is generally at about eight years of age, although it can begin anywhere between four and sixteen, affecting girls and boys in equal proportions. Rarely, babies of eighteen months have been diagnosed. When the onset is early, two-thirds of affected children are likely to deteriorate finally to a stage when wheelchairs will become necessary.

Initially, weakness is noticed during walking and signified by increasing stumbling and awkwardness. It may be thought that there will be no further progression of the disease but inevitably hands lose power and it becomes more difficult to write and to hold utensils, cups and cutlery.

Doctors encourage physiotherapy, since this does delay the worst effects and gives children more of a sense of well-being. Parents learn massage techniques and this helps the circulatory problems as mobility lessens. Swimming is regarded as a helpful exercise and it is important that bedrest is never prolonged since it is difficult to regain lost strength. There is no cure as yet.

Some ten per cent of these children develop diabetes and must diet carefully. Friedrich's Ataxia does not cause any impairment or deterioration of mental powers. Researchers are hopeful that they will shortly discover the responsible gene and be able to identify carriers.

8 Haemophilia

A mother carrying the haemophilia gene suffers no ill effects since she is protected by the sex-linked 'X' chromosome described earlier. A man bearing this gene will have haemophilia. When female carriers and normal males produce children, fifty per cent have a chance of being affected, the girls becoming carriers and the boys developing the disease. An affected man cannot transmit haemophilia to his sons, but all of his daughters will be carriers.

Diagnosis usually follows a minor injury during the first two years when bleeding continues beyond the usual clotting time. Following bruising, bleeding may occur beneath the skin into tissue or joints, the knees being particularly vulnerable. Recurrent episodes may lead to joint damage and chronic disability. Because the blood takes longer to clot there may be sufficient loss internally or into the joints to require transfusions.

The difficulty is to encourage these children to lead active lives whilst protecting them from trauma. It is important to ensure that preventive dental care, dental work, and in particular extractions, are performed with due caution. As boys grow the episodes of bleeding generally become less severe, possibly because they learn to be careful. Regional centres have been established to provide skilled care for haemophiliacs, the detection of women who carry the gene and counselling.

A few young haemophiliacs have been given Aids through blood transfusion before there was awareness of the possibility of infection. This is only possible through sexual relations, injection or transfusion. Blood or bodily fluids do not infect orally, and breath contact is not a danger. There is no possible contagion from haemophilia itself.

9 Blindness and Impaired Vision

Whether a child is born with visual defects or acquires them later, the news comes as a painful blow. Blindness seems to strike more fear than any other malady and until recently was thought to be an appalling tragedy, making one helpless and an object of pity.

Many deaf people, however, will argue that loss of hearing is a more isolating impairment. Either or both of these disabilities will mean that life is going to be hard, but it can nevertheless be enjoyable. Visiting blind schools and watching children without sight run about and play confidently out of doors despite this handicap provides an uplifting experience.

Symptoms

When no abnormality is apparent at birth it is assumed that all is well. It may be weeks before parents begin to suspect that their baby cannot see. Happy children who are responsive to sound, enjoy being cuddled and talked to, but do not reach to play with mobile toys, their toes, or towards people nearby, must cause worry and a suspicion that something is wrong.

Compensating with Other Senses

Blind babies cannot respond in quite the same way as sighted infants, but need love, contact with humans and lots of cuddles just as much as, if not more than, sighted babies. They may need help to use their hearing to compensate for their lack of sight and should be given encouragement to crawl, to reach out for things and to make responses.

It is surprising to sighted people to realise how much the blind can know about their surroundings and how capably even young children can use their senses to make up for the one they lack.

The child who can see is motivated by curiosity to touch and explore objects within vision. For the child with impaired vision behaviour is different, and touching what they cannot see may produce fear or evidence of dislike. The toddler should be encouraged to explore freely and to examine objects by touch. Much can be learnt about the extent of the child's vision from these behaviour patterns.

Upwards of three-and-a-half years children use other senses to support their curiosity, they listen with great care, defining sounds and using smell and touch to identify and classify things around them.

Causes

It is a relief to record that many causes of blindness no longer offer the threat they once did. Cases due to smallpox, eye infection and inflammation are now extremely rare. A relatively high incidence of visual impairment occurred in the 1940s and 1950s in low birthweight infants. It was suggested that the high level of oxygen given to these babies in the hope of preventing disability might in fact have caused the damage.

Tiny babies are susceptible to convulsions and this may lead to sight impairment. The expert intensive care given today to premature infants and those whose birthweights are lower than they should be means that such problems are less common.

Another cause of sight damage in the new-born is that of rubella, more commonly known as German measles. If every schoolgirl were to be vaccinated against this disease then another potential danger would be virtually eradicated.

Inherited Factors

Damage to sight may be due to an inherited factor. When there is a sight problem in either or both of the parents, or elsewhere in the family, then a visual handicap in a child may come as a deep disappointment – but not as a completely unexpected shock.

When a blind child is born to normally sighted parents it could mean that recessive genes have been carried forward and are present in both mother and father, despite the fact that neither of them has a sight problem. This is not only a shattering piece of news but means that any future children have a chance of inheriting the same disability.

Recent discoveries in genetics have dramatically altered the outlook for the prevention of the birth of children having severe visual defects. This is possible through genetic counselling when parents at risk are given the opportunity to decide whether they should chance having children with visual problems. Prevention is also possible in some disorders by the recognition of affected foetuses and counselling which may result in advice to terminate the pregnancy.

Visually handicapped youngsters should always receive genetic counselling alongside accurate diagnosis of their own problems. They can then embark on parenthood knowing with a high degree of certainty what the visual health of their future offspring will be.

Low Incidence of Blindness

Since the main cause of blindness in children today is genetic disease there should be a steady reduction in the birth of children with this disability provided that advantage is taken of this new knowledge. Happily, sight impairment is already a handicap of low incidence, occurring in approximately one child in 10,000 of the population.

New discoveries not only reveal which genes are affected

but give promise of further progress and perhaps, one day, a treatment which will prevent the damage.

Damage at Birth and After

For a few babies damage is caused in some way at the time of birth, and it may not be immediately recognised. Standards of maternity care in developed countries are now high and the proportion of problems at birth is low.

Following birth there are illnesses which can cause blindness as well as other impairment. Meningitis is one of these, but prompt treatment can usually prevent damage of a serious and permanent nature.

The older child who has acquired blindness through accident or viral disease does have an advantage compared to the child who has never been sighted. Visual memory of things seen remains although it may recede as time goes by. Most children registered blind do have partial sight which enables them to distinguish objects, and there is a wide variation in degree of vision. The advice of professionals is necessary and they will consider all the facts, and then advise according to the individual needs of a child.

Multiple Disabilities

A considerable number of children with visual problems do have additional impairment, and it is important that an assessment should discover all of these. Assessing vision in children without language is difficult and it might be concluded that there is low intelligence where in fact poor hearing is the answer. Greater stress is now laid upon both training and postgraduate work for doctors so that they are better prepared to make correct diagnosis of handicap. Accuracy is imperative so that remedial treatment and training can begin, and appropriate genetic counselling can be given.

Potential Problems

The maximum age incidence of the onset of squinting is about two-and-a-half years. At this age mothers tend to bring their children to see the doctor less often so defects are not noted as soon as they might be. Earliest possible referrals to an ophthalmologist are desirable whenever problems are suspected in order to avoid serious complications later on.

There is a high proportion of eye squints in children when they commence school, almost one in fifteen. Any child with this symptom should immediately be referred to an eye specialist. Treatment at five or earlier can avoid serious complications whilst leaving matters untreated for years can result in permanent damage and possibly the loss of sight in an eye. It is common to treat young children by using an eye patch and although this is not popular with child or parents the results are worthwhile.

It is usually easy to remove a foreign body from the eye, but if there is any difficulty at all in getting the object out it is best to cover the eye and immediately get the child to the doctor or a hospital. If a fragment has entered the eye at speed then immediate referral to a specialist is imperative.

Regular Assessment

The general development of children with visual impairment calls for specialised training. Whilst children do fall into patterns and grades of ability they need individual assessment by experienced personnel. Some deviation from the accepted norms are nevertheless recognised as right and natural.

Tests are made with a view to remedial training and treatment. The assessing team must take into account the child's environment and family, whether there is an extended family which is helpful and which relationships are the most important to the child. When the fullest information is compiled about everyone involved, the team is in a position to offer practical advice and to gauge future needs. Guidance of the utmost benefit to the whole family is thus made available.

The degree of sight loss will be regularly assessed so that appropriate care is given, and treatment varied as necessary. Some conditions will require regular hospital treatment and children, if they are of an age to understand, should be prepared in advance for this possibly traumatic experience.

Cornea transplant is possible for some children, and when this is suitable they are given a high priority on waiting-lists.

A new method for storing corneas for up to a month instead of the traditional forty-eight hours has been pioneered at Bristol Eye Hospital. This means that transplant operations can be carried out routinely rather than as emergencies; the extra time allows for necessary checks to be made to ensure that the corneas used are free from disease and also match the recipient.

Counselling Essential

Following diagnosis ample time should be allowed for counselling. Many questions will surface – why us, what have we done, what good can life be, what future is there? Parents may be so shocked that they do not register responses and need to be given information again.

They should write down all the things they want to know so that they do not leave counselling sessions having forgotten important points they had wanted to raise. They will want to know the exact nature of the problem and what the effects will be. Will it affect the child's development? How many other children have this particular sight problem? What happens about education? – and so on.

There should always be the closest collaboration between medical, social and educational advisers. Conflicting information causes confusion and additional stress that affected families can well do without.

It is established that babies with visual handicaps need and will get referral to specialists, but the parents themselves must form part of the team which considers the child's welfare. No one sees the child more often than parents do, and their observations are invaluable. In addition, the care team will have an opportunity to observe the relationship between child and parents, and this is always useful.

Early Training by Parents

Of all our senses, sight is said to be the one which co-ordinates the others. If we hear a sound, we look towards it, if we feel something we look at it and we make eye contact with people we speak to. The loss or absence of vision places an intensely emotional strain on the whole of the family. But we do have another four senses and can do very well in life with these.

The attitude of parents and family is all important to the child's future and much depends on the early pre-school opportunities for learning. Parents who develop a positive and encouraging attitude will reap benefits as their child overcomes the disability and learns to communicate.

It is important to recognise the good sense of teaching any child independence, and for the visually handicapped child it is vital. Time must be given to encourage movement, to explore surroundings and find things that have been dropped. Conversation must be constant so that images can be evoked about what is going on. The kettle is boiling, the bread is toasting, an aeroplane is flying over, the milkman is in the road, daddy is coming downstairs . . . a constant flow of words will give the child interest and make up for the loss of vision. Soundless approach is scary to a blind child and some warning sound should be made, especially on sound-deadening carpet.

Confidence in the environment must be learnt. Walking tall and fearlessly will become natural as awareness develops and children begin to know their districts.

Furniture and household objects should reliably be found in their accustomed places. Keeping toys tidy is easily and readily learned, this box for soft toys, that one for plasticine, this shelf for braille books and that one for mother's books.

All young children enjoy having a regular story-time and benefit from it. Reading stories and poems to poorly sighted children is especially rewarding for they frequently have better concentration and memories than sighted children. Certain books are better for these children because they appeal to senses other than sight. Books are available which are printed both in braille and normal type.

Eating Out

Teaching any young child to feed independently is going to mean a lot of mess, but the blind child soon learns the art of scooping food out of dishes. Quite young children can be taken to their friends' birthday parties and to restaurants without people generally being aware that they have disability.

A warm and loving family giving sensible encouragement and support to the visually handicapped child can provide a great start in life, and when at times the disability is forgotten and the family feels like any other, having fun and laughing, then things are not turning out too badly after all.

Separation from Family

The mother is the foremost need of any baby, but it must be said that often the father undertakes and does the job very well. The idea of separating any child from a close, loving parent is not a good one. It should only be considered if circumstances demand that such a decision must be taken. Certainly if the mother is ill or living in difficult accommodation and already has a number of children, she may be unable to care adequately for a blind child and then it could be in the best interests of a greater number of people to send the child away.

Children under five are known to suffer from such a break in relationship, needing to form an emotional attachment to one person. Older children who are happy and secure in the knowledge that they are loved and who have developed a sense of their own value can successfully accept separation from their families. They can then benefit from admission to a residential blind school.

The Child's Future

Parents often believe at first that their child is going to be severely limited in what he will manage at school and later on in jobs. But blind people take up a number of professions successfully; they make good lawyers, musicians, teachers, therapists, switchboard operators and computer programmers.

They manage businesses and engage in many other occupations. There is a wide range of equipment, such as enlarging screens for print, which is designed for use by poorly sighted children and adults. Optacon machines enable the blind to read print or writing; a tiny camera focuses on the print which is transferred into a raised letter and 'read' by the fingers. These and other devices help to overcome disability.

Agency Support

For the parents of a visually handicapped child the future seems at times difficult and bleak, but it need no longer be thought of as an insurmountable tragedy to be without sight.

There is a great deal of support to be had from the health visitor, who is a trained nurse, from the family doctor and a number of local agencies. These are able to send experienced counsellors to the home, bringing with them useful items on loan or trial as well as recommended reading material.

Blind Mothers

When one considers that a number of blind mothers have children they successfully take care of, then it can be appreciated that loss of vision does not mean the end of the world. Such a mother can be quite independent, keeping her house in order, going out shopping, walking in familiar parks and even sharing books which her child looks at whilst she reads a braille version. Considering the way they cope, one can appreciate that a very good quality of life is possible for blind people.

One of the best ways for families to learn about dealing with their new problems is to meet with people who have had similar experiences. The story of Judith and the accident which blinded her illustrates how she, and her family, overcame their problems.

Judith was already at a school for the blind when I met her and her family. We sat in the grounds of a substantial house set among groups of old trees, the leaves of which varied in shade from gold to dark green. Rose bushes bloomed in a variety of colours, but the children playing on the lawn saw nothing of this. They could, however, feel the peace and beauty of the place. The scents and shapes of the trees, bushes and flowers were familiar to them. They saw with their fingers and moved confidently outside in the gardens as well as inside the house. It was open day and the visiting parents were charmed by the gracious old house and soothed by the serenity of the pleasant environment.

Peter talked about his ten-year-old daughter, Judith, and the accident that had changed life for the whole family. Peter was a teacher at a comprehensive school and his wife, Sarah, had given up her teaching job when their second child was born. Judith was playing in the front garden when a heavy corner tile slipped from the roof and crashed on to her. The five-year-old girl was knocked unconscious. She was rushed to hospital and underwent surgery. Her general recovery was good, but there was bad news. Her sight was gone.

In the period that followed Sarah nursed her daughter like a baby. She did everything for her and could not bear her to be away from her side. It was Peter who realised that Judith could never learn to be independent whilst living with the family. It took months to persuade his wife that Judith needed specialist teaching away from the home, but eventually the mother gave in and Judith went to a school for the blind.

She came home for holidays a different child. She was confident, learning to read her favourite books in braille and her teachers were delighted with her progress. Sarah recognised the improvement and, despite her unhappiness at her daughter's necessary absence, agreed that she should continue with residential schooling.

The Conclusions

An accident like this devastates a family. The heart-break is followed by self-doubts, guilt and depression. Fortunately, the father was strong enough to make sensible decisions about his daughter's future and events proved him right. Both parents and an elder brother came to terms with the tragedy and were able to feel proud of the child's accomplishments at school.

Judith is now nineteen. She is a telephone receptionist and has mastered the Optacon machine which she carries with her. She travels around the country extensively, and is very independent.

10 Hearing Loss

People generally do not appreciate what a severe handicap deafness can be or understand that speech and communication depend upon hearing.

The deaf child lives in a silent and often quite incomprehensible world. But once deafness is recognised, the type of abnormality known and the extent of the hearing loss measured, then treatment can begin. The child can make the most of residual hearing and become part of the everyday world.

Early Diagnosis Vital

There is increased awareness about child development which has led to the earlier diagnosis of deafness. It is unusual nowadays to find that children from two to four, and even five, years of age remain undiagnosed even though quite severely deaf. But it *still* happens too often.

There is a statutory obligation for health visitors to examine babies' hearing at eight months. However, it is certainly recommended that this should never inhibit earlier referral whenever parents feel concerned. By the age of eight months a baby may have lost valuable hearing time. Infant deafness is not very common and consequently is not readily recognised. Many parents of hearing impaired children say that their children's problems would have been far less if they could have been diagnosed earlier.

Early Sound Awareness

Tests have shown that even prior to birth babies are aware of sound. Following birth they respond as they hear the sound of the mother's approach. At eight to ten weeks babies will turn their heads towards the source of sounds. They will make copying noises and musical gurgles and a mother who suspects that her baby is not hearing properly should get an assessment at the earliest opportunity.

During the first months a great store of sounds is accepted by the brain and categorised. Pleasant or unpleasant, loud or soft, angry or soothing. The recognition of noise is an essential step in the process of learning and taking normal part in family and community life.

Some areas have walk-in clinics where parents can take children for hearing assessment. Sophisticated equipment is available and carefully prepared screening techniques are employed once a problem is suspected.

Loss of Tones

If we do not hear clearly our understanding may be limited quite severely. We do not, for example, speak in monotones. Our voices go up and down, loud and soft. If we are robbed of part of the range it becomes difficult to comprehend what is said to us.

Parents Know

Parents are the most practised and motivated observers of their own offspring and should be made aware of what to look for when hearing is faulty. What does a deaf baby do? What noises can a deaf baby hear? The mother's sneeze or cough may sound just the same as the baby's own name.

The fact that a hearing problem exists may have evidenced itself in several ways and these signs may have been ignored. It is easier for some of us to quieten fears than to face unpalatable truth; easier to accept an opinion that all is well because that is what one would wish. When an assessment establishes that there is deafness parents feel a great burden of responsibility. A frequent reaction is an unwillingness to accept the diagnosis. But the first step to helping the child is to *face reality*.

Facing Facts

Hearing loss will not go away and parents can best help the child by accepting a challenge and a long-term commitment. Help will be forthcoming. Professional advice will reduce or overcome problems. Immediately the diagnosis is made and hearing loss measured then hearing-aids will be properly fitted by experts, and the child's listening age established. This starts when the child begins to hear. The months or years of loss of hearing are subtracted from the child's actual age. A four-year-old fitted with a hearing-aid at two will have a listening age of two years.

The question of why a child is deaf is extremely important to the whole family. If there is a genetic problem, then the sooner that is recognised the better. The family must understand what the chances are that the deafness will occur in additional children.

If hearing is to be normal then there must be a perfect functioning of the outer, middle and inner ears. Sound is conducted along the channel of the outer or middle ear and if something prevents vibration and transmission of sound then a hearing problem will result and is known as conductive deafness. It is usually regarded as curable or partially curable. The hearing loss involved is somewhat less serious and may go undetected for some time.

If the abnormality occurs beyond the middle ear along the pathway known as the inner ear, nerve deafness is caused, known as sensori-neural deafness.

Sensori-Neural Deafness

This is a difficult condition and is not capable of correction. The degree of damage varies from mild loss to a complete loss of hearing and the cause may never be known.

What Causes Deafness

There are three main causes of deafness; pre-natal damage to the ear as the baby develops, damage at the time of birth, and impairment due to an inherited defect.

When the child is growing in the womb it sometimes happens that imperfections occur causing hearing loss. These rare malformations usually affect one ear only, and the child will manage perfectly well. Corrective operations, whether for hearing or cosmetic reasons, can be considered when the child is older.

At the time of birth, damage may be unavoidable or due to mismanagement and if there is any degree of impairment to the brain, loss of hearing may result.

Hereditary Deafness

Hereditary or familial deafness is handed down from parents or from ancestors. Where both parents of a deaf child have normal hearing they are described as having dominant hearing factors, but they may carry recessive genes which will produce deafness in their offspring. If the mother carries a recessive sensori-neural deaf factor and marries a man with no such recessive factor then the dominant normal factor will override and the child is safe from damage.

However, in those rare cases where both normal hearing parents carry recessive hearing loss factors each of their children faces a twenty-five per cent chance of inheriting a pair of sensori-neural deaf genes which will cause deafness.

Genetic Counselling

Those parents whose child has impaired hearing for some unknown or hereditary cause should seek advice from a genetic counsellor. These specialists can explain how disabilities arise and what chance there is of another child in the family inheriting the deafness. The child too will want to know, when he is adult and considering marriage and parenthood, about the likelihood of the problem passing to the next generation.

Acquired Deafness

Blood tests to assure would-be mothers whether rubella antibodies are present can easily be carried out, removing the fears of a child being born with defects from this cause. Take-up figures for inoculations against rubella should be higher than they are. This particular handicap could be so easily eradicated.

Proper antenatal care will ensure that the mother is either inoculated or aware that she must immediately report to her doctor any undue symptoms — however slight. The risk for the child is greatest during the first three months of pregnancy.

Jaundice and Viral Causes

Jaundice due to various factors may occur, resulting in impairment to the hearing nerve. This is more likely to occur in premature and undersized for date babies. Rhesus incompatibility can produce injury to hearing mechanism, but this is now extremely rare since preventive measures are taken wherever required.

Deafness in older children may result from viral infection. Very rarely, measles has caused sensori-neural deafness and sometimes mumps will cause heavy loss of hearing in one ear. Even influenza has been known to cause damage to the delicate cochlea within the ear resulting in impaired hearing.

A significant cause of sensori-neural deafness is meningitis. This inflammation of the membrane covering the brain can leave damage to the fragile cochlea. The danger of permanent impairment is averted in most cases due to the prompt use of antibiotics.

Some of the acquired forms of deafness have to be regarded as permanent and no operation or treatment currently available can correct the condition. Perhaps scientific research will one day make implantation of new cochleae or auditory nerves possible.

Avoidable Dangers

Young babies and children are liable to ear infections and it is as well to understand how they may be caused and how some of them may be avoided. Each ear leads through a passage called the outer ear to the inner drum. On the other side of this is an area called the middle ear which leads to the back of the throat via small tubes. Because young babies spend a lot of time lying down infections can spread along this route.

Letting a baby feed from a bottle while lying flat may free a parent to get on with other tasks, but it is not a good idea. Milk or vomit may travel up the tubes to the middle ear giving rise to infection or even danger of suffocation.

Wax in the Ears

Wax is a natural secretion in the ear and performs a necessary task, lubricating, waterproofing and protecting the inner parts. Ears should never be probed.

Wax on the outer edges can be gently removed. Any foreign bodies should be floated out or removed by a doctor.

Glue Ear

Numbers of children in schools across the country suffer from an often undiagnosed condition. These children lose a great deal of what is going on in the classroom and consequently they fall behind other pupils. They flounder on trying to comprehend what other children find so easy, and their school work and social development are affected.

What happens is that mucus collects in the middle ear and the condition is known as glue ear. Any adults concerned with children, their parents, family, doctors, nurses or teachers should be alert to the possibility that hearing is impaired. Glue ear occurs more commonly in children from deprived areas where it is less likely to be diagnosed and treated.

Residual Hearing

Whatever causes the hearing loss, the task remains for everyone concerned with the welfare of the deaf child to achieve the maximum potential possible from any residual hearing. It is the child who is important as well as the disability which can be overcome. Finding the best way to do this will involve parents, family, doctors and associated medical workers who form a team. There should be equal partnership at discussions, although much of the work will fall upon the parents for they are with the child for the greatest time.

It is unlikely that there will ever be a sufficient provision of speech therapists. The number of therapists who work solely with children has reduced in recent years, and is now below what is thought to be an acceptable level. In fact, no professional can possibly give enough time to enable any single child to reach the full potential attainable.

Speech Development

Whichever form deafness takes it is obviously an urgent matter to have a proper assessment at an audiological centre. Corrective action may be taken and management of the child's disability considered so that there is the least possible loss of language and comprehension.

The age at which children begin to speak varies a great

deal. Speech is such a landmark in development that there is often needless anxiety if there appears to be delay. In most cases there is no cause for alarm. Babies who are hearing clear speech will build up memories of sound and in their own time will speak.

Teaching Skills to Parents

Parents have more resources and useful knowledge within themselves than they ever take credit for. They have to be taught by therapists how to put that know-how to good use and make their child oral.

They will learn to speak clearly, preferably with child and parent face-to-face; to make comments familiar through daily use, to read and use pictures to describe activities. This repetitive constant teaching pays dividends.

Radio and TV are no substitute for personal attention and will not give equivalent results. The normal hearing child has heard many thousands of hours of talking. There is a lot of catching up to do for children disadvantaged by lack of diagnosis of hearing loss.

However, once a parent has learned enough to teach the child and has the commitment and determination to ensure that discipline is maintained, then that child has a very good chance of achieving normal speech. Some parents will say that they feel useless. No parents are useless and they will soon come to realise that they can do a great deal.

Education

There is more chance now than ever before that hearing impaired pupils will spend at least part of their school lives working with normal hearing pupils.

The isolation of children into deaf schools set a pattern that tended to repeat throughout life. Segregation in most cases is no longer thought necessary and normal children who work alongside impaired children have the opportunity to know and understand each other. This welcome change in educational policy is just one of the reasons why children with serious deafness have a better chance of achieving clear speech and good education.

Obviously, children with disabilities do have special needs and these may best be met by having certain lessons separately. Units within normal schools are set up so that these children can benefit from appropriate education according to those needs. Residential colleges for deaf children may be thought advisable for some part of school life. These are discussed in the chapter on education.

Discipline Needed

It is not helpful to be over-protective and try to compensate children for handicap by letting them off homework or household duties. Hearing impaired children may seem immature for their years. The loss of hearing and learning time and the lack of communication impose a severe strain on the young child. Living in a silent world or a world where sounds cannot be interpreted can mean intense frustration.

It is not unnatural that deaf children suffer uncontrollable bouts of ill temper and bad behaviour. Sometimes parents do feel hopeless and perhaps momentarily regret that their child was ever born or that they ever met their spouse, let alone married them. But such feelings pass and when understanding of language and skills of speech develop it becomes easier to teach socially acceptable manners. Bouts of obstreperous behaviour lessen until eventually the reasons for them disappear and a happy child emerges.

As the successes continue and speech is learned, as communication becomes normal, so the relationships within the family become more positive and meaningful. Love and affection grow, strains reduce and life becomes enjoyable.

Cost of Handicap

Undoubtedly there is additional strain on families having children with any kind of handicap. There is less freedom for the parents themselves and a greater proportion of time and finance goes to the handicapped child. Siblings see this as unfair unless they understand clearly the reasons why one child is singled out.

Children will copy the attitudes of adults and any feelings of resentment shown by an adult towards a child who requires extra attention will be mirrored by the other children. On the other hand, care that is too zealous can lead to over-protective attitudes on the part of the parents, older sisters and brothers, and could prevent the deaf child from developing the necessary independence.

Recognising All the Problems

The external influences around the family need to be known so that problems can be fully appreciated by advisers.

Is there an extended family living nearby and are they helpful? Do grandparents blame their children's wives or husbands for the handicap? Are there complaints that the child is given too much time? Are families getting the right kind of support, whether financial or emotional? Is there a problem with the hearing-aid or has the child been teased or bullied at school?

It needs patience to detect the problems and more patience to find the answers.

Marital Counselling

If there is already a weakness in the relationship between husband and wife, breaking point may be reached when new strains are imposed. Counselling by trained personnel may reveal why things have been going wrong and can result in greater understanding, and the renewal of happiness between the parents.

Children with special needs should have the loving support of both their parents. It is not always possible to resolve differences, but at least efforts should be made to reach agreement. If outside help is needed it should be sought and used by both partners.

Family doctors recognise and understand what strains are put upon families with a handicapped member and can provide sympathetic and practical advice. They can also recommend associations where useful advice can be given. Community medical services vary from district to district. Groups like the National Deaf Children's Society know what is available and where. Useful addresses and telephone numbers are given later in this book.

Value of Shared Experience

Parents often say how much they benefit when they can talk to someone who has been through the trauma of having a deaf child. Learning informally with others about dealing with problems is easier and knowing that other parents came through their experiences successfully gives them hope and the courage to go on.

The experience of Karen and her family demonstrates both the depths of despair as well as the satisfaction and joy of success which go along with having a severely deaf child. Karen appeared to be a bright baby, but, although she sat and crawled early and walked at a year, she didn't seem keen to start talking and sometimes was not responsive. Susan and Charles, her parents, felt concerned, but everyone else in the family seemed to think there was nothing unusual about the child.

In response to Susan's worry, Karen had taken three tests by the age of two-and-a-half years. Her mother felt sure that something was wrong and became increasingly worried, despite the child's apparent good health and intelligence. Karen had fits of bad temper and would bang her head on the wall if she didn't get her own way. She seemed self-willed and obstinate and did not always respond when called. By now there was a second child, a boy, who at a year was making sounds his sister had never made.

Susan returned to her doctor yet again asking for another hearing assessment for the little girl. 'Are you sure,' the doctor asked, 'that you are not worrying over nothing? She's very healthy and she does have a baby brother to concentrate on.' The mother was obdurate. 'Doctor, I know that something is wrong. Please, please let her be tested for hearing.' The doctor walked behind Karen and rattled some keys. The child turned at once and Susan's heart jumped. She felt mixed relief and pessimism. 'Doctor, she doesn't always respond. Please!'

At the hospital the waiting-room was full. Susan couldn't take her eyes from a boy of about five years who sat with his mother. He wore a black box-like hearing-aid on his chest and each time he fiddled with it his mother gently chided him. There were other children there and as Susan listened to their flat voices she knew that they were deaf. Karen joined them in play and her mother felt that she surely could not be deaf, she was so bright and alert. Only her talking was delayed.

Susan's turn came and picking up her little daughter she walked into the room and sat in the indicated chair. The lady doctor smiled at her reassuringly saying, 'We are going to test Karen for the high and low sounds which are present in ordinary speech. Please hold her quite naturally on your lap but don't move or react yourself in any way to anything we do or say.' The minutes ticked slowly away. Half an hour went by. Still the tests went on.

Susan described to her husband what had happened. 'First she was on my lap; a nurse attracted her attention with a toy whilst the doctor made noises behind us. The noises got louder and louder but Karen didn't respond.

'They put her on the floor with some blocks and showed her what to do when they signalled. She caught on quickly. They signalled first in her left ear and then her right ear with various degrees of noises. I could not believe she didn't hear. Only at the loudest did she turn.

'Then they tested her using an audiometer. I knew it had to be bad news. She was playing on the floor and I just let the tears come. The doctor came, took my hands in hers and told me that Karen was very deaf. I felt so bad. How could this happen to us?'

Susan reproached herself. 'We thought she was self-willed and obstinate, but the poor baby didn't hear us. They said her condition was inoperable and gave me this hearing-aid. All the way home I thought, "She can't hear the traffic, she can't hear the birds, she can't hear that car door banging or those children shouting. Or the television, or the radio. All those lullabies we sang to her at night. She never heard us. She only watched us. No wonder she never talked".'

Charles and Susan were stunned by this confirmation of their worst fears. They had felt relief when tests showed that she had no problem; inaccurate tests that gave an incorrect diagnosis.

Children like Karen need to have deafness assessed at the earliest possible age. Training can commence straight away to compensate for the hearing loss and valuable months are not then wasted. By the age of two years hearing children have already accumulated a store of sounds and understand many words.

The deaf child has no way of knowing what anyone or anything is called or indeed that everyone and everything has a name. The loss of some of the tones can mean that many noises sound exactly the same. Parents feel bitter and angry that their children's opportunities to learn language are lost through inept testing. Whenever hearing loss is suspected expert testing must be available on demand. And in most districts it is.

The cause of some forms of deafness may remain unknown. In the case of Karen the condition was diagnosed as sensori-neural and may have been present before her birth. The cause might have been due to an inherited genetic factor although a second child was unaffected. Since neither parent had any hearing problems and there was no traceable hearing problem in any branch of the family it could only be assumed that Karen's defective hearing was congenital, that is to say, present at birth but for unknown reasons.

Karen grew to speak well. This was due to the determined efforts put into her training by speech therapists, teachers and both of her parents which have enabled her to enter normal hearing school. She lip-reads, benefits from the most up-to-date hearing-aids and, with the sympathetic collaboration of her schoolfriends and teachers, is academically successful.

Karen has been fortunate. The commitment of her family ensured that she learned to speak well. The struggles that parents have before they acquire the services their children need make it clear that there are insufficient resources available in Britain. We lag behind other countries. In Sweden, for example, the right of deaf children to learn sign language as well as speech is established. Parents have the choice. The fact is that the quality and range of our deaf children's education must be decided not only by the experts but by parents as well.

11   Profound and Multiple Handicap

It is rare for a child to have a single handicap uncomplicated by additional problems. In the sense that cystic fibrosis is a breathing problem but also produces digestive problems it is a multiple handicap. Other inherited diseases like muscular dystrophy produce many disorders as the disease progresses and functions fail consecutively or collectively.

Loss of vision can mean there is delayed mobility because there is no desire on the part of a child who cannot see, to crawl or walk. Loss of hearing means loss of speech development and frequently such a degree of frustration that in addition there are problems of behaviour.

Multiple Handicap at Birth

For many children profound and multiple handicap is evident at birth. The cause may not immediately or indeed ever be clear. Perhaps there is an inherited factor, a dominant gene passing directly from a parent. Or perhaps the child has linked to an ancestor via a recessive gene that has been carried forward, unnoticed and ineffective until now.

Some recognisable forms of damage give rise to the suspicion that there will be other forms of handicap to watch out for, so that, for example, sight and hearing loss may occur together. The part of the brain responsible for one sensation may be so close to another that a second impairment is likely to be caused. Such children at least have the advantage that they will be properly assessed and quickly diagnosed.

Viral or Accidental Causes

The disabilities may be caused by a virus or drug or some

mishap during pre-natal growth. And perhaps there has been mismanagement at birth or some unavoidable occurrence. Following birth the reason for disability is usually evident, attributable to infection or accident.

Disabilities like rheumatic fever, which, although now rare in this country, is still responsible for much acquired heart disease in the world's children, can result in multiple problems. Accidents involving spinal injury may mean either the loss of function or a reduction in ability of more than one part of the body.

Regular Assessment

Whatever the cause may be, however it has happened, it is important that for such children accurate diagnosis is made of each and every disability at the earliest possible time. Regular reassessments must be arranged.

Three-quarters of the children who have cerebral palsy also have problems with speech or feeding because of a lack of co-ordination of the tongue and lip muscles. It is the area of the brain in which damage occurs which determines what and where the malfunction will be.

Parents Recognising Symptoms

Mothers who recognise additional problems in an already handicapped child must have the confidence in themselves and their doctors to express their fears, and know that they will be listened to. A troubled mother may say, 'I know it is his legs that are the problem, but he's now taking a long time to chew his food.' Telling her not to be silly and to change her child's diet is no help at all. An acknowledgement that her fears may be justified and that steps will be taken to investigate the new problem comforts the mother, making her feel that her opinion counts, that she and her doctor are doing the best that can be done for the child.

Of course, there are fathers and mothers who separately

or jointly worry unduly, but they are fewer than is supposed. Parents are the experts about their own children, they have them constantly under their care and their observations are invaluable. The medical profession is coming to accept this and to take the parents' judgement into account when evaluating a child's condition.

Handicap Affects Staff

The first news of handicap is distressing not only to the family but also to doctors and nurses. Medical staff feel personally involved at the birth of a child and bad news affects them deeply. When it is immediately apparent following birth that a baby is profoundly impaired it is not just the parents who are upset. Doctors and nurses who were present when thalidomide infants were delivered with limb deficiencies told of the distress and shock they felt at the time and of how those memories stayed to trouble them for many years.

Parents can be comforted by knowing that their distress is shared by medical personnel. A cold and clinical approach seems so heartless, deepening pain. There should be an opportunity for families to talk to experienced counsellers about their child as soon as possible after the birth. It is at this time that suffering and confusion are felt and resentment can arise from which both parents and child may take years to recover. Care should be taken so that the weeks, months and years ahead are viewed in a positive way.

Negative Outlook

Pregnancy should be a time for dreaming of a bright future with a child who will bring cause for pride and happiness. These dreams may seem to end with the birth of a profoundly handicapped infant. Years of caring loom ahead. People cannot imagine how they will cope and may feel anger that such a big problem has entered their lives.

A Positive Side

There is certainly, however, a positive side and happiness and success come to profoundly handicapped people and their families too, bringing a satisfying sense of achievement.

Reactions to the news of disability vary from one person to another. Some cannot accept that a child has the least imperfection whilst others can only think of ways to help their baby, no matter how disabled the child may be. They feel amply rewarded for all the hard work involved in the nursing, caring and education by each small improvement of the child's behaviour or health.

Coping

Coming to terms with disability, accepting whatever that may entail, is essential. So often I marvel at the serenity and contentment in a household with a child whose disabilities make for constant sacrifice and hard work. These are families who may not have taken a single day's respite from their duties in many years and yet they bear themselves with equanimity, making the best of everything. Often these are families with firm religious faith who accept a child with very special needs as a sacred charge and not as a burden.

The Fethneys are one such family who have brought up three profoundly and multiply disabled children as well as two who are able-bodied. They have founded a charity, CRYPT, which encourages artistic talent in handicapped people, providing accommodation and independent living as well as tuition. It is a real privilege to know them and to acknowledge the contribution they have made, improving the lives of many handicapped children and adults alike.

The Questions

Parents have many questions to ask about children with

handicap. What help is available? How do we tell other people? Explain to other people? What about education? What specialists can we see? What will the future hold? They need full and frank answers.

It is not always possible to forecast what the future will hold. So many parents have been told that their children will be unable to speak or walk, only to find that the years do bring improvement and that perhaps their child has managed after all to walk with callipers and go to normal school. Doctors don't like to be optimistic and then have parents blame them for raising their hopes unduly. They are understandably reluctant to anticipate what the outcome will be.

The wisest thing is to establish those aspects of a child which are normal. Families need time to become accustomed to the idea of an extremely disabled child growing up in their midst, but if they have some positive factor to encourage them then they are better able to cope.

The Ideal Community

A handicapped child who could be accepted into a community which showed compassionate understanding and the desire to share the care and the burdens, financial or otherwise, would have comparatively few problems. Families would have an easier time, everyone would share the duties of caring for special needs as a matter of course and no one would look askance at another person. There would be dignity and a good quality of life for all, a regard for the ability of anyone who might be handicapped rather than for their disability.

But how often does one find such an ideal and enlightened community? Attitudes are changing, but not quickly enough to benefit our handicapped neighbours. Some people are so ignorant of handicap and have so little understanding as to be cruel – knowingly or unknowingly.

A Street Experience

I met a mother by appointment in the street who handed her child to me as she got the pushchair out of her car. The little girl was seven years old with severe cerebral palsy. I cradled her in my arms and kissed her forehead, a greeting which she liked. Her facial muscles were not easily controllable, but I knew that her expression passed for a smile.

A passer-by paused, watched as we placed her in the pram, muttered 'That ought to be put down,' and walked away. I registered shock and anger but the mother restrained me. 'You get used to it,' she said. 'It's no use telling someone like that how much we love this child. And how she loves us.'

That little girl was very handicapped. The youngest of five children, she was cherished by the whole family. She enjoyed television and had her favourite programmes, loved ice-cream and hated bananas. She had her own distinct personality and within her family and her special school she was accorded the respect due to her. Outside she needed protection from the abuse of ignorant people.

Education

For children like this, special schools probably remain the way to provide the best possible training and education, but there should not be total separation from normal children.

The integration of handicapped children within normal schools (even though in special units) is, in my view, the way forward, but it is essential that there be an adequate provision of staff and equipment. Able-bodied children can then understand at first hand what it means to be handicapped and learn how people who are affected can best be helped. Thus enlightened they can get to know the disabled children in their own communities, and can include them in their activities and friendships. And they grow to be tolerant and compassionate adults.

Those children who must be sent to special schools outside of their own areas do not get the same opportunities to strike up acquaintances or enter into friendships locally. They remain lonely and unknown by the neighbourhood children. Small wonder that they and their parents sometimes feel ostracised.

Family Involvement

When children with very special and demanding needs are in a family of a few brothers and sisters, sharing their parents' time and possessions, problems do arise.

It matters where in the family such children come. If they are the youngest then other children have had a chance to be the important, attention-taking members and may resent a new baby who demands such a large share of adults' time. But they may, as I have seen, welcome the addition and cherish the child in a protective fashion, each becoming adept at nursing and caring.

As far as possible it is a good idea to involve non-handicapped brothers and sisters in the caring duties and the teaching. Giving them responsibility removes some of the feeling of neglect they may experience. They can share in the sense of achievement when there is progress, take pleasure in their personal involvement and feel pride in having a disabled brother or sister who is overcoming handicap. Sharing the burden lightens the load and a sense of fun and pleasure enters the training sessions.

When there is laughter things don't seem so worrying and everyone in the family takes a more positive attitude. The views and ideas of even young children can be surprisingly helpful and wise. Discussions about any future plans should take place within the family circle so that everyone is encouraged to feel equally important. Parents need a lot of professional counselling to help them to cope with the pressures that arise not only in relation to their children, but also in their personal roles as husbands and wives.

Family Unity is Needed

Multiply handicapped children need both of their parents as much as and more than their normal siblings, but that need is not enough to hold an insecure relationship together. A well-founded marriage which has stood for some time is better able to withstand the heavy demands made upon it.

Parents find that there are so many unexpected and new factors to learn about; so much that seems bewildering. Their own self images as independent parents vanish as they find themselves leaning upon therapists, teachers, counsellors and other professionals for advice on what to do and when to do it. They feel guilty about their other children and the lack of time to give them the attention they need. They have to learn specific techniques and how to use them to educate their handicapped children whilst still finding time for others in the family.

Community Should Share the Problem

It is up to the community to share in the tremendous task of caring for a child with special needs. Neighbours can offer a baby-sitting rota so that mothers are free to shop or to take a break. Proper support has to be provided to families so that they never feel friendless or alone.

The GP is a key figure whose interest and support are vital. He or she will be sure to have a knowledge of local social service and voluntary provision and will ensure that the family who needs such provision gets it. Referrals to specialist assessment units, occupational, physio and speech therapy training in sufficient quantity, home helps, respite care, all must be provided if community care is to become a reality.

Benefits and Allowances

A number of benefits are available and parents need to know what can be claimed and at what age and what other relevant criteria needs to be detailed.

Citizens Advice Bureaux are a useful source of advice and information and can provide support for clients at times of stress.

Social Workers

Social services are always under pressure, but those families with children having special needs take a high priority on their list of clients. Social workers will give practical as well as sympathetic advice and part of their job is to ensure the well-being of all the children in their area. They also know about special services and can make recommendations for holidays and respite care placement to their authorities.

In addition they concern themselves with the provision of services and equipment and will undertake fund raising when this is necessary. They become involved and concerned about the families allotted to them and can get as frustrated as anyone at the limitations on provision of essential needs.

Inadequate Resources

Profoundly and multiply handicapped children were thought at one time to be ineducable and parents had to find private resources to pay for the education of their children. The 1970 Education Act required the Department of Education and Science to make provision for the education of all children regardless of the severity of their handicap. This has led to a more satisfactory state of affairs, but there is by no means sufficient finance allotted to give these children the best chance of development.

There is a limit to the amount of money the Government

is prepared to put in. Until the day when public attitudes have changed further, demanding that adequate provision should be a priority, such children will continue to be denied the opportunity to reach their maximum potential and they and their parents will continue to be frustrated and disappointed.

Expert Diagnosis

Where there is multiple impairment careful diagnosis must be made of each handicapping condition by professionals whose training ensures that they are up-to-date and aware of the latest methods of assessment.

Cost of Disability

The cost to the community of a multiply handicapped person is very high. Demand in health and education fields will always exceed resources, but it seems wise to press for more research that will show how to reduce the chance of handicap as well as to find better ways of relieving disabilities once they have occurred.

Charities, businesses and drug companies do contribute considerable sums to research projects. Government ministers must constantly weigh the priorities when considering where and how money should best be spent – never an easy task.

Prevention

Prevention of the birth of multiply handicapped babies is possible where a recognisable family genetic factor is known to have caused the fault. Amniocentesis involves the withdrawal and testing of a sample of the fluid surrounding the foetus to determine whether the child will inherit a familial problem. Positive identification of handicap may result in advice to terminate the pregnancy.

Whenever a mother contracts German measles (as rubella is known), medical advice should be sought immediately. Unfortunately it is not always recognised when this disease is present since it may be of only a few days' duration and characterised by the slightest of symptoms. This is why all schoolgirls should be immunised.

Rubella children, fortunately few in number because of immunisation, are generally anticipated to have hearing and sight problems, so there is little doubt about their benefiting from correct early diagnosis and referrals for remedial treatment.

A Rubella Baby of Yesteryear

Thirty years ago Anna was born, a severely affected rubella child whose birth emotionally disturbed the entire family. She needed an immediate heart operation and recovered well. Her hearing and sight were poor and the day school she went to was not able to give her sufficient teaching time to encourage her progress.

After two normal siblings had arrived it was decided that it was in everyone's best interests for the little girl to go to a residential school. She was taught basic skills and there she made her home, acknowledging her family who visit regularly – but she is unable to communicate to any useful degree.

Opportunities Today

Today's sophisticated hearing-aids and contact lenses as well as new training methods might have helped Anna. Some of the habits which such children adopt, such as eye-poking, staring at lights, rocking and head banging might never have developed.

Anna could possibly have remained part of her family, her parents receiving instruction in an early teaching programme while she had the stimulation of special therapy. She might have succeeded in gaining admission in due course to a school unit for those having moderate learning difficulties.

It has been recommended that there should be screening of all of those births considered to be at risk, whatever the reason. In addition, there should not only be an expansion of the health visitors' domiciliary service, as well as more practice nurses employed in surgeries, but GPs should extend their range of services. Health education, pre-pregnancy advice and antenatal care are all part of the support the good GP will offer.

It is essential that more help and advice should be given to handicapped patients and their families.

Special Needs of the Blind and Deaf

Children who have hearing and sight problems alongside physical disablement are deemed to be multiply handi-capped in another sense because their problems require a special form of education and training. If a child has experienced normal sight and hearing even for a year there are memories of vision and sound which help the hearing process.

A child who has begun to speak may never lose the ability. But children who have neither sight nor hearing, nor memories of these, may need time away in a residential school in order to benefit to the maximum from the educational programmes.

Loss of Hearing

The earliest possible diagnosis is vital when hearing problems are suspected. I have stressed before that the neglect or misdiagnosis of deafness is inexcusable bearing in mind that a child learns such an enormous amount in the first months of life. This loss of learning time may never quite be made up.

Parents feel fortunate when they have early diagnosis for their deaf children, especially when they later meet parents whose children were not diagnosed as deaf for two and even three years. They can appreciate the extra problems such families bear and realise that their anger and distress are warranted.

Disabilities may then be put into order of precedence and the child can be directed towards the most suitable school. The aptitudes and abilities of individual children should be considered by a team which includes parents as well as professionals so that everyone involved understands the reasoning behind decisions.

All resources provided in the home area must be considered too. Families have been known to move to districts where their children would benefit from a particular school or where the local councils would be more sympathetic to their needs.

A Profoundly Handicapped Child

One has to get to know profoundly handicapped children to realise what attractive characters they can be. One boy I have known for some years is now eleven. He is the most engaging child, who loves his books and enjoys learning, has an infectious laugh and a mischievous sense of humour.

He and his parents never talk of problems, they say they don't have time for depression and are always fund raising for this or that charity. Their son has little vision and wears heavy spectacles too big for his little nose to support and which are secured by a band round his head. He also wears hearing-aids for both ears because he is profoundly deaf. But that is not all. At the age of six he had to have total amputation of one leg and so wears a false limb.

He seems to have an instinctive knowledge of what is happening around him so that despite his visual handicap he is well aware of everything going on. He has been taught by splendid teachers to speak well. Will someone argue that

106

this courageous child is not worth every penny spent on his care and education?

Recognising the Disability

So many children could be written off as severely mentally disabled when in fact they are merely deaf. They may never have realised that language exists or that people and objects have names – and they live in a confusing world of silence.

Visual problems are more apparent and the loss of sight cannot be masked. Observation of a child serves to tell whether or not vision is impaired. The baby in arms may not seem to have any problems, but an infant who does not reach towards or turn to the mother when she silently approaches should be checked out by the doctor. Children who have squints should not be neglected as these may be an early indication of serious problems later.

Support Services

Profound and multiple handicaps in a child mean that the family will need every bit of support that can be given. Fortunately there are many resources to call on in our society. There is, however, no room for complacency and the balance of care needs to be tipped further to provide adequate back-up. Training, therapy and equipment are all needed for profoundly handicapped children. These needs *must* be met and adequate finance allotted.

Teams Include Parents

Parents become part of teams which may include consultants in relevant specialities such as audiology and ophthalmology as well as GPs, health visitors and physio-, speech and occupational therapists and social workers.

Emotional balance and a positive outlook are important

adjuncts to progress and so psychologists and genetic experts are often brought in to help to achieve this.

Doctors and Patients Learn Together

Many professional people will never previously have encountered a profoundly handicapped child and they and parents learn together by experience what is possible for the child in their care. Extended family members may be found who can provide valuable support; nothing can beat the devotion of a loving grandparent.

Once the child begins school, teachers become part of the scene and need a good understanding of the background in order to counter problems and achieve the best results for the children in their classes.

Music Therapy

Music often releases pent-up emotions in severely handicapped children, producing reactions which they may never previously have experienced. The concentration, absorption and interest exhibited by these children when attending concerts show that they become unusually stimulated. Musicians and singers are able to establish and hold eye contact with them, and music is widely recognised as a valuable form of therapy which should be fully exploited.

For many years The Wingfield Trust, through its volunteers, has bought musical instruments for children with the idea of compensating for their disabilities. For example, a child with asthma would be taught to use a wind instrument.

These youngsters have given public performances and no orchestra ever played with more delight, no audience ever gave a warmer reception. They were under the direction of Bert Lyon, and until his untimely death many handicapped children benefited from his enthusiasm, not only for the music but also for his designs of tricycles which gave so many children mobility. The work of the Trust continues under the capable direction of Barbara Cooke, herself wheelchair-bound since the age of ten.

The Down's Syndrome Child

Down's syndrome children certainly suffer from multiple disadvantages. The difference in these children is complex and is traced to a chromosome variation. Normal cells contain forty-six chromosomes in twenty-three pairs. Down's syndrome children have an extra number twenty-one, and this is not something that can be corrected. What are the effects on the child? They may be varied and include anaemia so acute as to require complete blood replacement. They may have digestive, bladder or bowel problems, but on the other hand may be quite well.

Physically, they are markedly different from other children but in common with each other they have a Mongoloid appearance. This so sets them apart that it can be a serious disadvantage, predisposing people to think that they all have the same limitations. Cosmetic operations have been performed which change these facial characteristics removing what many parents and children believe to be the stigma of the Down's look. However, as children develop, this becomes less noticeable and, what is more important, many of these children are educable, learning to read and write and to undertake household duties and responsibilities outside the home.

Throughout infancy most children and certainly Down's syndrome children learn through mimicry. They can, and do, benefit from integration with ordinary children.

One Down's girl I know was twelve when her mother died. She undertook the care of her father, keeping the house in impeccable order, helping with cooking as well as going to school. She was chosen to take part in a television play and learned her lines with great pride. She may be slower than most normal children and, perhaps, she will never get O levels, but she is a lovely and loving, sociable girl.

Given that there is the will on the part of school authorities, many of these children are capable of learning and keeping up with their normal peers. They benefit from the stimulation of ordinary children and I support the stand of the Down's Syndrome Association which claims that every child should get the chance of normal education. It was no surprise to me to read that a Down's girl of nineteen had got her driving licence and was driving herself to her job daily.

Disabled Does Not Mean Dull

It is a false assumption that handicap and in particular profound multiple handicap necessarily means dull intellect. There are projects where profoundly and multiply handicapped people are housed in independent units where they are assisted in their daily needs by able-bodied neighbouring staff.

Within the project are offices where businesses have been set up by these disabled members of the community. In one room I met a man busy editing a magazine specialising in office equipment. He was well liked, respected, with wide interests and knowledge. He could hardly have been more disabled, having the use of one hand only and being dependent on an electric wheelchair for his mobility. How proud his family must have been of someone who did not allow severe cerebral palsy to prevent his success.

The Carers

The task of caring for the severely multiply disabled is made worthwhile when progress is seen. The discouragement felt by teachers, therapists and parents when an infection or illness sets in to undo weeks or months of therapy and learning can be so disappointing as to cause despair to everyone concerned.

Teachers will say that they felt like changing jobs into some kind of work that offered more chance of success. The determination to go on is eroded when there are repeated set-backs until hope evaporates and people do give up. Parents need support more than ever, their willingness to give their time and devotion to children, to try in all directions to give their children a quality of life, shows a faith and courage of the highest order.

Hospital beds are taken up for months and sometimes years by children so handicapped that their families cannot undertake the degree of care required. The cost is enormous. But what kind of quality of life can these children experience in such circumstances?

Whether at home or in hospital such children require 24-hour care and their lives depend upon the quality of nursing they get. It is not always the parents who provide such devotion. There are many grandparents who, for one reason or another, find themselves as the only support of a severely handicapped child.

The frustration of the child who is given up as ineducable and incapable of any intelligent function whilst having understanding locked within is unbearable to contemplate.

It is estimated that there are 3,000 children in the UK whose severe multiple handicaps are such that they cannot communicate or learn. Sometimes they vent their frustrations by biting themselves, pulling clumps of hair out and self-inflicting other damage. The needs of such children have never yet been met.

Many devoted parents say that they know that their children have knowledge, understanding and intelligence which they cannot transmit by normal means. They themselves establish communication with their child, but are reluctant to take breaks because of what the loss of this would mean to the child.

A Grandmother's Experience

Teresa was three years old and spending the weekend with

her maternal grandparents when she had an epileptic fit. The little girl suffered brain damage which left her incapable of speech or movement. Her mother could not care for her and the grandmother determined to restore her to health.

During all the years while she grew to be a tall and handsome girl the care continued. Birthday parties and Christmas gatherings of the family were centred around the beautifully dressed child who showed pleasure by laughing and smiling but who could not otherwise join in, could never again speak or walk.

The grandmother's care has sustained her, and considerable local and national resources have supported the little family. The early hope that she would one day recover has long gone. No hospital or nursing home, however good, could replace such devotion. The grandmother worries about what will happen when she can no longer care for Teresa.

Support in the Community

It is always hoped that profoundly handicapped children will be enabled to live the richest lives possible and that they and their families will receive the utmost support. They are severely limited in what they can do, they are very dependent on others for their needs, and as children reach adolescence their restricted ability is felt more keenly.

Everyone concerned with the health and well-being of the entire family should be made aware of every possible advantage, either monetary or in services, whether statutory or voluntary. There is no question of charity, only of entitlement. It may be for help with a car through Motability, a holiday, a special wheelchair, a standing frame or respite care. And there is need and entitlement to counselling too, so that worries and emotions, whatever the nature of the feelings on the part of a child or a member of the family, can be expressed and discussed freely.

The responsibility and commitment of carers in these

situations is great. Despondency will be felt at times and it is not only the doctors, nurses, social workers, therapists and teachers but also the extended family, friends, relatives, neighbours and society in general who must make life for our most disadvantaged members as happy as possible.

ACQUIRED DISABILITIES

12 Acquired Disabilities

Statistical figures relating to morbidity and mortality in children in England and Wales show that there are three major influencing factors. They account for almost two-thirds of sickness, disability and death for children aged between one and fourteen years. These factors are accidents, respiratory and viral diseases, and cancers. In addition, despite all precautions, handicaps do still occur in the new-born for reasons which include infection transmitted by the mother prior to birth.

Some malformations seem unavoidable, occurring for no apparent reason. Some are due to drugs or medicines taken by pregnant women perhaps before they realise that they are carrying a child. It is even thought that some substances could affect more distant future generations, altering genetic structures in some way. This may have happened in the past and could explain some of today's problems.

It is logical to recognise that emotional states could conceivably influence the make-up of an unborn child. Hormones, naturally produced might, for example, irritate the foetus, affecting a new-born baby.

The position the baby takes in the womb sometimes affects growth and accounts for malformations like hip displacement or a foot turned the wrong way. Growth is rapid and any interference pre-natally, may result in impairment.

Generally speaking, the baby is very secure within the womb and it is comforting to remember that despite all the hazards most babies grow to full term without any problems during pregnancy or at birth. Among the small percentage who are imperfect are those who pick up infections from the mother via the birth canal.

Infectious diseases scarcely trouble most children, but in

117

a few cases crippling effects are seen, some of which may be reversible whilst others linger on, producing multiple problems which may become permanent disabilities.

Immunisation of children against some common ailments causes a very low percentage of injuries, but the damage through failure to vaccinate would be considerably more. On balance, the risk is well worth taking.

The effects of allergy-producing substances can cause profoundly disabling results and may be due to foods, additives, chemicals and sometimes to medicines. Researchers all over the world compete as well as collaborate to find the reasons for, and the answers to, these and many other related problems. Drug companies support research and continually produce new medicines, some of which are extremely beneficial although they have to be stringently tested before being passed as safe for use.

Nowadays doctors have an immense choice of drugs and procedures which can delay the worst of symptoms, relieving pain, sustaining life and sometimes achieving a complete cure. But they must be monitored carefully for undesirable side-effects in individual cases. Many diseases have been wiped out and it is certain that each decade will bring knowledge that will eradicate more.

The care in this country for children involved in accidents is of a very good standard, but we need to direct more resources to the prevention of accidents for the number who are injured is unacceptably high. Yet statistics show that these numbers are repeated year after year. Since the disappearance of many of the killer diseases of the recent past, accidents are responsible for more deaths and disabilities than any other cause.

Statistics tell us that annually a thousand children lose their lives through drowning while many hundreds die in fires. Cases of accidental poisoning and suffocation, falls, cuts, blows and choking, account for a further 2,000 lives.

It seems incredible to most people that any adult could show violence to their own or anyone else's child, and such behaviour is regarded with abhorrence. Occasionally newspapers will highlight a particularly repugnant case.

But violence within the family and directed at children is not easy to discover or to deal with. What is known is that each and every week on average in the UK, eight children actually die as a result of inflicted violence although not necessarily from within the family.

The incidence of acquired disabilities resulting from all these causes fluctuates very little over periods of years. We know from official statistics that for every child who dies, many more survive, some to recover completely, but many to face permanent disablement.

13   Cerebral Palsy

It is thought that a minority of cerebral palsy cases may be caused through inheritance of defective genes, but almost ninety per cent are reckoned to be acquired otherwise.

The damage can happen prior to the baby's birth but in many cases, although it may be no one's fault, the abnormality is caused at childbirth. Whilst it is rare, it does happen that through human error circumstances combine to produce a damaged child. If this can be proved, then parents can claim on the child's behalf for damages from the Health Authority.

It is not Contagious

Cerebral palsy is neither an illness nor a disease and it certainly is *not* contagious.

The term describes a neurological condition where there has been damage to the developing brain. This results in a disorder of movement and posture, and may lead to either spasticity when there is alternative rigidity and floppiness, athetosis which increases involuntary muscular activity, or ataxia which means there is poor balance and unsteady gait.

Some children have a mixture of two or more of these disorders.

What are the Main Causes?

The reasons for CP are not always easily explained. The damage may occur in a number of ways, quite apart from that minor percentage of cases thought to be due to an inheritance factor. If there should be a lack of oxygen to the brain at any time during pregnancy, damage may occur. There can be a restriction of nutrition passing to the baby. It has been shown that even modest alcoholic drinking may interrupt foetal growth and it is wise to remain teetotal during pregnancy.

If the mother contracts German measles or other infections during the first weeks of pregnancy, the growth of the foetus may be seriously affected in a number of ways causing physical deformity; any abnormalities of blood clots, haemorrhage or malformation can affect the brain – resulting in damage.

Cerebral palsy occurs in about one in every 300 live births and similar conditions are responsible for some of those babies who are stillborn.

It is important to note that a third of all cerebral palsy children are of low birthweight. This is simply because they are not fully developed, are weaker and more easily subject to viral attacks and damage at birth. Better pre-natal care, health education, attention to diet and genetic counselling will reduce the incidence of cerebral palsy, with all its tragic consequences.

It is now possible to recognise some disorders and damage to the foetus early enough in pregnancy to offer termination. This presents both doctor and parents with that most difficult of choices, and all circumstances must be taken into account before making a decision.

Difficulties of Diagnosis

Suspicion that something is wrong may be aroused soon after birth when it is noted that there is poor sucking response or altered muscle tone. The doubts pose a problem for the maternity team who will be reluctant to alarm the parents needlessly.

When doctors find that there is suspicion of disability following birth they hope against hope that those suspicions are groundless, and so often decide to say nothing. And it is sometimes the parents of new babies who find themselves anxious and frustrated by a feeling that all is not well, that something is wrong with their child. They look at other babies and note their growth, development and activities, and make unfavourable comparisons. The family doctor or health visitor should be consulted so that the parents fears may be put at rest; or if confirmed, then specialist opinion can be sought to resolve any doubts about the baby. An early diagnosis is important so that remedial treatment can begin and help to lessen any long term damage.

Life is never going to be quite the same again for the parents whose child is confirmed as having handicap. There cannot be an easy way to break the news to parents that their child is not normal. They have a double shock to bear. First the loss of the perfect baby they have awaited with joyful anticipation during the pregnancy. And then the possession of a child they have mixed feelings about. Dread, dislike, shame, guilt, fear . . . the whole episode is like a nightmare from which there is no awakening. And if no one talks to these parents, tells them that it is all right to feel this way, that these feelings will pass and things will seem brighter, that there is a lot of help to count on, then strain and depression set in and may continue for many weeks or months. Medical advisers have a great responsibility in these situations, and a positive and compassionate family doctor can make all the difference – and give people the courage to go on.

The News is a Shock

There are still medical professional people who think that news of handicap had better be given as quickly as possible, never mind how. One young mother whose child was twenty-four hours old was having her morning tea when the consultant called and said, 'Mrs D., your little girl has cerebral palsy. I shall be coming along to speak to you about it later'.

This mother was in total shock, could hardly speak and had the job of telling her husband this totally unexpected news. How much better if that consultant had made sure that both parents could be told together, given immediate comfort and an opportunity to ask all the questions. And then to ask them all over again, for shock takes away the ability to absorb information.

The feeling of being left alone, almost of being shunned is unbearable. It is a relief to hear parents say that they were given the kindest of care and treated with the utmost concern when they had bad news about their baby.

Early Diagnosis

It can be seen why cerebral palsy, generally referred to as CP, is not always immediately recognisable in young babies. They spend most of their lives sleeping and damage may not be apparent. Any child who fails to kick and move its legs could have a problem. This condition may be suspected within a few days of birth if there are problems in feeding and a lack of movement.

Once home, the mother may feel worried by a lack of development in her child and if by six months there is poor head control or difficulty in sitting up unaided then cerebral palsy is likely to be diagnosed. The term 'floppy baby' is often used. Any anxiety should be freely expressed to the health visitor who is trained in the development of babies and can allay any fears or arrange for the baby to be seen by a consultant.

Coming to Terms with Handicap

The emotional strain of worrying for months that something is amiss is replaced by a feeling almost of relief when a diagnosis is finally made, even though the news is bad. Provided that there is a sense that everything possible is being done to help the child, parents do feel better.

News of disability hits hard, but where a doctor gives time, understanding and sympathy, people feel more hopeful and can adapt to the new situation while preparing to help their baby. The knowledge that people are around who will help – and who care – makes all the difference in the world.

Normal Development

A baby's movements in the first hours and days are not co-ordinated and they simply respond involuntarily. As the child develops, these primitive reflexes become controllable. The eyes focus, neck muscles strengthen and the head can be lifted at will. Hands and arms can grasp objects, and back muscles are strong enough to enable the child to sit. Finally the leg muscles permit standing and walking.

Brain Damage Can Affect Movement

The problems in cerebral palsy do not stem from the nerves or muscles. There is damage to different parts of the brain although there may be no damage to intellect. In order for movement to take place the brain has to give the command for muscles to act, some to tighten and some to let go, all in a co-ordinated fashion. If the information is incorrectly interpreted by the brain then the wanted movement cannot happen.

The brain receives all its messages from its base and any damage in this vulnerable area can result in signals becoming scrambled so that a wish to move a leg might produce movement in an arm and a spasmodic reaction throughout the body; the tongue moves involuntarily in and out, making chewing and swalling difficult.

Everything is out of control, moving at different speeds and in unwanted directions. Unsteady gait and poor balance make walking difficult. If the muscles all stiffen at the same time the child is termed spastic. If the damage has affected that part of the brain which controls balance then the child is unsteady and ataxic.

If one side of the brain has been damaged, it is the

opposite side which will be adversely affected, the condition being known as hemiplegia. When legs are more severely affected than arms it is called diplegia, and when all four limbs are involved the condition is known as quadriplegia.

Half of the children affected by CP have resistant muscles which are stiff and tense, although they may begin as floppy babies, having little or no head control. It is hard for parents to realise the problems these children have. They can lack the ability to feel hot or cold, may not feel pain to the skin, and the facial muscles may not reflect the intelligence of the child.

Sight and Hearing Loss

The areas of the brain which control hearing are so close to those associated with CP that it is important to assess for deafness. Once deaf children receive hearing-aids their educational and social progress is rapid.

Sight problems are more apparent and remedial treatment and glasses can be provided.

Perceptual Damage

Perceptual damage can result in children being unable to tell the difference between large and small things. They may put their clothes on the wrong way round and feel puzzled by the resulting look, read well yet be unable to draw or write legibly.

It takes a lot of patience, understanding and persistent training but improvement does come, making the child, teachers and parents feel well rewarded.

Speech Problems

Speech therapists are essential to the correct development of the CP child because they can work wonders with speech and breathing problems. Chewing food and talking may not be easy and it is intensely frustrating to an intelligent child not to be able to perform functions which come so naturally to most of us.

Parents have to learn therapeutic techniques, for busy professionals can never provide enough time to ensure the child's maximum progress.

The Team Approach

These problems are best dealt with by a team which includes parents so that everyone involved can freely discuss all areas of difficulty. Often the mother, father or another member of the family becomes very knowledgeable and, on encouragement by the doctor and therapists, can make practical and useful suggestions.

A well informed family which understands the reasons for treatment and the physical capabilities of a CP child, and learns how exercises can improve and increase power, is in a better position to help.

Assessing Intelligence

The progress of a young baby is based on performance, but this does not and cannot assess intelligence. It is one of the duties of health visitors to check babies' development. They know that children who cannot walk or talk may well have good levels of comprehension and the ability to learn to do many things which will enable them to achieve a fair degree of independence.

It should not be assumed that the brain damaged child is mentally subnormal. So many parents are told early on that their children can never amount to anything, only to find in later years – as these children develop well – that their advisers were wrong. Many CP children do achieve far beyond what was hoped for them and they need the constant encouragement and assistance of professionals as well as their families, to make the best progress possible.

In general doctors give necessary time and attention and parents are unstinting in their gratitude and praise. But still there are parents who are less fortunate in their medical advisers and who say that doctors give ill-considered advice and seem to regard their opinions and themselves as more important than their patients.

Counselling for Parents

Parents need assurance about their own ability to cope and advice about anything troubling them. It is essential to provide time for discussion to allay doubts and worries. With sufficient professional expertise and good standards of support, most parents, as well as children, come to terms with their disabilities, adjust and make the best of things. The CP child, who is encouraged at home and is bolstered by the love and pride of the family, has a good chance of doing well.

The relationship between professional advisers and parents needs to be strengthened. Parents' experiences and intuitions regarding their own children permit them to make judgements often every bit as good as those of the professional. Parents, and as soon as possible children themselves, should voice their opinions and make known their needs and wishes. Families must have the confidence to consider and examine the effectiveness of advice and services.

Improvement is unlikely to emerge, or to be effective, from individual opinions and must come from group pressure. The Spastics Society is a powerful and influential body which has done a great deal to improve resources for children with a wide range of disabilities. The Cerebral Palsy Society is also able to bring pressure to bear to achieve progress.

Training for Parents

Learning special ways to hold a child, giving manipulative

exercises to develop movement, and positioning children to reduce problems are all skills which therapists can teach to parents. Families who undertake the care of their CP children must not only have considerable support and be included in assessment teams, but need those assessment on a broad base.

Treatment and rehabilitation must be directed towards making the most of all residual ability, resulting in maximum independence. And it must all start early. Children need to be able to share and work in the home whenever it is feasible, using equipment like telephones, radios, televisions and video-recorders. If they are able to use the kitchen and join in cookery and washing-up, then they can feel useful and develop independence. This shared experience within the family helps to bind everyone together and lessens the feeling the disabled child has of being left out.

Prevention of CP

The tragedy of a handicap is heightened when it is needless and caused either by human error, deficiencies in the diet or the poor environment of the least well off families. The need is for more special care units and the nurses to staff them, education about diets beginning at school age and better housing. All of these factors need to be constantly monitored and corrected.

When there is doubt about the cause of handicap added to the suspicion of the parents that human error is involved, bitter feelings grow and every effort should be made to talk to the parents, to explain what has happened and why.

The Cost of Handicap

Leaving aside the emotional cost to the families, to doctors and to paramedical workers the financial burden that is incurred in caring for a severely handicapped individual is very high. Carers within a family may be loving and prepared to give their whole lives to the care of their disabled relatives. This kind of sacrifice has to be eased by a public ready to share their time and money with those who are less fortunate than themselves. More sympathy out in the street from the people, more practical help and understanding, are all needed. The health and happiness of disabled children must be the prime objective of any self-respecting and caring society.

Communication Aids

A variety of communication aids can be recommended by specialist assessment units set up around the country and even the most disabled of children can operate computers which enable them to translate their thoughts into words.

More information about equipment is given later in this book.

Mobility Aids

The provision of mobility aids is necessary for children who cannot walk or stand; there is a wide range of equipment on the market. It is essential to have the best advice in order to decide what is most appropriate.

The natural ability of the child must be encouraged whilst recognising that in order to get around, wheelchairs may have to be used for some of the time. Rollaters encourage independent movement, and there are bracing devices which give structural support allowing joint movement for walking as well as sitting. These are discussed later in the chapter on equipment.

Is CP Progressive?

Provided no new damage occurs there is no reason why the

disability should get worse. However, other functions close to the area of brain damaged could be affected. Non-co-ordination of muscles in the tongue and vocal cords may cause difficulties with speech.

Depending on the site of damage there may be visual problems or a degree of mental retardation, and hearing may be affected. Again, I stress this should not be automatically assumed since intelligence is often present, but cannot be expressed. Once remedial work begins and better communication is established a realistic assessment can be made of the child's capabilities.

Learning Ability

Many extremely handicapped children are bright and respond eagerly to education and training. It is vital that this should be recognised. So many people without experience of handicap cannot absorb the fact that physically disabled children may well be highly intelligent. The fact is that physical disability can often mean that energy is directed to academic prowess and accomplishments, which in normal health would have been dissipated otherwise – possibly in sport or entertainment.

One thirteen-year-old girl is doing well with her studies despite severe handicap, and is determined to follow her parents by becoming a lawyer. Her school work is promising. Her teachers expect that she will succeed in her ambitions.

A boy of eleven, finally able to communicate, composed this poem for the charity who had bought him a specially adapted typewriter.

> I couldn't speak, I couldn't write
> I know they thought 'He isn't bright'
> And all the time I prayed one day
> To have a voice and have my say.
> They made machines, now I can talk
> Say thanks to mum for that nice walk
> Tell dad that I enjoyed his joke

Say many things to many folk
And now I say my thanks to you
For making all those dreams come true.

This was a child who had been thought to be retarded – but who proved otherwise.

Failures of Judgement

When a child is born it is the duty of doctors and nurses to ensure that, as far as possible, their judgements are sound and that no action can occur which might endanger mother or child. The high standards of professional training generally ensure that nothing goes wrong. But they are human and they do make mistakes, perhaps without realising that harm has been done.

A young nurse was left with a mother in labour and knowing that the senior consultant wanted to be present at the birth begged the mother not to bear down. When the baby's head appeared she pushed it back. The child was born with the imprint of five fingers indented on its head. This bright child has never walked and it is always questionable as to whether damage was incurred when that pressure was placed on the head.

A Mother Remembers

Barbara came from Ireland to train as a nurse. She qualified as an SRN, married a laboratory technician and returned to her own hospital to have their first baby. She was a robust girl who had never known a day's illness and thought that having a baby was the most natural thing in the world.

Medical staff know very well that not all babies are perfect, but Barbara had no misgivings about her own child and thought that her baby would be perfectly normal and healthy. She felt confident that nothing would go wrong for her in the experienced care of the maternity team. Later, when she went back over events as they had occurred she felt that her training enabled her to judge that mistakes had been made. She tells her story.

'My daughter has cerebral palsy, diagnosed at six months. Not that anyone said anything to me personally. No one *ever* said anything to me.

'I had twenty-two hours in labour after induction. I had quite a fever and the baby had too. There were twenty-two hours of suffering. Agony for me and the baby – as well as for my husband. He was there too, all those hours, falling asleep or holding my hand. We were just left by ourselves almost the whole time.

'A registrar put his head round the door, but when he heard that I was a special staff patient and under the consultant he backed out. No one dared come near me it seemed. I'd have been far better off with a junior registrar, or a midwife. The consultant looked in a couple of times and just went away, giving his orders. I was left too long. Even the sister didn't question those orders. He was too important, that consultant.

'We are so angry – we've always felt angry. I've thought . . . I could bear it if she had spina bifida or something genetic, but I think this is human error. I can't bear mistakes – not ones that could do this.

'In the end I had a vacuum delivery. Poor baby, her head was black and blue, and she shouted when she was born. Shouted! I never heard anything like it – I went rigid with fright. Is she handicapped? I pushed the dreadful thought away.

'She was eight pounds and three ounces. She cried and grumbled a lot. She fed well, but her head was so sore. You couldn't touch it. She'd pull away. All round the fontanelle it was bruised and angry looking.

'Nobody said anything – nothing. At eight days we went home and she slept, ate well, was terribly sensitive to noise. "Come back in three weeks," they said. Then a further three months, and never any comments. Six months after her

132

examination I was told she needed physiotherapy and handed a card to take to the department. On the card it said CP. That's how I knew. She was lively and slept well at night. We thought, well she's not *very* handicapped.

'I breast-fed her. That was the only time I could cuddle her. At six months we were referred to a treatment centre. I learned to do her physiotherapy and did it every day. At two years of age she went daily to the centre. She wasn't walking and, still, nobody asked what had happened or anything. We took her to a homeopathic hospital. I told them what had happened at her birth. "Could that have caused her to be cerebral palsied?" I asked. They were cautious but "Yes, it could," they said. I know it was human error that caused the damage – I could burst with anger. Why didn't they speak to me about it? It was so unnatural, just letting me go home with my damaged baby.

'Linda is eight now. She's realising she can't do things her brother does. He's six and fine. He loves her, but she is jealous and thinks we love him better. I do nag her. She's supposed to sit straight, stretch her legs. She won't, and I'm frightened she'll lose hard-won improvement and get worse.

'I hate the worry, the problems, the exercises. She doesn't co-operate. At school she's fine, they say. Maybe my attitude is wrong. I need sorting out. I want her fit and well and I know it can't happen.

'We had so little outside support. No relatives around or neighbours that were interested. Now it's better because we're in a baby-sitting circle and one of the mothers is really good. She makes all the others understand my special problems.'

Few Cases of Complaint

The Health Service has a splendid record and complaints are few. We have not heard the other side of this story. Is this a case where the hospital failed? This mother should have had professional counselling as soon as it was realised that there were special difficulties. Putting her in touch with a local group of mothers with handicapped children might have been helpful. She has resisted the label of handicap, hoping and believing her child would improve and grow out of the difficulties.

It should have been possible to let her know the hospital side of the story, so that she had a more balanced view. The anger that she and her husband feel has been so bad for them both. They have been unable to come to terms with the degree of disability, but have managed to cope with it.

Sympathetic support and expert counselling is recognised as vital for those families who receive devastating news which is going to alter their lives. The number of divorces in families with handicapped children is evidence in itself of the stress they go through. Society owes a great debt to people who undertake the care of their handicapped children. Even those children regarded as being mildly affected still need a lot more attention than children born without problems.

Management of Cerebral Palsy

The management of a cerebral palsy child is not easy. The earliest possible assessment has to be made so that additional problems may be anticipated. Epilepsy and fits can occur, possibly producing mental handicap. The right medication may prevent these. Disordered spastic movements can be damaging, causing joint deformity. There may be sensory damage and the testing of vision, hearing and intelligence is necessary.

A knowledge of the child's background is required to make correct assessment. Emotional problems could indicate that professional counselling should be sought and there must be recognition that no one needs security more than the handicapped child.

Quality of Life

Some parents say that given the choice again they would not

put the child, or themselves, through the trauma of life with handicap. Other parents say that their children enjoy life and the hard work of caring is worthwhile.

What quality of life can be enjoyed? Will there be support for the child? What share of resources can be directed to support that single severely handicapped child? Will an unfair share of resources be directed to a single child when many might otherwise benefit?

These are some of the questions that are asked when the matter of termination of pregnancy is considered.

There is also much concern about the welfare of children when the parents die, the feeling that even adequate care cannot replace family love.

Some cerebral palsy children grow into adulthood and achieve success against all odds. One young man is a computer expert, has difficult speech, limited physical ability and writes with his foot, but be can solve most computer problems. He has impressed the business world and changed the attitudes of many people towards handicap. And it is attitudes which often prove to be the greatest barriers of all.

14 Spina Bifida and Hydrocephalus

During the early weeks of pregnancy the spinal cord of the infant grows rapidly, and any interference in development at this stage can mean malformation. The brain and spinal cord are each protected by bone, the skull of the head and the vertebrae of the spine. Further protection is afforded by layers of fluid, tissue and the skin.

Any damage to these coverings resulting in exposure of the spinal cord is very serious and potentially damaging. The degree of severity varies according to the site of exposure, and there may be loss of function and feeling in the body below that level. When this occurs the condition is known as spina bifida.

The News Comes as a Shock

The news to parents that their new-born child has suffered this kind of impairment is agonising. Adjustment takes time and feelings of fright and isolation, anger, rejection and failure are natural. Professional and kindly support should be convened to help people through this dark period in their lives.

Where there has been time to know and to love a child it is far easier to accept handicap. An unknown baby may be looked upon only from the point of view of the impairment and regarded with revulsion. The parents could feel additional guilt because of this reaction. Once they can accept the little person that the child is and begin to understand that the handicap is no one's fault, then there is every chance that a good, close relationship will develop and work can begin to help the baby on.

The GP's Role

Doctors are in a position to encourage and support the family. The general practitioner knows how much both parents are needed to provide the child, and each other, with that sheltering and protective unit which is a close family.

At no time is this undivided strength more essential than when a damaged child is born. Parents cannot imagine how they will cope and the support of their GP at this time is enormously helpful.

No Known Cause

At present it is not known for certain how spina bifida can be avoided. It is thought that there may be a genetic link, but it may be that a simple vitamin deficiency is the cause. However, in the UK, where malnutrition cannot be the worst in the world, there is one of the highest rates of this disorder. To counter any deficiency, additional vitamins may be taken but only on medical advice at any time during pregnancy, and especially during the early months when the foetus is extremely susceptible and could be affected.

The Damage of Spina Bifida

Medical advances have reduced some handicap and made possible the existence of children who would otherwise have died, amongst whom are those born with spina bifida.

An operation can be performed to close the opening over the spine but any damage already done is irreparable and the child will suffer a degree of paralysis. The higher in the back the lesion occurs, the greater the handicap. Consideration has to be given as to what quality of life there is to be enjoyed before the life-saving operation is attempted. In deciding this factor doctors and parents face making a most difficult judgement.

Hydrocephalus and the Spitz-Holter Valve

The complication of hydrocephalus, resulting in an excess of fluid which leads to pressure on the brain, often goes with spina bifida. The normally soft fontanelle feels hard from this pressure and does not pulsate.

It is treated by the insertion of a narrow tube tucked away behind the ear under the skin. This reduces the high pressure and ensures that the excess cerebro-spinal fluid is diverted from the brain outwards. To make certain that it does not return, a tiny plastic valve is secured inside the tube.

Before surgical intervention there was brain damage resulting in mental handicap and the head might grow to a massive forty inches, the child rarely surviving. The invention of the Spitz-Holter valve by an engineer (himself the parent of a child with the problem) and a surgeon, has saved the lives and intelligence of countless babies. This minor operation may need to be repeated as the child grows or if blockages occur.

What are the Effects?

The destruction of nerves can make it impossible for the child ever to walk, and paralysis usually involves the loss of control of bladder and rectum with attendant danger to kidneys.

Those muscles which are supplied by damaged nerves are weak and one or both legs may be affected. This can lead to deformities of the joints and, in particular, of feet and hips. Whether walking is ever possible depends largely upon the site of the lesion. Physiotherapy will help to strengthen existing muscles, the aim being always to give the child independent mobility, if possible.

It may be necessary to provide a wheelchair, however. Electric wheelchairs are discouraged if the arms can be used to turn wheels. However, battery power may be needed for outdoor mobility because no one wants, for example, to go shopping or for longer walks with family and friends and depend upon the arms to propel chairs for great distances.

Another problem to watch out for is the lack of feeling and reaction that some children have on their skin. Scalds or bruises may not cause pain.

Parents need to understand special procedures to empty bladder and bowels until the child is old enough and able to handle such problems. Since circulation is poor in affected areas, pressure sores must be avoided and any red patches should be treated. Scoliosis sometimes develops but severe curving of the back can usually be prevented. Any child with limited mobility must be on a careful diet to avoid putting on too much weight.

Coming to Terms with Handicap

Disabled children come to terms with their condition and are, on the whole, quite happy. I have known twin girls, one of whom is handicapped by spina bifida whilst the other is perfectly formed. It might be expected that problems of jealousy and unhappiness would arise, but they never did.

Where there is good support and understanding by the parents then there is generally an acceptance of the situation. That is not to say that things are always perfect. Of course, bitter feelings do surface at times, but given that they can be talked through then they can be kept in perspective. Emotional problems need to be discussed and professional advice sought when relevant.

The Health Visitor

Once the baby is home the attention of the health visitor and family doctor will boost the confidence of the parents at an anxious time. They will have been advised to look out for infections which may be pointers to serious setbacks involving kidneys or blocked Spitz-Holter valves. The need to rush off to hospital at intervals adds to the stress and the natural joys of parenthood are touched by pain and anxiety.

Hope is an effervescent characteristic of people and there

is much happiness and satisfaction in bringing up a child. Even when there is the most severe disability parents hope for the best. One mother remembers after years the anger and distress felt when a friend told her not to mind too much as the child would probably not live for very long. That was no comfort at all. She wanted and needed to hope for a good outcome. The health visitor understands the feelings of parents, her encouraging role is very important and she comes to be regarded as a dependable friend.

Encouraging the Family

Every facet of knowledge about spina bifida is important to the family and they will certainly ask about the expected progress of the child's condition and long-term treatment.

The need for continuing professional observation is accepted, giving a feeling of security. When careful assessment is provided, taking into account all physical, sensory and psychological elements, then the family carries on, buoyed up by the feeling that everything possible is being done for their child.

Regular Assessment

Paediatric assessment should take place at a specialist unit and a number of these exist which offer high standards. Parents draw comfort from having access to a unit where there is a relaxed atmosphere, and enough time is given to recognise what a child is capable of doing and what problems have been encountered. Time is needed to ask questions and digest advice, and parents can contribute their own views.

Assessment teams will identify the damage suffered more exactly. Signs and symptoms noted by the family will be taken into account, and the child will be considered in the round, as part of a family unit. Then the management of problems can be discussed and solutions examined.

Education

For many spina bifida children normal school can be attended if there is provision for their special needs, and access for those who have wheelchairs. Most of these children have normal intelligence. Those with hydrocephalus may be slower and lack concentration. Considering what they go through with visits to hospitals, operations and physiotherapy, it is not to be wondered at. For the children whose conditions are complicated by additional disabilities, special schools or units within ordinary schools will be best.

Segregating children from the neighbourhood community however, can only compound the problems. Children who are taught to understand about their disabled neighbours can be very supportive and understanding. It is hard when despairing parents must recognise extra problems, but the right support makes all the difference. The hard work is worthwhile, for despite the many drawbacks of handicap these children can be happy, lovable and valued members of their families and of the community.

Social Development

It is impossible to generalise about feelings, but one thing we can say about everyone, including the handicapped, is that we all have emotional problems. Obviously anyone with a disability has certain disadvantages and every effort should be made to minimise these. Adolescents need very understanding adults around who will appreciate their frustrations and their feelings. They should be given every opportunity to enjoy friendships in a natural way.

There are girls with spina bifida who have made successful and happy marriages and produced fine, healthy children. The boys have the disadvantage that they cannot father children other than in rare circumstances, but this has not prevented many of them from entering into loving relationships.

Other People's Experience

The advice of families who have had similar experience to one's own is extremely valuable, and the voluntary groups that have been formed offer excellent advice and support.

The difficulty and trauma of coping before such support became commonplace is illustrated by the case of a baby girl born in 1964. Following birth she was rushed to a specialist children's hospital where they operated to close the opening over the spinal cord and to have the life-saving Spitz-Holter valve inserted. The family consisted of the mother and daughter. Their story follows.

A Personal Experience

Stella was thirty-eight when she became pregnant. The father could not marry her or offer her support and she knew that the responsibility of parenthood would rest with her alone.

What she was not prepared for was the baby's imperfection. The doctor told her that her little girl had been taken to another hospital for an operation. For the next forty-eight hours there was little news and she hardly dared hope that her baby would survive. The sense of relief when she knew that the baby was recovering well overwhelmed her and even the knowledge that it had spina bifida and hydrocephalus scarcely marred her joy.

She knew nothing about these conditions, only that she loved her baby. The consultant explained about the operation and that the child would never walk.

Her health visitor proved a tower of strength in the months that followed. Mary was as content as any other baby, but as she grew she remained in nappies. With callipers and elbow crutches she walked a little but felt more comfortable in a self-propelled wheelchair. A bright child, she read a good deal and was very patient about the exercises that the physiotherapist had taught her mother to do for her.

142

Mary remembers her tenth birthday. 'Mum told me that I could have an operation and would never need nappies again. I thought it was wonderful. I hated those nappies more than anything. I didn't mind the operation and it went well. I knew the hospital and the nurses were my friends. Then, when I was eleven something went wrong with me – I began to drop things. My body had rejected my Spitz-Holter valve and I had to have it changed. After that I felt fine, and told mum I was going to work hard on my exercises and that by fifteen I would dance. But I never did.

'Mum and I joined a music club for the handicapped, the Wingfield Trust, and I learned to play the trumpet, which helped my breathing. I still go and teach young children. I have a boy-friend there who is also in a wheelchair. We talk of getting married, but I doubt that we'll make it. I've had three cardiac arrests and each time they rushed me to hospital. A few years ago a charity bought me an electric wheelchair so I am able to go out alone.

'Oh yes, how could I forget? At sixteen I started college, and had a wonderful two years there – taking maths, English and typing. I have had some jobs, but my health is so unpredictable that I can't blame employers when they won't chance taking me on.'

Stella and Mary take life day by day. They are members of ASBAH, the Association of Spina Bifida and Hydrocephalus. Stella has often been called upon to visit families with new babies who have the problem she is so familiar with.

For Stella life changed dramatically when her child was born. A single parent in the 1960s experienced far more difficulties than would be known today. She never doubted for an instant that she would take the baby home regardless of its condition. She recalls the days in hospital when the child was removed for the operation as the worst she ever knew. Today, arrangements would be made for mother and baby to stay together, to ensure that a loving, natural bonding can occur.

When the nature of the disability was fully realised, Stella felt fears for their future. Having no one to share the burden of sorrow, let alone the burden of caring, made things much worse.

The years ahead loomed in a terrifying way, but as time went by the nightmare receded. Reality was not awful, or even bad. Mary was a beautiful child and she and her mother shared a loving relationship. Stella was able to continue her job part-time once her little girl started school. This, coupled with the fact that she found the music club so beneficial socially, enabled her to maintain a balanced and contented outlook.

Research into Spina Bifida

The damage to the central nervous system which produces spina bifida and hydrocephalus could be caused in a number of ways, but nothing has so far been proven. There does seem to be some evidence supporting the view that supplementary vitamins taken by the parents for some months prior to conception may avoid spina bifida in a second child, but these must only be taken on a doctor's advice.

A simple blood test can be carried out on every pregnant woman which can indicate whether further tests for spina bifida are warranted. If those tests confirm the worst fears then a difficult decision has to be made. Parents and doctors have to consider all factors in deciding whether or not to terminate the pregnancy.

Provision Today

Today there are fieldworkers employed by a registered charity, The Association of Spina Bifida and Hydro-cephalus, who ensure that the 15,000 people in the UK, including children, who suffer from these conditions get all possible support. The association supports training for the employment of disabled youngsters, research into the treatment and management of the spinal defects, and ways of improving the quality of life for those who are disabled.

At their residential centre they offer activity holidays and courses in independent living. Children with this disability now have every opportunity to enjoy a full life and take their place in the community. It is up to the community to welcome them.

15   Cleft Palate
or Cleft Lip

One of the most distressing abnormalities to be seen in a baby is a cleft lip or palate – or both. This congenital abnormality occurs in about one in every 700 children. The reasons it occurs are not known except that where there is already a case in the family it is thought that there must be a genetic link.

What is certain is that something happens during the early weeks of pregnancy to prevent the union of the two halves of the palate or the joining of the parts of the lip. In the more severe cases the cleft is extensive, reaching into the nose.

The Causes

Whenever the reasons for disability are unclear, it is thought that influencing factors may have been environmental ones such as infection or drugs, as with thalidomide. Perhaps genetics are partly to blame, needing only some triggering agent to interfere in the baby's development.

Mothers will backtrack to try to find the reasons for their child's imperfection. One grandmother confided her fear that a genetic mutation had taken place, due to her own long-term intake of medicines. This she felt had been transmitted to her daughter without apparent damage, but then to her grandson who was anencephalic, with an undeveloped brain.

A young woman told me in her grief for her stillborn child that she had sprayed the garden with insecticides, inhaling the chemicals, and knew from that moment that her expected baby was doomed. Another, a hairdresser, thought that the sprays and preparations she used caused her baby's blindness. And a nurse who assisted with X-rays wondered if this work could have been the reason for her baby's cleft palate.

Speech Therapy

Speech problems for the child with a cleft palate were once grave. Speech sounded funny and caused amusement in other children who mocked and mimicked. Today, techniques are so good and speech therapy begun so early that there is every chance that these children will find that they do not have such serious problems.

Operations are necessary and these are usually carried out quite early, the aim being to enable the child to feed as easily as possible and also to get things right before speech begins. The timing of operations may vary since much depends upon the child's condition and the views of the medical team. There are numbers of doctors who must be involved and who agree a programme; ear, nose and throat specialists, dentists, audiologists, speech therapists and plastic surgeons whose microsurgery expertise is essential for initial operations and finally so valuable in making the child look more presentable.

Parents are very anxious from the birth on. All the feelings of shame, guilt, fear and revulsion are shared by mother and father. One father told me he wanted to smother his affected baby and had to be physically restrained from doing so. Staff have to decide whether parents are able to take the shock of their baby's malformation. Sometimes parents recognise immediately what is wrong. In some cases the nurses have taken the child away and the parents only see the baby after many days.

It is dreadful to bear the news of handicap, but it is also intensely worrying to have the child removed immediately following birth. On balance, it is not considered advisable to separate the parents and their child. Parents need a lot of help and ongoing support, especially when they may never have previously encountered such a condition. Producing photographs which illustrate what plastic surgery can do is helpful at this stage.

The nurse whose child had a cleft palate told of how she had put on a brave face because that was the way she was trained. But inside, like anyone else, she too was frightened and prayed that someone would treat her like the other mothers, taking the trouble to speak to her and counsel her. At night she and her husband cried like children and wondered how they would survive the days and weeks ahead.

Their little girl is now a year old. It has been a year of remedial operations, of trying out every known feeding bottle on the market and braving outings with their daughter. They are anxious about her and what the future will hold for them all.

Although there is no such condition in any member of either family they are too nervous to chance another baby, feeling that there may be a genetic link and that future children would be at risk.

Their child may have no other difficulties and may be quite bright. There could be problems of hearing and these should be dealt with early so that the child does not lose language assimilation. The important thing will be for her to be treated normally, for then psychological damage will be minimal. That is up to the people she will meet, out in the streets, in the shops, and at school. I hope that she gets a fair chance.

16   Viral Damage

Most infections are mild and of brief duration, but some are recognised to be potentially dangerous and can have long-term or irreversibly damaging effects.

Viral diseases such as mumps, influenza, measles and German measles usually take a mild form but when they are contracted by the mother in the early formative weeks of pregnancy they are associated with an incidence of miscarriages and stillbirths. In addition to causing this loss of life they also account for a number of deformities in babies.

Antenatal Care

In recent years there has been considerable improvement in antenatal care. Women are recommended and encouraged to attend clinics where they can receive counsel both prior to and during pregnancy.

Despite all precautions handicaps do still occur for which there is no apparent reason.

Foetal Damage

The developing foetus is most vulnerable during the early weeks when pregnancy may not have been confirmed or sometimes even suspected. Rubella is well known to be potentially harmful in the first months of pregnancy, but may cause only the most moderate symptoms in the mother.

One such mother ignored a mild headache and rash which disappeared after a day. She was six weeks into pregnancy and felt so well that she ignored these slight signs. In fact she had contracted German measles and her daughter was born with profound and multiple handicap, having damage to the heart and brain, affecting her sight and hearing.

This mother had never been inoculated against rubella, which could and should be eradicated. The vaccine is now offered to schoolgirls aged between eleven and fourteen and immunity should last for several years. No vaccination can take place once pregnancy is confirmed, but pre-pregnancy or pre-natal care should establish whether there is still immunity.

Impairment Without Known Cause

When there has been no apparent infection nor any other known cause and yet a child is born with severe impairment it is difficult for parents to understand why this has happened.

Reactions vary and may be angry, sad or bitter. One father rejected his religion following the birth of his son without legs. There were a number of associated problems for the child and operations were needed. These were successful and the boy grew stronger each year. He is able to wear artificial legs, albeit reluctantly for they are heavy, and he goes to a normal school.

A thoughtful little boy, he was delighted when his sister was born and was curious about her and the completeness of her body.

I wrote the following lines to illustrate a conversation that he had one day with his mother.

'Would you prefer,' her small son said,
'If I'd been born with feet?'
His little face was serious,
Her sad heart skipped a beat.
'It's true when I first saw you
That I felt a bit afraid
And wished you had been born more like
Most other kids are made.
But you're a very special boy,
Such happiness you bring.
You're clever, bright, you love your life.
I wouldn't change a thing.'

This child has integrated well at school and has many friends. He is popular, too, with his teachers and whilst his parents are very supportive of him he is not in the least spoiled and undertakes his share of duties. The family provides the right balance of loving care and discipline.

Combating Infection

We live with bacteria and viruses and usually our systems can cope with them when they offer danger to our health. Viruses are different from bacteria, they do not feed or move independently – nor do they reproduce. They can be conveyed by droplet infection on the breath and they invade healthy cells which manufacture more viruses.

The body's defences can usually offer protection in the same way that they combat bacteria, but a child born with an infection such as rubella may continue to produce the virus and further damage can occur. Care must be taken, for infectious diseases are common in young babies and scrupulous cleanliness is necessary. When unwelcome bacteria and viruses enter the body and multiply they cause damage and sickness.

Antibiotics can be used to combat bacteria, but viral diseases must be tackled by the body's own immune system.

Pregnant women are particularly vulnerable and must avoid the possibility of infection whenever possible. Most babies are born perfectly healthy and I would never suggest that women cocoon themselves, but sensible precautions are wise.

Most inherited disabling conditions will increase a child's susceptibility to infection whilst poor housing and crowded conditions can only add to problems causing repeated illness and additional disability.

There are some rare disorders which account for a lack of resistance and the family doctor can determine the likelihood that these exist so that relevant precautions may be taken.

Natural Abortion

A high proportion of natural abortions occur with babies who would have been handicapped. Some mothers feel poorly during pregnancy and as though abortion is threatening – yet at full term they may be delivered of perfect infants. Others feel sure that something is wrong and events prove that their fears were justified.

One mother of a child with severe cerebral palsy said, 'I knew that something had to be wrong. I had such bad flu and felt awful, it never seemed to clear up all through the pregnancy. It was not like my other pregnancies. I kept feeling that there was something wrong with my baby.'

Undersized Babies

Premature babies or those termed undersized are especially vulnerable to infection and need careful nursing and the benefit of specialised equipment if they are to have the best chance. Some hospitals provide mobile intensive cot-care equipment which can pick up newly born babies at risk and transport them to units where they have the maximum opportunity, not only for survival but also of unimpaired good health.

An American couple on holiday in London and expecting their first child in another two-and-a-half months were dismayed when the wife began labour. They felt sure that their child was lost. The baby was born in Westminster Hospital, London, and placed in a special care unit. Consultant paediatrician Leonard Sinclair, head of the unit, stresses how vital it is that a baby born so early should receive care and round the clock attention within a unit equipped to deal with every emergency so that life is preserved and no handicap suffered.

This little baby weighed barely two pounds but survived and was able to go home with her mother two months later, having then achieved normal birthweight. Mr Sinclair has said that such small babies may remain vulnerable as they grow into school age, needing greater care than babies of more average size.

Immunisation

Health visitors will advise about ordinary immunisation from the common diseases from which children need protection. Measles is mostly a mild illness but occasionally produces serious complications. Diphtheria is almost unheard of now but once caused the death of almost fifty children each week in the UK alone. Tetanus still occurs, taking the lives of a few of our children annually.

We can never be complacent about these diseases and continued vaccination against them, as well as against other commonly transmitted viruses, is to be recommended. Travelling abroad increases the chance of infection and it is undoubtedly wise to accept advice about inoculation.

Tuberculosis is still rife in some countries and older children are offered BCG vaccinations. If someone in the family has had the disease younger children are included in the vaccination programme. Tuberculosis once caused grave illness, consuming the lungs, causing great and distressing weakness and was often fatal.

Poliomyelitis is a viral infection of the nerves in the spinal cord which results in paralysis. It begins with a fever and headache and general malaise. Paralysis develops soon afterwards, ranging in degree of severity. Some of the wheelchair-bound members of our population were the victims of this infection in their earlier years.

Overcoming Disability

Nancy and Andrew Robertson were both affected by polio in their teens and each soon became wheelchair-bound. They have been happily married for twenty-six years and have each achieved success in their careers, she as Director of the Prince's Trust and he as an editor and writer.

They produced a fine son of whom they are justifiably proud. But he is even prouder of them and the way in which they have disregarded and overcome disability.

Meningitis

Meningitis is always suspected whenever there is unexplained fever, loss of appetite and a general air of listlessness. It is a life-threatening condition which may result in brain damage and multiple handicap. Children have symptoms of fever followed by headache and sleepiness, a miserable air and neck stiffness. Correct diagnosis and treatment are urgent because convulsions may occur with a lapse into unconsciousness. And it is possible that inflammation will affect the brain with resultant impairment.

The watchful parent and careful GP will be on the look-out for any complications but lack of attention to a child who shows these symptoms can be very dangerous indeed.

Whilst meningitis can be the result of a viral or bacterial infection transmitted through mouth or nose it is possible that the meningitis can develop at the site of a head injury which has penetrated bone. When infection develops in this way in babies, the fontanelle becomes firm and may bulge. Whenever multiple symptoms are present without obvious cause the doctor will not delay in taking a lumbar puncture.

Such a test is used to confirm diagnosis. After local anaesthetic, fluid is drawn from the spine and is then examined for evidence of meningitis. Treatment is by antibiotics and recovery nowadays is usually straightforward.

Osteomyelitis

Another infection which must be accurately diagnosed is acute osteomyelitis. The child who tells of sudden severe pain in the long bone of a limb, pain which worsens and feels hot, should be regarded as in need of emergency treatment. These symptoms alone are sufficient to warrant investigation, which will include throat swabs and blood tests, and which will reveal whether there is an infection.

X-rays will show any abnormalities. At this stage some

conditions will clear up and all will be well. Often, however, osteomyelitis is present, and if it is not recognised as the cause of the symptoms, as distinct from a bang or a kick in the area of pain, if it is not distinguished from arthritis or polio, then the wrong treatment may be given. There is not time for erroneous diagnosis, or to wait and see if things settle. The results for the child can be disastrous.

Immediate Action Essential

The symptoms have been recognised for some years by doctors and nurses and the form of treatment is well established, but painful areas which are attributed to growing pains may be ignored for months. It is sensible to investigate a suspect symptom rather than risk the possible complications. Uneven growth of limbs, stiffened joints, and even amputations can result when the condition has been left untreated.

Parents must be aware that there are some signs which indicate that expert help is needed without delay and insufficient treatment can lead to a chronic form of the disease. If there has not been complete healing then relapses can persist and the bones are weakened by infection. It is then that joints become involved. Responsible adults who see a child regularly should never ignore symptoms of pain or ongoing discomfort – permanent disability can result from neglect. Children in larger or poorer families where moderate symptoms of pain and fever are overlooked may well be left too long before the doctor is called in.

17   Still's Disease

'But It's an Old Person's Disease'

It is hardly believable to people to be told that their child has arthritis, for it does sound like a disease of the elderly.

The name Still's disease is given to arthritic conditions which affect one child in every thousand.

The Diagnosis

Diagnosis must be made on all the evidence available, for there is no foolproof test to definitely pin-point the condition. Other diseases must be ruled out and children have to undergo a number of tests.

Arthritis

In some forms of arthritis there is a risk of eye disease. Since it is not noticeable, the expertise of an ophthalmologist is required to check the child's eyes regularly. If the eye problem is not discovered and treated it can lead to serious eye defects.

Stills begins at around one to four years with an infection and a persistent high temperature; the child is lethargic, losing appetite and weight. There is excessive perspiring, joints may feel hot and painful to the touch and, in time, they swell and movement becomes restricted. The resultant discomfort makes a child very miserable and reluctant to move or to be touched and this makes the job of nursing hard. It is particularly wearing and disheartening to care for a child in constant pain and for whom little can be done.

However, the disease does burn itself out in the end. There are periods of remission, followed by fresh flare-ups, but after some months, or, in the case of some forms of arthritis, even years, it ends.

There will be some children who are left with impairment. Some may need hip replacements, have damage internally, or detectable changes in the hands or in the length and shape of a leg. But many of the children who develop Stills can look forward to leading relatively normal and independent lives when they grow up.

Treatment

In addition to certain drugs, physiotherapy is regarded as essential, both to prevent deformities and to keep joints supple. A programme of graduated exercises will be prepared by the physiotherapist who will supervise and teach parents how these should be done, and how to avoid putting excessive strain on joints.

Advice will also be given on the correct use of walking aids, supportive clothing, neck collars and resting splints. A simple wrist splint can make it easier to use the hands and hold a pen, knife or fork with more comfort. It may be advised that a splint should be worn temporarily at night to keep the fingers or other joints in the best position.

Regular exercise will help to minimise the damage that is caused, so unless there is pain it is well worth persisting even when the child does not feel like co-operating. Introducing games and simple equipment will help. It may become boring but the value of a twice-daily routine at home will pay dividends and beats the few sessions which can be offered at hospital.

Mobility is obviously important to any child and tricycles are popular both to maintain flexibility and because they are fun. Any toys should be checked for safety and tricycles should be solid as well as balanced, and the child taught how to stop them. Runaway tricycles going down an incline are dangerous, particularly if near traffic. Swimming is an enjoyable as well as useful activity and should be encouraged as soon as the child is well enough.

Is There Permanent Damage?

In general the outlook is good and the loss of movement can be minimal. But if there is involvement of many joints and muscles there may be muscle wastage sufficient to cause a measure of permanent disability. The nursing care that the child receives will determine to a large extent just how good the recovery will be.

Gina was only ten months old when she became feverish and fretful, and soon she was diagnosed as having Still's disease. By the age of five she was in constant pain and could scarcely walk. Her despairing parents sold their home abroad and the mother brought the child to England.

There was no quick cure available and although different drugs and therapy were attempted Gina showed little improvement. Funds ran out and they returned home. News of a new treatment in Los Angeles filtered through and again Gina was off abroad, but to little avail.

The disease simply had to burn itself out and when I last saw Gina she was a happy child of twelve, having had two pain-free years, and although left with slight impairment she was able to walk and was preparing to write a book about her experiences.

Rheumatoid Arthritis

This is very similar to Still's disease and is merely a juvenile form of the well-known adult variety. Girls seem to be affected more than boys and the condition occurs in all age groups from infancy on.

The onset is usually recognisable so that parents can describe precisely when it began. There is a high fever which subsides only to rise again and at first there may be little pain. Attacks go from joint to joint, first this one and then another. In the next stage the pain settles in the hands, wrists and elbows or knees and ankles, and the skin over the affected and swollen joints is stretched and shiny. There may be involvement of one joint or many which can cause problems of diagnosis.

Sometimes the spine is affected and scoliosis may result, but treatment can prevent deformity. When muscle wastage occurs there is distressing loss of mobility although every effort will be made to prevent this becoming permanent. Frequently there is remission for a while and the aches and pain subside as the joint swelling goes down, but it is possible that some residual damage will remain. A relapse may follow during which the pain returns with a flare-up of the fever and renewed swelling of the joints. An accurate diagnosis must be made so that the proper treatment can be given.

Drug Warning

A recent report claims that the danger of anti-arthritic drugs has not been sufficiently emphasized. Paul Dieppe, professor of rheumatology, said at a British Medical Association conference that doctors should be more cautious in their prescribing habits. He warned that the question of drugs contributing to progressive disease must be carefully considered. In urging doctors to rely less on drugs, Professor Dieppe said that more traditional remedies such as warm water bathing should be employed as they could be effective in reducing pain.

It may well be that pain relieving drugs could be blocking the natural repairing mechanisms of the body.

Systemic Lupus Erythematosus

SLE is becoming better known and more frequently diagnosed. The symptoms are so similar to many other illnesses that it has often been misunderstood. It is another disease which affects girls far more often than boys and can be extremely disabling. It is rarely found before the age of eight years, but when it strikes it causes children to be so ill that they miss a lot of schooling.

It is known as the butterfly disease because of the shape of the rash which spreads over the nose and cheeks. Since SLE attacks all organs, the effects are varied and may cause intense pain and misery. A good deal of research goes on in this field and it is hoped that more effective treatments will be found. Sufferers are advised to stay out of the sun. Remission of considerable periods occurs, but the patient with SLE is watchful for attacks at any time.

18 Asthma and Eczema

Among the conditions which are said to run in families, but are triggered off by an external factor, are asthma and eczema. It is frequently found that a parent with eczema has a child with asthmatic problems, whilst the child of an asthmatic parent may have eczema. If it is known what the familial tendencies are then factors known to be common triggers can be avoided, if that is possible. Sometimes ordinary childhood infections like measles or whooping cough can precipitate asthma, but it can also be triggered by stress. Children who are handicapped are often delicate and may be subject to chesty conditions or skin problems, developing these in addition to their other problems.

Some babies with an inborn sensitivity will occasionally have irritating blotches on the face, and this sensitive reaction may follow a change from breast to cow's milk. It seems worthwhile to extend breast-feeding for extra weeks in the hope that this avoids the initial mechanism that triggers the alarm and begins allergies. It is important to try to find and eliminate the offending substance because the child with eczema does have a miserable time. The same cause may bring on asthma.

Degree of Disablement

Children who have only mild asthmatic reactions may never be correctly diagnosed. No one likes to label children with diseases which they are likely to grow out of and, indeed, many of the children who do have asthma and eczema will grow out of it as they reach adulthood.

For some children asthma can become a life-threatening condition and it is alarming to see a child in the midst of an

161

attack, struggling to breathe, wheezing and coughing. They endeavour to help themselves by pushing their hands against a firm surface to try to force air out of their lungs. It is important that parents and patients understand what is happening so that they can prevent or help overcome attacks. Doctors are only too familiar with asthmatic conditions and can prescribe helpful drugs and give advice which will avoid potentially dangerous situations.

Following Infection

For the asthmatic child chest infections are likely to be followed by attacks, especially during cold weather when the airways respond to the change in temperature.

It will probably occur to parents that their child is having an attack of wheezy bronchitis or a cold that has gone to the chest. If this happens frequently such attacks should be noted and discussed with the doctor in case the diagnosis is asthma.

Allergies and Asthma

Many children who are asthmatic react to the presence of pollen. It is fairly easy to recognise this since attacks come at the time of year when pollen is heavy and follows trips to the park or play in the garden. Another cause of asthma is the common house-mite which should be suspected if there is wheezing at night or in the morning. Skin tests may confirm an allergy, but it is not always a single factor which brings about an attack.

It is puzzling when children react occasionally to specific items and yet at other times appear unaffected. There may be two or three agents which together produce the reaction. Some foods and colourants provoke a variety of adverse responses in children and all suspect factors need to be removed and reintroduced singly to discover which one or which combination causes the problem.

Emotional or Nervous Asthma

An episode causing deep agitation or worry may promote an initial attack and the anxiety of a possible repeat can be sufficient to cause further problems. Yoga has been used to teach children how to breathe with gentle rhythm so that they can control asthmatic attacks from the outset. An understanding of what is happening in the chest is important and quite young children respond intelligently using self-control to reduce the panic which can only make things worse.

An Additional Cause

Involuntary smoking can cause problems for the families of smokers. Children are known to have increased risks of chest diseases and studies have revealed a direct relationship between passive smoking and childhood asthma in the first and second years of life.

A child is entitled to live in a smoke-free atmosphere.

Exercise

Children are encouraged to exercise to develop their lungs and although this may precipitate wheeziness at first it can be helpful in the long term. Swimming is an excellent sport for asthmatics and children should be encouraged to go regularly and so improve stamina. The warm and moist air in a swimming bath enables them to exert themselves with greater ease and comfort.

Breathing exercises are certainly useful, so parents should try to institute a regular regime of therapy as advised by the doctor. Caring for a delicate child can make the carer fraught with anxiety, but an intelligent approach is needed. Mollycoddling and fussing can be counter-productive, leading to fear and anxiety in the child, and the temptation to be over-protective should be resisted.

Severe Attacks

The danger of severe attacks which have continued for some hours is considerable, hence children must be taken to hospital. Oxygen may be needed if drugs have failed to alleviate the condition. Other treatment is available in hospital in emergencies. The very fact that parent and child arrive in hospital seems to bring about a reduction of symptoms which confirms that worry and fear have something to do with the severity of an attack.

Repeated attacks of frightening episodes may lead to chronic chest conditions and frailty. It is occasionally recommended that children be sent to boarding-schools where such conditions are treated. The Invalid Children's Aid Association runs one of these on the coast where the fresh air and regular regimes are helpful and where staff are on the alert to prevent attacks before they reach dangerous proportions.

Undiagnosed Asthma

Speaking to the European Society of Pneumology at a meeting in Amsterdam, consultant paediatrician at the Brompton Hospital, Dr John Warner, said that in a survey of seven-year-old schoolchildren in Newcastle, eleven per cent were found to have asthma. 'Half of them,' reported Dr Warner, 'had not been diagnosed as being asthmatic before. Many had been diagnosed as having wheezy bronchitis and only twenty per cent who had a non-specific diagnosis had received appropriate treatment compared to more than seventy per cent of those correctly diagnosed with asthma.' Dr Warner maintains that patients who present with over-inflated chests and growth retardation are a failure of diagnosis and management.

In a New Zealand study of more than a thousand children, followed up for twelve years, the incidence of asthma was increased in boys whose parents had eczema, stated University of Melbourne paediatrician Dr Peter

Phelan. But the same is not true of girls, although the reason for this is not known.

It is recommended by chest physicians that all pre-school children should be screened for asthma. They claim that this would give a high yield of untreated diseases and assert that any asthmatic children, or those who have wheezing bronchitis or nocturnal coughing, should have peak expiratory flow tests routinely measured.

In case there is ever delay in getting a doctor it is best to know where the nearest hospital accident and emergency department is. Not all hospitals have such departments, although any general practitioner is required to give emergency treatment whether the patient is registered or not. Early medication can avoid the dangers and improve recovery times.

In the future when all children have early diagnosis and preventive care the thin asthmatic child with pigeon-shaped chest should no longer be a feature of asthma. By following doctor's instructions, physiotherapist's advice and keeping strictly to prescribed medicines and recommended exercise, children can remain fit and healthy, escaping the limitations of this handicap.

Asthma is sometimes replaced by eczema which needs careful and patient treatment. It most often appears on the hands, head or body in young children, but I have seen it cover a child. It can be intensely irritating and it may become necessary to put cotton mittens on the hands to prevent the child scratching and infecting cracks. Cotton clothing is best – anything woolly tending to aggravate the skin.

Allergies to various substances may cause attacks of eczema and antihistamines can be prescribed. It is best to try and find out if there are any offending materials which touch the skin and cause outbreaks. Soap powders may have to be changed and clothes rinsed very thoroughly to remove residual irritating substances.

Eczema may not be life threatening, but it can be a very disabling and miserable condition, difficult to live with at home and at school – giving rise to emotional problems which make the condition worse. Stress often plays a part in producing rashes that may be conveyed from parents to children – sometimes through misunderstanding. One child overheard her parents discussing their wills, and thought this meant that they were going to die. She broke out in a severe neck rash and it was weeks before she could bear to ask her parents how long they had to live. Explanations relieved the child's anguish and the rash disappeared.

A full discussion with the doctor and careful heed to advice usually leads to improvement. With good management the child will get better as time goes on.

19   Crohn's Disease

Chronic Inflammatory Bowel Disease

This is a group of illnesses in which there is inflammation of any part of the gastro-intestinal tract, more commonly known as the alimentary tract, extending from mouth to anus.

One of the most important of this group is Crohn's disease which is characterised by inflammation of one or more parts of the tract.

It occurs in the youngest of children, schoolchildren and adolescents, as well as in adults, and in most races. The early signs mimic other more common conditions, and it is therefore not readily diagnosed.

Crohn's disease has been a comparatively rare condition until recent years, affecting only one in 25,000 of the population, but it is now found in increasing numbers. There are at present a considerable number of children with this complaint in the UK. For example, in one London hospital 250 children attend the special clinic dealing with this problem. The marked increase in incidence has not been attributed to improved diagnosis. It appears to strike more often in urban areas for some reason and there seems to be a distinct familial tendency, many children having a close relation with the same disability.

How does it Affect Children?

The problem of Crohn's disease in children is urgent for it can affect emotional and physical growth and development and is becoming more widespread among adults.

The symptoms begin with stomach pains, diarrhoea and weight loss and the miserable feeling of being generally ill. Later symptoms include fever, weakness and swelling of legs. In young teenagers puberty is delayed. If Crohn's disease is suspected the patient must have barium enema and barium meal X-rays in hospital. Confirmation is sad news for the child and parents since this condition can mean restricted activity and a reduction in the quality of life.

During relapses a child may be severely debilitated by malnutrition, and so incapacitated as to need a wheelchair. When flare-ups of internal ulcers occur there is failure by the system to absorb nutrition and colostomy may have to be considered.

Control of the Condition

Although there is no known cure for this inflammatory disease, there are procedures which can be considered to calm the inflammation. Steps must be taken to improve and maintain good nutrition with a balanced diet, and to find the medication which best holds the disease in check. An operation may become necessary to remove the most severely affected parts of the intestine so as to alleviate discomfort. Considerable research is in progress on both sides of the Atlantic and the results have encouraged further expansion of projects. It is conjectured that a single virus may well be the cause but that a pre-disposition to this illness runs in families. Allergies should be considered as the cause or as a contributory factor. It is not, however, due to poor diet or a lack of care in upbringing. There is fear that it is cancer, but this is not so.

Lyndsay has grown up with Crohn's and was first diagnosed with the disease at eight years of age. Her parents have no knowledge of anyone in the family suffering with this or similar problems. They have found that certain foods will sometimes make her feel worse and these have been eliminated from her diet. She has maintained reasonable health on steroids and although hospital admissions have been necessary she leads a full and active life, but she and her family are constantly wary in case attacks recur.

With her teacher's co-operation she has kept up with school work, her friends know about the problems and are understanding and helpful.

Many children grow out of the disease achieving late growth and good health with no apparent ill-effects whatsoever. One youth having had a delicate and sickly childhood with retarded growth suddenly recovered at the late age of nineteen, put on a spurt of inches, gained weight and is now perfectly fit.

Coeliac

Some babies are extremely sensitive to gluten and the inability to recognise such sensitivity has resulted in life-threatening illness. Gluten is present in cereals and so there is no problem until the baby's diet includes these foods. The intolerance is thought to be due to an enzyme defect in the intestinal wall.

Coeliac babies react to the gluten in wheat, rye and other cereals by failing to thrive. They are irritable, with vomiting and diarrhoea. There is soon a noticeable loss of weight, retarded growth and a marked pallor.

Diagnosis and Treatment

The diagnosis will require a considerable number of investigations to be done to eliminate the possibility of other illness. Where there has been failure to recognise a problem, and the child has simply gone on being ill for a long while, dwarfism has resulted and sexual maturity has been delayed.

The treatment requires that all forms of gluten must be excluded from the diet and any breads, cakes and biscuits have to be made with a gluten-free flour. The response to a gluten-free diet is dramatic – the child gaining height, weight and having an improvement in general disposition and health. Oddly enough this disease appears to be selective, affecting children who are fair and have long eyelashes.

20 Drugs

Whatever characteristics we may inherit through our genes there are other factors which influence our growth and health. Drugs and chemicals are important elements which concern us directly or indirectly. When the air we breathe is altered we can be adversely affected as was recognised when thick fogs used to hang over London. Many people died or developed chest diseases and bronchitis from the noxious fumes.

It makes a difference to children when they are brought up in overcrowded, underprivileged areas, and a poor environment generally means slower growth and a greater likelihood of ill-health. The children of unemployed and low income parents generally do less well than those in better circumstances. There may be a genetic limit to our physical size and we may be potentially bright and talented or dull-witted, but the maximum and minimum possibilities of attainment depend upon our homes, accessibility to sunlight and clear fresh air as well as the quality and type of food we get.

In the wider sense, our environment is altered by chemical crop sprays which spread over greater areas than intended and by incidents such as atomic disasters or the nuclear tests still carried out by some countries. Clusters of children born with malformations suggest that there is a common external cause. Mothers of such children search their backgrounds for the reasons why such tragedies have happened.

There is evidence that children living near to old nuclear sites suffer a higher percentage of sickness than children living elsewhere. It has been shown that certain chemicals drained from factories can be a health hazard. There will, no doubt, be proof in the future that other substances which spread in our environment can cause problems.

The medicines and drugs that we take influence our

health, and not always in the way that was intended. Additives to our foods can cause unpleasant reactions and sometimes quite dangerous illnesses. All of these factors can affect children at any age, but they can also affect our children before they are born. A group called Foresight or the Association for the Promotion of Pre-Conceptual Care has already been mentioned. They have interesting ideas and a growing supply of evidence that health care prior to conception leads to healthy children. It is certainly advocated that no pregnant woman should take any medicines or drugs without medical advice.

Drugs, Good and Ill Effects

Drugs are either natural or synthetic chemical substances which can be used to keep us well, affecting the processes of our bodies and minds. For some they are essential to life, and many people are dependent upon daily injections as, for example, diabetics.

The number of drugs available for medicinal and therapeutic purposes increases each year. Some of these are beneficial or life-saving and can delay the progress of illness, others can alleviate symptoms. There are few drugs which do not also have side-effects, some of which are undesirable.

Drug Abusers

This term is given to those who use drugs improperly, either as a new experience when they are bored or to block out an unpleasant phase in life which they are finding hard to bear. However it may begin, misuse has sad endings. Dependency can mean that supplies of the addictive drug are all important and finding the cash to pay for a drug habit can occupy the addict totally. Young children are exposed to the temptation and offered drugs, ruining their lives by becoming habituated. It is all too easy to begin, but addicts end by risking ill-health of body and mind, and death by infection or overdose.

The addicted youngster is the saddest sight. The ruination of a young life so needlessly is a tragedy and anyone who engages in the sale of drugs for profit or to encourage drug abuse deserves the most severe penalties.

It is generally wiser to avoid taking any medication unless it is recommended by the GP who knows his patient and has become acquainted with details of present and past history. Chemists' shops are full of remedies for every conceivable ailment and the temptation to try them out often overrides caution. But caution is essential whenever the purchase of these products is considered over the counter, and especially when it is proposed to take them in addition to prescribed medicines. Singly they may be useful, but together they can work against the health of the patient and the pharmacist's advice should be sought.

Essential Medicines Only

Considering that much illness is self-limiting and will run its course after a brief period, whilst other illness is self-imposed by bad habits, we should look twice at our individual lifestyles before taking medicines which are not strictly necessary.

Whenever I hear from patients that they feel cross because they have doctors who refuse to prescribe medicines I tell them that they are fortunate. Such doctors usually give more time and more considered advice. Reaching for the prescription pad in order to please the patient or to abbreviate the interview is not what good general practice is about.

Effects of Chemicals

Evolution has enabled us to adapt to different foods as they were introduced to our diets and to a changing environment. But we have not had time in the last centuries to adapt to the vast increase in chemical pollution of our food, air and water.

Our systems can become upset, we may become chronically ill and future generations may suffer too, from present conditions.

Allergies

Adverse reactions to substances may be described as allergies. Children who display symptoms of severe pain, irregular heartbeat or abnormal behaviour without apparent reason should be tested for allergies.

Some children produce symptoms of acute arthritis due to sensitivity to milk products or eggs. Others have hay fever through pollen or asthmatic responses to other foods or chemicals. In some children a dramatic change in behaviour can be traced to certain foods.

Edward's parents were at their wits' end to find out what was the matter with their son. For two years, from the age of four he had exhibited bouts of wild behaviour, tearing the wallpaper, pulling up floor covering, biting and scratching. Other children were afraid of him during these unpredictable attacks, and his parents found him almost impossible to control. Doctors feared brain damage although he seemed physically fit and between the hyperactive periods he was a normal and pleasant little six year old. He was finally given controlled allergy tests and found to be extremely affected by certain vegetables and drinks with added colouring. The removal of these from his diet ended the demented behaviour and he is growing up calm and normal.

Dr Jean Munro became interested in coeliac children and the dangerous effect wheat had upon them. This led her to switch her studies into allergies, and she is now an authority on the subject. Numbers of patients under her care have been helped by discovering the substances causing adverse reactions through controlled testing and using a desensitising programme.

Drug Testing

All new drugs which go on the market for use by the public, whether on prescription or not, must undergo the most careful testing. So many problems have been caused by medicinal remedies that the most stringent regulations have been introduced governing the use and prescription of products. Following the introduction of thalidomide and its tragic effect on unborn children, pregnant women are advised to take no drugs whatsoever unless they are vital to the health of the mother and are advised by a doctor who is aware of the pregnancy.

Although it was once thought possible that a fright or burn or other injury to the mother might affect the unborn child, stunting growth or producing malformation, no one dreamed that any substance taken by the mother could affect the baby secure in the womb.

However, when numbers of children were born with serious deformities whose mothers had all taken the same drug prescribed by their doctors for the relief of morning sickness, it became clear where the fault lay. These perfectly fit and healthy parents produced children who had in common a specific disability. The drug had passed the tests required at that time and was released for use in 1956. Doctors were pleased to add to their lists this medicine which alleviated the symptoms of morning sickness and had, it was believed, no unpleasant side-effects.

Thalidomide

The defects caused by the drug thalidomide are familiar in each of those countries where it was marketed and prescribed to pregnant women for alleviating sickness. The drug companies accepted responsibility and agreed settlements with the families of affected children. Money was paid out for their immediate needs and a trust established for their future benefit.

However, no amount of money could recompense for the

damage suffered. Certainly the modest sums awarded in each case could in no way make up for the heartache and misery that were caused.

The dismay felt by medical staff who brought thalidomide children into the world was never to be erased from their memories. The shock and heartbreak of the parents was immense and even the passage of years has failed to dilute the sadness for some of those families.

Children were born with missing or foreshortened limbs, or deformed joints. For some the defects were minor, for others there were grave disabilities. In America thousands of children were spared profound handicap when the executive responsible, Frances Kelsey, refused to license the product.

When Jim and Sheila Bickers were expecting their first child they welcomed a drug that reduced Sheila's morning sickness. She had no suspicion that anything would be wrong with her baby. Following the birth she realised from the staff reaction that there must be something wrong. And there was. Her baby's limbs were foreshortened, almost completely missing.

Theirs was one of the earliest cases of thalidomide. At first they agonised, wondering what could have caused the tragic deformities and could not imagine what kind of life this child could look forward to. They felt the greatest pity and were determined to give him their devotion and loving care. David rewarded them with his sunny nature. He loved to be out of doors and his parents, supporting each other, braved the looks and whispers as they walked in the streets and took him to the parks. He had a lively intelligence and curiosity, wanted to know about everything.

He was provided with a wheelchair, custom-made and designed by Eric Booth, an engineer dedicated to helping children like David, and went to a normal school where his problems were explained to the pupils, and they responded with understanding and friendship, helping him in every way that they could.

The boy was intelligent and cheerfully found the means to achieve independence in every way possible.

David passed six O levels including English, maths, computer science and journalism. He is a popular member of local youth clubs and raises funds for those less fortunate – as he says – than he is.

For some years he worked as a reporter for a magazine for the blind, successfully auditioned for work with Radio 4 and plans to submit material to local radio stations across the country. Recently, he was commissioned to take part in a TV programme on the long term outcome of thalidomide. Now twenty-seven, he is an able computer operator and has set up his own printing company, to produce only the highest quality work. He holds an advanced driver's certificate and was awarded the Gold Class Certificate in RoSPA's demanding test drive.

He is very enjoyable company. In restaurants, I have watched him put people at ease, bantering with waiters and enjoying his meal. He is so positive, so laughter loving, so full of life.

His mother and I were talking recently, and I gave voice to the hope that one day David will marry. 'I hope so', she said 'I do hope so'.

A world that accepts David for the fine person that he is and disregards his disability can only be enriched by his presence, his spirited outlook and his ability.

Outings with the Baby

It is generally agreed that when a severely handicapped baby is born it is best to let everyone in the family know as soon as possible. Delays only make it harder, and have led in the past to secreting the child.

When the first outings are made with the baby it is always best if the parents go out together or, at least, go accompanied. People in the street may react with shock, but once they know the child they become helpful and understanding. Handicapped children must be part of society from their earliest years so that they and the community accept and respect each other.

Medicines

The human body has a natural system of healing and can take care of its ills. Doctors want to encourage natural healing to take place, but if they think that medicines are necessary to alleviate a condition or help the healing process then they will prescribe them. However, medicines taken frequently generally become less effective and should not be used indiscriminately.

Patients often leave surgeries without taking in the importance of advice regarding prescriptions. They pick up their prescribed medicines, then take doses or give them to children in a haphazard fashion.

Careful regard must be paid to directions on taking medicine, otherwise the effects will either be lost, be unpleasant or may cause illness.

The dosage is important and the child's age must be known to the doctor, as well as any background information so that proper account can be taken of all the facts before medicines are recommended.

Pharmacists are expert about medicines, frequently advising doctors and can be helpful about minor problems. It is, however, the doctors who must know the whole history of their patients and who will decide to recommend medicines when he, or she, thinks that they are necessary.

21 Cancers

Cancer in children is rare but it is still a major cause of death and takes many forms, the most common being leukaemia. The diagnosis of any kind of cancer is often difficult since many trivial conditions give rise to similar symptoms.

The very young child tends to ignore or accept aches and pains, and cannot in any case explain what is happening. Where they occur most malignancies seem to develop in children before the age of ten, the higher proportion at five or under.

What is Cancer?

Cancer is characterised by the abnormal behaviour of cells. They are like riotous weeds which grow in and around plants, choking some out of existence.

Any, and every, part of the body can be struck by cancer.

Symptoms

No doctor would thank me for providing a long list of symptoms which would bring mothers rushing to the surgery unnecessarily. But in the interest of early diagnosis I list some of the symptoms provided for me by a consultant paediatrician specialising in childhood cancers, each of which could warrant a professional opinion.

Such referral should be made if a child has one or more of these symptoms for a week or longer: pain in any extremity with swelling; a milky-white look in the eye; a visible swelling felt in the abdomen; unusual enlargement of glands; tendency to bleed along with pinky discolouration of the skin; an unusual and enduring pallor; difficulty in swallowing or breathing; an unabating cough

178

which does not improve; persistent stomach pains for unexplained reasons and unaccompanied by infection or inflammation; a fever which continues and changes for the worse and is signified by apathy, loss of appetite and weight loss. Then, if only for the sake of peace of mind, it is worthwhile letting the doctor check them out.

The key to control of cancer is early diagnosis and prompt treatment. On the rare occasions when cancer strikes in children it moves fast. Recognising symptoms and taking immediate action is the responsibility of the child's adults.

Tumours

Tumours are collections of fast growing cells which form a lump. They are not all dangerous and many are benign and harmless, but those which invade or destroy healthy cells are malignant. Once they begin to develop the growth usually continues, either slowly or rapidly.

Some of these malignancies remain confined to one area whilst some spread through the blood system or lymphatic stream and may invade the entire body. This very dangerous and life-threatening condition is known as metastases.

Types of Cancer

There are three types of cancer – carcinomas, sarcomas and leukaemias.

Carcinomas affect the skin or tissues such as the lining of the lungs. Sarcomas affect bones, fat and cartilege. Leukaemias affect the blood.

Osteogenic Sarcoma

Gillian was eleven when I visited her in hospital. She had

been diagnosed with osteogenic sarcoma, and an amputation of one leg had been necessary to prevent the spread of disease. Her mother told me how a painful swelling had developed only months before and the doctors had taken X-rays showing where there was destruction of bone.

Gillian was brave and knew that her life was in danger because she had heard talk whilst she was anaesthetised and although no one thought this possible she did repeat phrases which they agreed had been used.

She felt concern for her parents and said how good they had been and how happy they had made her. 'I am sorry this is happening to them,' she said, never seeming to consider her own suffering. Gillian did not, unfortunately, survive for very long, but her courage was impressive and typical of many children whose lives are endangered by illness.

It is a feature of this condition that it occurs slightly less in lower social classes and there is evidence that increased incidence of the disease is associated with any excess of radiation. Patients who have X-ray treatments over long periods and radiologists are afflicted more often when compared with other members of the public or other health workers. It is thought wise not to X-ray pregnant women.

Leukaemia

Leukaemia is usually described as cancer of the blood. There are several types, but the important thing is to determine whether the form is acute or chronic. The acute variety is rapid and the chronic form slower to develop. Leukaemia diagnosed in children is likely to be an acute variety, so urgent treatment is necessary.

Blood is composed of plasma which is fluid, and of cells which move in the plasma. The cells are of three types each with a specific job to do. Red cells circulate oxygen, white cells combat infection, and the third kind are platelets which stop bleeding. These cells are made in bone marrow and when this productive system goes wrong and out of control one kind of cell proliferates and takes over; children either become anaemic through lack of red cells, subject to infection through lack of white cells or subject to excessive bleeding through lack of platelets.

The Causes

Leukaemia is comparatively rare occurring in about one in 25,000 children. They are mostly between the ages of two and five, but increased numbers of cases affecting children under ten have been found in areas close to pre-1955 nuclear installations in the UK, whilst later modern plants indicate no such rises. Sir Richard Doll of the Imperial Cancer Research Fund told of a four-fold increase in deaths from leukaemia in children living close to old installation areas as compared to children from other similar housing areas.

In the face of evidence mentioned previously and of reports collected by the cancer research bodies, as well as the development of leukaemia in people of all ages following the devastating explosion of an atomic bomb on Hiroshima, it is accepted that excessive radiation predisposes towards leukaemia. The dangers of the nuclear age cannot be overstated.

The exact causes of most cancers are not known. Children may be born with abnormal cells which could always remain inactive. These cells may however suddenly begin to grow for reasons unknown. It is accepted that tobacco smoke causes cancer and that children whilst not smoking themselves can be adversely affected by smoke. Studies show that the lungs of children whose parents smoke have less capacity, and that these children are more prone to develop chest diseases and cancers in later life.

A study reported in the British medical magazine *The Lancet* revealed that the more cigarettes a mother smoked during pregnancy the more risk there was that her offspring might develop cancer. 'When all tumour sites were considered,' it was reported, 'the overall risk for cancer in children whose mothers smoked ten or more cigarettes a day during pregnancy increased by fifty per cent.' The effects of even one cigarette a day are carried in the blood for eleven hours, sufficient time to be damaging.

Surgery and Chemotherapy

The best treatment for cancer is one that removes cancerous tissue leaving behind healthy and undamaged tissue, but this often involves extensive surgery. Chemotherapy uses drugs which actively seek out and destroy malignant cells. More often these days chemotherapy, surgery and irradiation are used in combination and despite the often unpleasant side-effects they can be worthwhile, sometimes providing a cure or at the least an extension of life.

Whilst treatment can be offered for all forms of leukaemia and remission can be secured for many children it is best not to consider cases as cured completely. Survival beyond four or five years is very encouraging and may mean that there will never be a recurrence, but medical knowledge has not advanced sufficiently to be totally sure that a cure is complete.

The treatment by chemotherapy involves the use of powerful drugs and procedures which themselves produce distressing symptoms. One side-effect of all treatment is loss of hair, but this is recovered after a few months. Various combinations of therapy are tried and may differ from one child to another. Curing leukaemia cells whilst leaving healthy cells undamaged and untouched is not easy. There must be constant monitoring for the effects on the system of the medication and treatment.

It is important to note that if the platelets are affected there must be no contact with infectious diseases since it could prove very dangerous for a child with leukaemia to contract any additional disease. Even the usually innocuous ones could prove life-threatening.

Bone Marrow Transplant

Some leukaemias are treatable by a change of bone marrow. A search is made for donors with matching tissue types and children undergoing the operation stay in sterile tents both before and for some weeks following the operation as they are so vulnerable to infection.

All care and nursing of the young patients is done though plastic sleeves from outside the tent. Precautions are very strictly observed and specially trained nursing staff are on duty round the clock.

The Outlook

The outlook is certainly better than it was forty years ago when it was rare for a child with leukaemia to survive beyond three years. Research produces new approaches to therapy all the time and the rate of survival will continue to improve. The strain for the family is great and they have to try to live like normal families. An older child with leukaemia may suspect the truth and direct questions pose everyone with a problem – whether or not to tell the child who is ill what the outcome may be.

Specialist counselling for this and other difficulties is required. All the uncertainties that families have to live with when a child has cancer can be emotionally draining. The family doctor is seen as a friend whose advice is welcome, but doctors too undergo strain when their patients endure such distressing circumstances and should share the burden with colleagues.

Jonathan was twelve years old when he went on a camping holiday with his parents. They noted his undue pallor and lethargy which was so marked that they felt it was an emergency situation and took him to a local doctor. An immediate blood test and bone marrow examination was arranged. The results were returned within their holiday period and they had the chilling news that Jonathan had leukaemia. The doctor himself visited the family to break the news and has maintained contact. The treatment resulted in immediate improvement and remission of the disease. After three years Jonathan is well, and there is no sign of recurrence. He is however monitored regularly, just to be on the safe side.

Jonathan is a promising artist, creating beautiful studies of birds. He is well aware of his condition and talks of his life since his remission as a bonus he means to use well. The family thinks it is best to be quite open in their discussions, feeling that this creates less problems.

We all hope that he will have a normal life-span. But however many the years they will be of good quality, happy and fulfilled.

For Andrew there was no such happy result. At seventeen he thought his tiredness was due to school work, but it was due to acute leukaemia and despite the care of his doctors, his own battle for life and the round the clock surveillance by his brothers and parents, the encroaching white cells took over. He died after a few months.

The work of paediatric oncologists, aided by the many other specialists involved, has produced better cure rates. The strides they have made in treating childhood cancers with new drugs and techniques means that many lives are saved. Inevitably, some of the cures are only achieved by accepting risks of problems in the future.

The loss of a child brings great sadness and the grief continues; but the present longer periods of treatment, and the uncertainty in the future of children deemed cured or in remission, means that a greater strain is placed on families. They need specially assigned social workers and nurses whose experience and understanding can help to diminish the stress, enable them to cope with life and to make the best of the situation.

Many self-help groups have been set up and these provide a real source of comfort to families. They can talk problems over with each other in an informal atmosphere of compassion and understanding.

22   Accidents and Child Abuse

The question of accidents to children becomes relatively more important as infectious diseases are wiped out by immunisation programmes and as more handicaps are prevented by improved pre-natal care and genetic counselling.

A greater proportion of accidents occur in the home which can be a dangerous place for young children.

Choking Incidents

Babies and toddlers choke on all sorts of objects which they inadvertently inhale or on unsuitable food which they are too young to chew and swallow. Older children do not recognise the dangers and offer them nuts, sweets and crisps. Even passers-by in the street offer momentarily unattended babies such items, not appreciating the danger.

Plastic bags can cause suffocation, either when children try chewing pieces of them which get trapped in the throat or put the bags over their heads cutting off air. These bags should never be left within reach of young children and are a regular cause of casualties.

In cots or prams healthy young babies can sleep comfortably and safely on their tummies, but sheets should be closely fitted and there should be no pillows or loose materials which can obstruct breathing. The health visitor's training and experience are invaluable regarding the care and safety of children. They are well-versed in the prevention of accidents and will recognise potential sources of trouble – and give sound advice.

Water Accidents

Children should be adequately supervised when near any expanses of water such as swimming pools or rivers and streams.

The best safeguard is to teach children to swim at an early age and to appreciate the dangers as well as the attractions of water. Life-jackets should always be worn when recommended.

Burns and Scalds

Fire is a very common cause of death and injury among children and the hazards should be recognised and precautions taken. Fire-guards are a must where there are any kinds of fires and they should be spark proof. Portable heaters, in particular, are a risk and guards should be securely fixed and at a sufficient distance from the fires to remain cool. Hot metal fire-guards are a danger in themselves.

Smokers can set themselves and their surroundings on fire by falling asleep while smoking or carelessly failing to stub out cigarettes.

Faulty electrical installations or old equipment can also cause fires. Electric sockets should be plugged because even babies at the crawling stage poke into them. Kettle leads which hang down within reach of toddlers are a hazard and should be fitted with flexes which take them out of danger. Cooker guards provide insurance against accidents which may cause disfiguring or life-threatening scalds from boiling water or soups.

Games with Fire

Matches produce results which are fascinating to children and one group of youngsters under ten devised a game whereby they burned lengths of wool in competition with each other. It was a miracle that none of them were burned.

Children learn by experimenting, but it can be impressed upon them that there are do's and don'ts.

Side-Effects

Some serious casualties occur due to the side-effects of moderate injuries. One child sat upon a hotplate which, although switched off, was hot enough to give him a nasty burn.

Although it was dealt with competently the boy became ill and feverish, and it was not recognised that he had dehydrated. Children quickly lose water content, but in a country of moderate temperatures dehydration is not a frequently encountered problem. In this case there were tragic consequences – this little boy of three died.

Poisonous Substances

Young children not only choke on pills, they are poisoned by them and by liquid medicine and chemicals they find and swallow. The hospital treatment which is necessary to rectify the damage can be frightening. It is sensible to look at all dangerous substances and consider whether the child could possibly get at them, either by climbing up to or inside cupboards and shelves.

Securely locked cabinets should house all potentially lethal materials. Child resistant packaging should further ensure the safety of children and avoid the dangers into which their natural curiosity may lead them. Many pills are made in bright attractive colours, looking and tasting just like sweets. Some parents do not realise how dangerous medicines, other than as prescribed, can be to children.

Avoiding Falls

There are many casualties to children who play on steps,

stairs and banisters. Younger children should be restrained by gates at the top and bottom of staircases and older children taught to climb up and descend stairs carefully, using handrails. Carpets should be fitted securely and worn carpet replaced.

Windows should never be left open where there are unattended young children. Enterprising toddlers learn to climb on furniture and can reach window-sills. Older children should know the great dangers of games involving ropes. Too often make-believe ends in tragic and unintentional reality. Knives and razors are useful tools, but they are also lethal toys and weapons. If guns are kept in a house they must be secure from children who should, in any case, be taught the danger of touching them.

Road Accidents

A news flash that told of the death of many hundreds of young would strike horror into the heart of the nation, yet in this country it is reported that a great number of deaths occur annually through direct vehicle collision with children. Even more are caused during, or as a direct result of, vehicles colliding with each other. How many families are bereaved and desolated through these causes alone each week? We have grown so accustomed to hearing these appalling figures that we hardly raise an eyebrow.

No child should travel in a car without a seat-belt. Too many parents live with constant self-reproach after their children have been sent flying through windscreens. It is essential to take the necessary precautions. Every child of school age should be well drilled in road safety and reminded of the hazards of traffic. Drivers should exercise greater caution, especially in streets which are so often the playgrounds of children.

The shock and horror in a family which receives news that a child has been the victim of an accident can be imagined. Life can never be the same again, each member of the family being affected by the incident. Although it is generally the mother who bears the greater burden of nursing care there are many fathers who give up work in order to share in the nursing and rehabilitation of the injured child.

Personality Change

The personality of a child who has acquired disability through an accident may appear unaltered but, in time, some changes are certain to be noted. Special needs must be satisfied and support provided to sustain the family through the first days and weeks when problem after problem must be dealt with. The loss to a child of its independence and the knowledge that one must place reliance upon others for daily needs is hard to bear.

Complete personality changes have been known to occur, particularly in adolescents. The loss of drive and ambition following severe disablement is not unexpected, and the subsequent despondency is hard to combat. Sometimes, however, and surprisingly, a relaxed and happy-go-lucky personality replaces a more serious one.

Graham was in a coma for many months following a car crash at the age of seventeen. It was a further year before he had recovered his ability to walk and speak. He had been a keen sportsman, thin and wiry with a burning ambition to succeed in business. Now he has changed, inclined to be plump, interested in watching but not joining in sports and of a jovial and relaxed nature. He took an undemanding job and although industrious he lacked his previous drive. Six years after his accident he married a bank clerk and now has a baby son and copes well with residual disability. His family are thankful for his recovery, but regret still the alteration from the boy they knew.

Clifford's family had a much greater change to accustom themselves to when he sustained a broken neck in a car collision. He recovered consciousness in a hospital ward to find that he could not move arms or legs. At fifteen Clifford had always shown a keen interest in school work and in his hobby of break dancing.

The damage to the spine was such that he was permanently disabled, unable to walk, write, feed or care for himself. His intellect is unimpaired and, although he is fully aware of the limitations now imposed upon him, he is hopeful that the future will be good.

It is ironic that the demanding break dance routines caused no problem whilst the moderate vehicle collision resulted in such devastating damage. Although Clifford talks cheerfully enough of his future, the brave front must hide occasional despair. His mother's sorrow is deep. 'My lad went off so full of health and energy.' she said. 'He is now turned back into a little baby, needing everything to be done for him.' Clifford will need 24-hour care, but has welcomed the provision of a wand attached to his head which enables him to operate a computer keyboard. He intends to continue his studies as a draughtsman and to take some qualifications which will give him a useful career.

His Family

Clifford is the third child of four brothers. Both of his parents work, his mother having taken a job in a canteen when the youngest son started school four years ago. She likes the work and the opportunity it gives her to get out of the house and, of course, she is glad of the extra money which makes it possible for her to buy luxuries they could not otherwise afford.

The father has a steady job and at forty-six has many more years before retirement. The eldest brother has left school and is working in a garage, whilst the second is still at school. The youngest is only nine years old.

This family has had to sit down and discuss how best they can cope with the new problem that has entered their lives. They are reluctant that the main burden of caring for Clifford should fall upon the mother once he comes home; she is anxious that her other sons should not be sacrificed and that her husband's job should not be jeopardised. It is almost inevitable that she will come to be the main carer.

The social worker on the case is already organising support and consulting with the GP so that physiotherapy and district nursing will begin as soon as Clifford is home. Voluntary services have been called in too so that the maximum support can be convened. Within the family, the tragedy is having its effect as this new problem pushes all others into the background.

Facing the Future

When a permanent injury has occurred, whatever the cause and whatever the age, the best way must be found of living with and overcoming disability once the initial grief and shock are over. No one can deny that things have changed. Parts of the body either do not work or are not as efficient as they used to be. But the qualities that contribute to a personality remain, the strengths and weaknesses, likes and dislikes, sense of fun, ambitions – these are all still there.

An important step towards regaining independence is to understand exactly what has happened to the body. When both parents and child know where and why things have gone wrong it is easier to use natural resources to assist healing. No doctor will deny that will-power is immensely powerful. We cannot expect to return to perfect health and strength where there has been irreparable damage, but children find ways of compensating for and sometimes overcoming seemingly insurmountable disabilities.

Anthony was involved in a car collision when he was five. His father was driving the car and was killed. The boy had multiple injuries, but recovered except that his sight was affected. It gradually deteriorated until by the time he was adolescent it failed completely and he could no longer see. I went with him and his mother to the eye specialist who examined him carefully and explained that the nerve behind his eyes was quite dead and could not be regenerated. His sight was irretrievably gone. Anthony himself asked many questions and then said confidently, 'I will see again.'

Subsequently, his mother took him to a faith healer on several occasions and some months later told me that his sight was returning, and he could distinguish colours and shapes.

Accident-Prone

Some children are more prone to accidents than others, being more awkward and unpredictable in their actions.

Jeremy was one of a pair of unalike twins, always mischievous whilst his brother was a quieter child. At the age of eight, Jeremy impetuously ran across the road and was knocked down by a car. It took months before he was able to return to school. Here he found difficulty in holding a pen and writing, but he learned to use an electric typewriter and by the age of sixteen he was expected to gain a number of O levels.

He still found difficulty in walking a distance, but used a cycle expertly. He was popular among his school friends and had ambitions to take up social work and help people with problems. His was a caring family who shared many activities.

When Jeremy was seventeen he suffered a tragic and fatal accident. He ran for a train and slipped beneath it. At his funeral the question was on everyone's lips; why did these things happen to him in particular?

Disadvantaged Families

Home circumstances can contribute to accidents. If the parents are very disadvantaged or preoccupied with problems then they show a reduced quality of care for their children.

Marlene was six years old when her mother claimed that she slipped into a bath of scalding water. When she went back to school the other children called her 'fried chicken' because of the shrivelled skin on her cheek and arm. She was eight when I took her to Max Factor's beauty salon where she was taught to use some make-up that disguised the scars and made them less obvious.

Some children suffer deliberate and intentional injury. A teacher showed me the shoulders of a five-year-old boy. They were scarred by marks caused by cigarette burns. He is apparently a happy child now and living with foster parents but what of the emotional damage that he has undoubtedly suffered? Can he ever recover? It seems that his mother who inflicted these burns had herself been wickedly treated when young.

No one can condone brutality to a child, but the facts are that although maltreatment of children occurs at all levels of society the majority of these cases occur in socially disadvantaged families whose lives are one long struggle. Many families with histories of maltreatment have been successfully rehabilitated and reunited with their children. Some parents form self-help groups to discuss their own problems and overwhelming impulses to injure their children.

They need help from doctors and social workers and the planners of our society. Decent housing, employment, a pleasant environment, are all basic needs if people are to enjoy good physical and mental health.

Assault

I met Sarah several months after an assault. She was slowly recovering from a blow on the head struck by a burglar when she was fourteen. Through brain damage she has partially lost the use of her right arm and leg, and walks with a limp. But she is fighting to recover her health and has learned to write with her left hand.

She and her physiotherapists are hoping that her eventual recovery will be complete.

193

Sports Injuries

Sports activities, unfortunately, result in many casualties. Whenever it is suspected that there are injuries to the spine it is best for the patient to be taken to a specialist unit where they have the optimum chance of recovery with the least permanent damage. The Spinal Injury Unit in Stanmore is an excellent example, where the Director, Ian Bailey, believes in treatment for the whole person, not just the injury.

Frank was injured whilst playing rugby and was fortunate to be taken to this unit where he underwent an operation on his spine to repair the damage. During the months of waiting for healing to take place, he lay in his bed studying for exams, aware that he might never walk again. The operation was a success and Frank's recovery has been uneventful.

Five children ran along a beach and shallow dived into the surf. One unlucky little chap didn't surface. He had struck his head on a submerged rock. His mother ran for him, carried him from the water and had enough first-aid knowledge to keep him perfectly still until medical help arrived. He was in hospital for many weeks and now walks with crutches. But things could have been worse. In many accidents much needless damage is caused by people anxious to be helpful and who move victims unnecessarily. The danger is that they can cause greater damage than was suffered originally.

Head Accidents

It has been estimated that a high proportion of accidents to children (from all causes) will involve injuries to the head. Significant damage will result in a stay in general hospital and the more serious cases will go to a specialist neurological centre.

Considering the danger inherent in any injury to the brain the greatest care should be exercised whenever a child has suffered head injury. The younger the child the more

194

vulnerable the brain will be. It is all too easy for a child to suffer severe injury. A head-on collision with a friend, a fall to the pavement from a tricycle or from a playground slide – quite apart from road or bicycle accidents. Any forceful blow to the child risks damaging the soft young brain, this most delicate organ within the bones of the head.

It is natural to rush to a child who has suffered an injury, pick it up and note with relief that there is no blood, that the child is conscious and that, after some tears, all seems well. But everyone concerned with that child should note carefully any changes in behaviour, and there should be close communication between family, school and hospital so that any differences can be noted and evaluated.

The child whose injuries result in problems such as a severe reduction in attention span or difficulties in learning new things needs specialist help and for the younger child, that help is even more essential. Small children have less accumulation of knowledge to draw on and if they receive injuries before all the stages of brain growth are complete, they may be retarded. Head damage might not actually damage the brain in its structure, but there is always a possibility of some disruption to function.

Restoring Confidence

It is important that the child's confidence should not be impaired. Difficulty with school work or a new inability to perform tasks previously found easy can be puzzling and worrying, and often results in cross behaviour and an unhappy child.

It is sometimes suggested that children should be referred for special schooling, but that it not necessarily right. The child who is known, or suspected to have received head injury of any significance should be seen by a doctor who will consider referral to appropriate specialists. Perhaps then a neuro-psychologist can visit and discuss all of the problems with a team which includes everyone concerned with the child. Decisions can then be made as to what can be done to help.

What of the Future?

It can never be easy to accept the loss of independence and the realisation that one must now rely upon others for personal and special needs. Impaired individuals have to accept their situation. But should society accept that so many avoidable accidents happen? The numbers of all of these acquired disabilities and the reasons for them should be considered far more closely. Why does the incidence of accidents remain so high? Why is it accepted that such great numbers of our children will be killed or maimed on our roads each year? We should not shrug off the casualties due to accidents in swimming pools, rivers and seas. Cases of poisoning are far too frequent.

There is still too much unsafe equipment in parks, play areas and playgrounds. There are poorly designed bikes which contribute to head and face injuries. Young children ride tricycles with no stop mechanism and from which it is easy to topple. Children are seen riding as passengers on bikes with no protection. Far too many children suffer emotional and physical damage through non-accidental abuse.

In any week it is certain that our hospital wards will contain numbers of children who will lie injured and morgues will hold some whose lives have been abruptly and needlessly curtailed through preventable causes.

Children's Rights

Children have basic rights and far too many have those rights ignored while their protests fall on unreceptive ears. We owe a debt to newspapers and television which draw attention to the plight of many children who are being sexually molested. No doubt some children cannot differentiate between affectionate or disciplinary treatment and abuse.

But surveys among responsible adults confirm that a high proportion of them were actually abused when young.

Young women told of years of forced sexual intercourse when they were children and of their hopelessness that anyone would believe them. There are some burdens which children carry which amount to handicap. And physically and mentally handicapped children do not escape this particular form of maltreatment. A child whose behaviour at school alters and who appears worried warrants close and sensitive investigation.

A Ministry for Children

Why not a ministry for the overall care and protection of children the aim of which is to bring down the statistics relating to acquired disability and abuse? Every child is entitled to a safe environment and the happiness and security of a home, love and care, preferably with their own parents. Thousands of children could be saved from preventable damage and their families spared the aftermath of their loss or handicap.

PROVISION IN BRITAIN TODAY

23   Health Care

The Right to be Well

The expectation of many people that they will be cured of every ill has come about since the Beveridge Report some forty years ago. Then it was thought that the provision of a comprehensive health service would result in a population so fit that the use of the service would lessen. But people's demands have risen and their self-dependence decreased. This tendency has begun to reverse with greater emphasis on healthy living. Recently, the importance and value of health education have been recognised and this, together with more health screening, is expected to produce encouraging results.

It is right that expectations for handicapped children and other disadvantaged sections should rise steadily. They start out with many problems and are owed special support. But for the community to have become so dependent on medical attention, so demanding of drugs to cure every ailment, cannot be right. In short, it cannot be healthy. Many of our ills are either self-limiting or self-imposed by unwise habits.

The provision of health care is dependent upon the needs of the people and the cost of meeting those needs. If the Government decides that the cost of proposed provision is more than can be allocated, then cuts have to be made. The whole process has to be continually revised and a balance achieved that is as fair as possible to everyone.

The Aims of a Health Service

The aims of any health service must be to bring about an observable improvement in health. There must be plans to prevent handicap and sickness, to diagnose early and to treat without delay. Planning must take place in close collaboration with other services, since social and environmental factors play an important part in health. Providing the conditions which enable people to lead lives of quality, dignity and independence, is the joint responsibility of all the services.

These aims are subject to complex factors; how many medical and paramedical staff are available, what finance can be allocated and what are the priorities and needs of the people?

National Health Service

The implementation of the NHS with its provisions for primary, secondary and community health care, has moved the nation towards better health. Today, standards of health are high; health education is given so that hygiene, immunisation and nutritional diets are recognised for their contribution to our well-being and people live longer. Our handicapped children are given special care from birth onwards and enjoy standards undreamed of years ago.

Whilst the health service has been subject to many modifications since its inception it remains basically the same today and is divided into three main parts. These are the primary care services provided by the general dental, medical, optical, and pharmaceutical professionals; community care which covers additional medical provision in schools, clinics and medical support services, and the secondary care offered in hospitals.

The Family Practitioner Committee

FPCs administer the contracts of all practitioners in their area – general dental, medical, opthalmic medical, optical and pharmaceutical – they control the numbers of doctors and pharmacies and have a clear responsibility to raise the quality of all services.

This duty they carry out in close collaboration with the local professional committees, which represent these practitioners. They are responsible for paying the practitioners, registering patients on doctors' lists and also deal with complaints from the public. Considering the huge number of consultations taking place daily, complaints are comparatively few and are dealt with as speedily as possible.

Registration

The name and birth date of every patient is recorded with the local FPC. These basic details are stored and registration with doctors noted. These records are kept up to date, with any notified change of doctor or name and address. All details are strictly confidential.

An example of the practical use which may be made of records is illustrated by the flagging up of children known to have suffered abuse who could be placed on 'at risk' registers. Such registers are at present kept by local authority social service departments. This would offer the child additional protection when the family moves, since, provided the previous doctor agrees, the new doctor could be advised of potential dangers and prepare to help the family.

Collaboration between FPCs, local authorities and DHAs ensures the maximum possible protection for children. With the danger safely passed the child's name would then be removed from the 'at risk' register. Useful information for GPs can be provided through registration data, for example, age and sex lists, so that particular age groups could be identified for treatment or perhaps immunisation.

The Committee

It is not generally recognised how much work is put in by Family Practitioner Committee members who voluntarily give time regularly. Apart from meetings they inspect surgeries, form panels to interview medical applicants for single-handed practices and agree extra partners, join working parties which prepare responses to government consultation documents, sit on service committees and hear complaints against practitioners from all services, and generally oversee the huge financial expenditure of their FPCs.

In undertaking these duties they are guided by an experienced administrator who has a considerable staff.

Independent Contractors

All practitioners are independent contractors and other than in District Health Authority health centres, they work from their own premises.

The FPC deals with them on all administrative and financial matters, and is directly responsible to the DHSS for doing so.

Dentists

Dental treatment and dentures are available either without charge or at reduced charges to children under sixteen years of age, older children still at school, expectant mothers and mothers with children under a year – as well as people living on low incomes.

Patients do not register with a dentist but it is better for families, including children, to go to the same one regularly and establish a rapport and a trust.

There is often difficulty in treating the teeth of handicapped children and it may be necessary to refer them to community or hospital dental departments. People are free to go to any dentist they choose, but should be clear as to whether the dentist is to provide private or NHS care by asking in advance. It is best to ask for an estimate for proposed treatment and for a second opinion if the proposed treatment is unexpected or worrying.

Dental standards for people have risen and, especially where there has been fluoridisation of water supplies, there is a substantial reduction in tooth decay. We should still see our dentists regularly and have our teeth checked to maintain both dental and general health.

Dental treatment recommended by the dentist on the NHS may have to be approved by the Dental Estimates Board. Payments for NHS treatment are administered by the Family Practitioners Committee, although part of the cost may be payable by the patient up to a prescribed amount. Any complaints about treatment or dentures are dealt with by specially appointed committees.

A fine reputation is deservedly enjoyed by the dental profession. Publicity has been given to a 'drill and fill' racket conducted by a few members who abuse the system. It is up to the profession to see that this is stamped out. Meanwhile, it pays the patient to be wary.

Ophthalmologists and Opticians

Sight can be tested only by an ophthalmic medical practitioner or ophthalmic optician. The sight test is at present paid for by the NHS, but it is proposed that a charge be introduced. If glasses are needed and the person qualifies they will be given a voucher to help pay for them. Otherwise the full charge for glasses is payable by the patient.

Vouchers can be claimed by anyone under sixteen, or under nineteen if in full-time education; the NHS also covers repairs for this group. Vouchers may also be given to anyone in receipt of Income Support which has replaced the familiar supplementary benefit and family income supplement. People on low income or anyone needing complex or powerful lenses may be able to claim allowances for them.

Opticians provide a valuable service because examination of the eye can reveal not only the eye problems but also the early stages of conditions needing medical treatment.

Certainly any child with squints or any other sight problems should be taken for checks without delay. Sight can be endangered if these are neglected.

Pharmacists

Pharmacists make up medicines prescribed by doctors, monitoring these in case of errors. They can also advise patients about medicines and give over-the-counter recommendations as well as warnings.

They can ensure that people understand the importance of directions for taking medicines. It is vital that instructions regarding correct dosage and times of taking medicine, whether before or following food, whether with water, are precisely understood by the patient and clearly written on the attached label. It is wise if the doctor puts the age of children on the prescription so that pharmacists can check that the dosage is correct.

The Nuffield Report of 1985 recommended that pharmacists should pursue their advisory role and that day-to-day dispensing should be undertaken by trained, but unqualified, personnel under the direct supervision of the pharmacist. The report recommended that pharmacists should provide a counselling room or area within the pharmacy in which to expand their advisory role and facilitate patient counselling.

The Government has been concernerd to bring down the cost of medicines paid for by the health service and to introduce a limited list. Provided that doctors are able to prescribe those drugs which will benefit their patients, this is sensible. Generic prescribing should be encouraged. Carbon copies of drugs in fancy packaging and with a variety of names do not enhance their basic value.

Contractual Duty of General Medical Practitioners

The contracts of GPs call for them to give 24-hour care.

They can, however, opt out of after-hours duty, but rarely do so.

They provide medical care to the patients on their list and to those patients who are temporarily in their area, and whom they are prepared to accept. They must also provide emergency treatment to anyone in need.

Maternity Services

GPs can elect to provide obstetric, that is maternity, services if they wish. Before admission to the obstetric list, however, they must prove they have considerable experience in maternity work. Those doctors who gain admission can provide maternity services to anyone.

Those not on the obstetric list can only provide services for their own patients. This means that the doctor who wishes to provide general maternity services must have had considerable home or hospital experience and sufficient births must be seen and worked with to warrant inclusion on the obstetric list. It also means that patients should feel confident of their doctor's maternity work experience before booking with them for births.

It is probably safer to choose a doctor on the obstetric list. This is not the time to be practised on.

Doctors' Manner of Approach

Patients sometimes complain of the manner in which they are treated. There is nothing in the doctor's contract which says, for example, that they must not be surly. I do believe however that patients are often so nervous of their doctors that an abrupt and rude manner can send them away depressed and more ill than ever, whereas a degree of charm and warmth can cheer a person and make them feel better.

The committed GP works hard and deserves not only the money earned but the respect that the medical profession is generally accorded. Patients who do not get good service can vote with their feet by going elsewhere. Doctors do not have to accept or keep patients on their lists; they are independent contractors and provided they render a service giving the due care required they may run their surgeries as they please.

Attitudes are extremely important. Doctors who do not look at patients during interviews or address them with terse remarks, without warmth or sympathy can hardly expect them to relax and confide their fears and ills. The way patients behave often depends on their past experience of doctors and their staff.

It is unfortunate that professionals who evoke aggressive attitudes in patients do not, or cannot, realise that they are at fault. A patient who has found it difficult to get an appointment at the surgery or for a home visit, may well exaggerate symptoms or adopt a militant attitude in order to secure attention to themselves.

Surgery staff who consistently cause dissatisfaction on the part of patients should have this called to their attention. And if there is no improvement they should be persuaded to change to another occupation where their attitudes may do less damage.

It is so easy to engage a patient's positive feelings by giving them simple courtesy and a little more time. Few people want to take up doctors' time unnecessarily and a relaxed doctor-patient relationship is good for everyone.

There are demanding patients and doctors have to learn how to cope with them as part of their training.

Families with handicapped children need special attention and warrant more time spent on them. Some parents may be over stressed by the unremitting care of a disabled child. The tension that such parents are under can erupt in unreasonable behaviour to the receptionist, who should always try to respond in a helpful way. Demanding patients may often just be people who are not very good at expressing themselves or who are simply so scared of health problems that they show their fear in anger.

What Makes a Good Patient?

Patients should arrive at their doctor's surgery punctually and with a brief written list of symptoms. They should be prepared to take no more than five to ten minutes of time unless the doctor extends it. They and their children should wear clothing that is quick to change out of. They should be thankful not to be prescribed medicines. The doctor will give them antibiotics if he believes this to be necessary.

They should be reasonable about seeing a partner if the usual doctor is unavailable. It is only polite to ask for a convenient time to phone and not expect the doctor to answer personally. Patients should not themselves suggest referrals to consultants unless there are very good reasons to do so. Patients are entitled to second opinions if they do not agree with a diagnosis, but GPs are doctor with years of training, just as consultants are. Patients should remember this and try to be reasonable in their requests.

Doctors' Referrals

Doctors can recommend patients to specialists for opinions and assessments.

It is important that no physically disabled child or adult should slip through the net and miss opportunities for the best of care.

GP's Responsibility to Young Disabled

A report by the Royal College of Physicians entitled 'Physical Disability in 1986 and Beyond' has described the general practitioner's role in this regard as becoming a much greater one. They should define the handicapped patients' problems in physical and psychological terms.

The report finds that in a group practice of, for example, 10,000 patients, 1,000 will be physically disabled, of whom about 200 will be severely disabled. Approximately seventy-two will have recourse to a wheelchair.

Disability Centres

The report recommends that there should be fifteen units in the country whose functions would include the assessment of severely physically disabled persons, the provision of appliances, aids and equipment as well as workshops where these may be modified. This is a recommendation with which I fully agree as there are still serious shortcomings to be overcome before it can be said that we are fulfilling the needs of the severely disabled in our community.

England and Wales do not have a medical speciality of physical medicine, and there are few rehabilitation consultants – hence the poor state of Medical Disability Services. We need more doctors with a formal professional commitment to the subject.

There is plainly a case for arguing for resources, particularly for those youngsters above the age of sixteen. This seems to be where the cut-off point comes and there is no co-ordinated care for the future concerning rehabilitation, further education, transport, housing, employment and leisure. Until this situation is remedied we have a doubly disadvantaged sector.

Changing Doctors

Patients often think that they sign on for life when they register with a doctor. They can certainly change, provided only that the new doctor agrees to take them. Sometimes, patients talk of doctors ganging up on them and not letting them on any list. This is most improbable. There should never be any agreement between doctors to limit the freedom of choice people have. If there appears to be a problem it is best to try and talk it out with the practice.

If the matter cannot be resolved then the FPC is empowered to place a patient with a doctor for a minimum period of seven days which often continues indefinitely. There are, of course, difficult patients, but these are people who need help more than most. Patients do tend to stick with the doctor they first register with and they do not normally change for flippant reasons.

When choosing a doctor it is wise to go along to the surgery and ask to look at the practice leaflet which sets out the services offered; it is far better for all concerned if the whole family signs on with the same GP.

Lists of doctors are to be found at FPCs and post offices, but recommendations to particular doctors cannot be given. For that kind of advice, the local Community Health Council may be helpful.

Surgery Premises

Health centres are provided in some areas by District Health Authorities from which doctors may practise single-handed or in groups. These centres are purpose-built and usually provide excellent accommodation. Many GP-owned premises are either purpose-built or adapted, and make inviting and efficient medical centres.

There are still some surgeries which are far from what I personally would call adequate; most GPs welcome the considerable experience which FPCs can provide, and will agree to improvements of their surgeries, towards which there are government grants. But if doctors resist change, and if the premises fulfil the modest basic requirements outlined in legislation, then improvement cannot be enforced. There are GPs who feel that they provide good care and prefer their premises to be left the way they are. Whilst numbers of their patients may agree with them there must be more who would be happy to have updated surgeries to visit.

Access for Wheelchairs

It is unlikely that there will be practices built in

the future which do not provide access for wheelchairs. It is regrettable that many handicapped people are discriminated against because this provision is lacking.

However, doctors with an inaccessible practice will visit any wheelchair patients who need to see them.

Shop Hours for Surgery

Ideally, surgeries should be open all day, even though the doctor cannot be there all the time. Someone can see the patients, make appointments for them, offer general advice, get another doctor in case of emergency or get the patient to hospital.

A surgery which is closed except for an hour or so morning and evening is not, in my view, providing a reasonable service – and does not inspire confidence. Patients will either go to the casualty department of a hospital or do without medical help until night when they often panic and make an emergency call.

Where surgeries have shop hours patients make far fewer requests for out of hours calls. In general, they are considerate and do not like to trouble their doctors unnecessarily, especially for late or night calls.

In an Emergency

Patients often find that in an emergency after surgery hours they have to make a number of phone calls in order to contact their doctor. Patients should be advised, in advance, of surgery arrangements when their own doctors are away or off duty, as they can become desperately anxious when emergencies arise. Doctors must have time off, but will arrange for other doctors or a deputising service to take their calls.

Sympathetic consideration can be given to a GP who has reached an age where it is wise to take things a bit easy or whose health requires that he or she must do less work. It is often hard for GPs who try to give good service and who come up against difficult local conditions. These are times of rising crime and violence and one would hope that doctors out on errands of mercy would be immune to attack. Sadly, they are not. Women doctors are particularly vulnerable and they need to be accompanied on house calls in certain areas or ask the families of patients for someone to come out to the car to escort them to and from the home.

Ancillary Staff

Ancillary staff help in the running and management of the surgery. There are receptionists, nurses, practice managers and others whose work involves the health care of the patient. It is the doctor though who is ultimately responsible for action taken by his staff.

Receptionists should be well trained and should receive patients with a pleasant manner. No longer are there dragons minding the surgery. There used to be stories of patients who trembled before them; of receptionists who gave medical advice and wrote out prescriptions without reference to their doctors and of some who threw patients off lists at a whim. But these ladies have disappeared – and not before time.

The Doctor Decides When to Visit

This was the experience of a family whose misfortune it is to suffer from bullosa nervosa. This miserable disorder causes the skin to break down on contact with virtually anything. Beryl's feet were affected and in the middle of an attack when she could scarcely tolerate shoes or slippers her baby ran a high temperature and Beryl requested a doctor's visit.

The receptionist was adamant and refused one, insisting that Beryl wrap the baby up and come to the surgery. The poor girl bandaged her feet and hobbled the half mile, arriving with bleeding feet. The doctor was appalled and drove her home. That receptionist was certainly in the wrong job.

Practice Nurses

These nurses ease the surgery work load by taking on some of the routine procedures for which they are qualified. They confer many advantages on both doctors and patients. They give treatment, inoculations, take blood-pressure, help to run the antenatal, infant welfare and childcare clinics, and whatever other services the practice is offering.

This kind of provision in a surgery can reduce the pressure on hospital departments, often taking on minor surgical treatment and the after-care of patients.

Staff Training

It is considered essential that doctors and their staff should take ongoing training so that they are kept up to date. Nurses can take courses which qualify them to target the high risk individuals on the practice lists and give preventive health education. It may be difficult for the busy practice to release staff for further education but it pays enormous dividends in the quality of care that a practice can offer.

Practice Managers

A large practice with five or six doctors can have as many as 12,000 patients. A good practice manager can see that everything runs smoothly. The responsibility is great; GP's daily instructions to be carried out, patients' queries dealt with and all the practice mail to be answered. Age and sex registers must be checked and elderly patients offered screening, children's assessment and immunisation programmes maintained, reminders to doctors for repeat prescriptions and so on.

The work is extensive. Practice managers must also prepare financial claims for the FPC so that the surgery income arrives without undue delay.

Attached Staff

Attached staff are employed by the District Health Authority (DHA). Health visitors are highly qualified nurses who besides being registered midwives also hold the health visitor's certificate. They have specific responsibilities; for example, they are statutorily obliged to screen babies at eight months for deafness and are generally responsible for family health. Their duty is to detect problems and advise about services available and, most importantly, to educate patients about keeping healthy.

Therapists are likely to be among staff attached to surgeries. Whilst drugs play an essential role in relieving and curing conditions, the management of sickness and disability also requires the experience of speech, occupational and physiotherapists. An anxious mother with a sick or handicapped child at home needs guidance about environment, diet, exercise and education.

Primary Contact is the GP

GPs are the first point of contact for all patients requiring NHS medical services, and they direct patients to the services required. They therefore play a leading role in ensuring that disabled patients receive all the facilities necessary and available.

In respect of general medical service, applications for admissions by doctors to practice as GPs are first vetted by the FPC in consultation with the Local Medical Committee

(LMC), and recommendations are then forwarded to the national Medical Practices Committee (MPC).

Medical Practices Committee

In order to achieve and maintain an even geographical distribution of doctors in England and Wales (Scotland and Northern Ireland have separate systems) the Secretary of State set up this important national committee. The MPC has nine members who come from all over the country bringing considerable local knowledge, expertise and views representative of the profession and of patients.

The MPC meets regularly to process applications from the ninety-eight FPCs. It must constantly note changes in areas and assess the ratios of GPs to people. Then, dependent upon a number of additional factors such as high density housing, multi-ethnic levels, unemployment, new developments, numbers of elderly, etc., the committee can decide whether that district is adequately medically served or not.

Regional Health Authorities

Regional Health Authorities (RHAs) are responsible for the planning of health services, all capital outlays on hospitals and other buildings, general postgraduate dental, medical and nursing training and for distributing finances to District Health Authorities. Their members regularly visit NHS, FPC and surgery premises so that they remain aware of the wide spread of services available to patients.

District Health Authorities

District Health Authorities (DHAs) have overall responsibility for hospital and community health services. Advisory subcommittees are responsible for seeing that there is close collaboration between health and local authorities. This ensures that consideration has been given to the most urgent priorities. There is an increasing tendency to develop health care in the community rather than in hospitals. This means that more dependence must be placed on support services supplied by local authorities and in particular by social service departments.

Handicapped children or other patients discharged from hospital whilst still needing some assistance require the support of their GP and must have sufficient home help and domiciliary nursing as well as the help of their families, good neighbours, and the support of voluntary organisations.

Community Medicine

This range of services is organised by the DHA and includes various clinics staffed by doctors, health visitors, nurses and therapists. In the child health clinics routine examinations are conducted to ensure the well-being of children, particularly in the first two years when they are most vulnerable. It is supplementary to the general medical practitioners' care, backing it up and ensuring that no one is lost to the system.

The school health service has an important role to play, particularly for children from poorer backgrounds who may not have had pre-school medical assessments. Such children see doctors less often, have less immunisation, a poorer diet and less healthy environment. Children who have problems which interfere with their educational progress, their physical development and their general well-being should be identified at some stage during their school years.

The partnership between parents, GPs and health and education authorities is ideally set to screen children through all stages of development, offering proper immunisation at the appropriate times.

Community Health Councils

These groups were introduced into health services in 1973.

In every District Health Authority district there is a Community Health Council.

They represent consumers' interests, ensuring that services develop according to people's needs. Members appointed make sure that they are aware of local priorities as well as any deficiencies in provision. The closest collaboration between all bodies involved in planning, provision or monitoring of services is vital so that resources are used in the best way.

The trend is growing for more primary health care to be delivered in the community rather than in hospitals, and Community Health Council members are invited to comment on family practitioner services, particularly medical and dental. The public must be admitted to meetings where agenda items for discussion might include the numbers of patients on doctor's lists, range and standards of service in surgeries and hospitals, patient facilities and amenities, the quality of catering in hospital, general areas of complaint and advice to individual patients and the effectiveness of health care throughout the service in the district.

Hospital Service

There must be provision for accidents and emergencies and these hospital departments are manned twenty-four hours a day. A number of beds are reserved for emergency admissions.

Referrals to consultants by general practitioners are made and appointments arranged according to the urgency of the case. There is generally a waiting-list for operations where delay does not threaten life.

The difficulties for young patients in hospital have long been recognised and the trauma of separation of child from mother is avoided whenever possible. Mothers can usually stay with children and overnight accommodation is often provided. Qualified staff are specially trained in the care of children and today's hospital wards have a very cheerful appearance. Teachers and play leaders help children with school work, continuing education and encouraging learning games. Children can establish relationships with staff so that the stress and strain through absence of the mother, if she cannot be there, is reduced.

Admissions to hospitals have been steadily increasing, older people generally making the greatest demands in relation to their numbers. The intention to put resources into preventing disability and sickness, promoting good health and making wider use of primary health care in the GPs surgeries should reduce demand on hospitals in the future.

The prevention of those diseases which may be dependent upon behaviour are to a certain degree the responsibility of the individual. There are surgeons who discourage smoking by refusing to operate unless the habit is discontinued. Excessive use of alcohol, drug dependency, obesity and diseases related to these habits are preventable and health education is important.

In Conclusion

There is ongoing collaboration between members of DHAs, FPCs and CHCs, and this is vital to ensure that there are neither gaps in provision nor unnecessary overlapping of services.

Patients get the best medical care that can be provided within allocated finance.

24 Alternative Medicine

Drug companies constantly devise new compounds which doctors are able to prescribe once these drugs have passed the strict controlling regulations of the Committee on the Safety of Medicines. These add to the wide range of medicines which are designed to alleviate some problems and cure others. But there are still many conditions which do not respond favourably to medicines and orthodox treatment. Patients may then turn for help to those who practise alternative medicine.

It is certain that some illnesses are self-limiting and if untreated will disappear of their own accord. Often, cures are attributed to alternative treatments when in fact they are more probably spontaneous. The natural defences of the body occasionally appear to have been overwhelmed by disease, but then find new strength and throw off invading causes of sickness and good health is restored.

Provided alternative methods do no harm and offer hope to patients there is no reason why they should not be tried. Some of the more popular forms of alternative medicine are outlined here and many children appear to have benefited from them.

Acupuncture

At the basis of Chinese therapeutics lie the principles of Yang and Yin, the former identified with masculinity, sun and heat, whilst Yin represents femininity, the cool and damp. Good health results from a proper balance of Yang and Yin.

These two forces are said to circulate throughout the body along twelve meridians and around more than three hundred and sixty-five points. When there is ill health, a needle is inserted at a precise place and this treatment has proved effective for some, although no reasoning convinces Western science that acupuncture can cure.

Allergies

A number of ills may be caused through allergies to certain chemicals and foods. It is recognised, for example, that a small percentage of children have arthritic type reactions to some foods. Allergy clinics generally provide the tests for a number of allergens whereby the skin of the arm is gently scratched and a number of suspect agents are applied. Some allergy specialists hold that these methods are not fully effective and they use either sublingual or subcutaneous testing with single substances diluted to various strengths. Once offending agents are identified sufferers can be desensitised.

There is increaseing interest in allergies which are associated with behaviour problems. Many mothers recognise that some substances affect their children adversely. The children become ill or hypersensitive, and it is best to eliminate any food and additives thought to aggravate the child and reintroduce them gradually, checking on any change of behaviour that might occur.

Aromatherapy

Pungent oils are used together with deep and prolonged massage of the body. The different varieties of oil have different attributes and can be used to achieve desired effects or improvements in well-being. It is a pleasant treatment, soothing and relaxing.

Massage has been used with some success at Charing Cross Hospital to reduce tension in patients with heart conditions. Children enjoy massage and it is beneficial, improving circulation for those who have little movement and are wheelchair-bound.

Cancer Help Centres

It is the belief of many that our systems are poisoned by the effect of environmental conditions added to our intake of chemicals in foods. The result is that we become ill. Cancers are treated by diets consisting of fresh fruit juice, fruit and vegetables which are eaten sparingly.

Once clear of poisons the body is again able to heal itself naturally. The Bristol Cancer Help Centre claims success for many of its cancer patients through the use of this diet.

Chiropractice

Chiropractors base their treatment on the belief that all medical problems stem from the spine. They practise deep massage and manipulation in this area. A few satisfying crunches appear to produce relief from backache as well as many other symptoms as varied as catarrh, stomach-ache or migraine.

Some young patients, as well as adults, have found that pain and chronic conditions can be alleviated by this treatment.

Faith Healing

Healers maintain that they have special powers which enable them to perform miracles by the laying on of hands or by absent healing through silent prayer.

Some healers claim to specialise and have particular success with certain disorders and organs of the body.

Herbal Medicine

Herbalism is used by many doctors practising traditional medicine who prefer natural remedies. Among many prescriptions, ginseng is held to be exceptional and effective for a variety of ailments. Practitioners must acquire a knowledge of herbs and their powers to heal, so as to produce the right medicine in suitable strength.

From time to time there are investigations regarding old wives' tales of herbs which heal. Some plants do contain powerful poisons and other substances which can affect humans. The absorption of such extracts, suitably controlled, appears to be curative in some cases.

Homoeopathy

Homoeopathists prescribe weak solutions of medicines and advise the intake of fresh natural foods combined with exercise.

This treatment is effective for some people, and there are many who are convinced of its value.

Hypnotism

Hypnotists attempt to instil total relaxation in their patients and then work on the subconscious mind by positive suggestion that ills can be removed or cured.

This method is commonly used to help cure addictive habits which cause ill health, such as smoking, excessive eating and drinking alcohol immoderately.

Naturopathy

Teachers eschew all forms of medicines, drugs or invasive treatment such as surgery. Patients are required to eat food free from additives and to give up tobacco and alcohol.

Moderate exercise, swimming and walking are advised – and exposing the body to sun and air is all part of the recommended way of life.

Osteopathy

A form of physiotherapy which achieves cures for some by

manipulation of the bones of the body. Such treatment is said to produce relief of muscle and joint problems.

Generally, half-hour sessions of any form of massage produce a feeling of well-being – so it is worth trying.

Reflexology

This press-point therapy is based on the assumption that nerve-like pathways in the feet connect to all parts of the body.

Allegedly, these pathways are easy to locate and treat in the feet. And when there is sickness the corresponding press-points are tender and can be gently massaged to produce improvements.

Yoga

A form of exercise, deep breathing, relaxation and meditation, this is a popular way to unwind and regain health.

Some children with cerebral palsy have been helped with yoga to control muscles, movement and to stabilise balance. Others with asthma have been trained to prevent and to regulate asthma attacks.

Summary . . .

These are some of the available forms of treatment. They do have one thing in common. Practitioners give their patients time. Time to sit, to relax, to talk and listen.

When traditional doctors can give their advice unhurriedly, allowing patients more time to unburden themselves of their problems, there is rarely a need to look elsewhere for treatment.

A Word of Warning!

Where there are serious or persistent symptoms always be sure to visit a GP for advice.

25 Social Services

The present provision of social services has only been achieved after many years of planning effort on the part of central government and local authorities.

Parliament is constantly busy debating a range of subjects and introducing new legislation, and it is the duty of members of parliament to ensure that the changes made result in improved conditions for the people.

Comparison with the Past

There is no doubt that conditions now bear favourable comparison with the past and handicapped children today can look forward to a quality of life they could not have dreamed of at the turn of the century.

One needs to consider conditions prevailing then and in the preceding hundred or so years to appreciate why and how living conditions arose and how they altered to become what is available today. There were changes in the way people earned their living and where they lived. People moved into crowded conditions, and there was little knowledge of hygiene. Children in particular ran a high risk of sickness, handicap and death.

Housing stock of the poorer classes was in bad condition without baths or toilets, and families often had only one bed, which they shared. Doctors knew better than anyone how people lived for they made so many home visits each day. Many children suffered from rheumatic fever and the damp housing many of them lived in gave them little opportunity to recover. Rheumatic heart-disease was common and those children affected lived out their lives as delicate invalids.

How These Conditions Came About

The nation's customs and living standards, which had been

static for centuries, with families living in isolated farming villages changed dramatically with the advent of the Industrial Revolution. At about that time preventive medicine had begun with Jenner's discovery in 1790 that an infection of cowpox was a protection against smallpox, although no one was quite sure how this was possible.

During the nineteenth century, advances in farming methods reduced agricultural employment, whilst at the same time mass production by factory machines was taking gainful occupation away from the villagers. Home crafts were no longer needed. People flocked to the new towns in search of work. There, they were compelled by circumstances to accept near starvation wages and to live in hastily constructed, inadequate housing which quickly deteriorated into slums. The combination of bad working conditions, overcrowded housing, poor hygiene and malnutrition caused much sickness and disability.

The tales of woe described by Dickens and contemporary authors shook the country into awareness of the plight of the poor. Ragged boys were being cuffed into subjection by bullying workhouse beadles and matrons and forced to climb chimneys as sweeps or do other unsuitable jobs. Scores of children were sleeping rough and scavenging for their food; little girls were put into kitchen service before they reached their teens.

Such suffering of children aroused the public conscience and by 1900 pioneering work by voluntary bodies like the National Society for the Prevention of Cruelty to Children (NSPCC), The National Children's Home (NCH), Dr Barnados, the Shaftesbury Homes and others had begun their work of alleviating hardship, taking destitute children off the street, educating and caring for them.

Poor Standards of Health

The realisation by the end of the Boer War in 1902 that half of the young men volunteering to fight were unfit to serve, shocked the Government into action.

It was realised that home living conditions and diet were supremely important to everyone, but in particular to the health of pregnant women; that the most dangerous period for a child was the first month of its life. As is still the case today.

Immunisation Began

It was during the Boer War that mass immunisation was introduced amongst soldiers following the discovery that inoculation of dead typhoid bacilli prevented the spread of typhoid. Subsequently the medical care of schoolchildren was advocated and examination of conditions in mines, factories and workshops was required.

The resulting reforms led to the first School Health Service and an expansion of health visiting at home. Much more prominence was to be given to the inspection of conditions for children in their homes, schools and places of employment.

Health Insurance for Workers

In 1911 a National Health Insurance scheme was introduced, contributed to by both employers and employees.

This gave domiciliary medical care to employees, but to them only – not to their families.

World Wars I and II

Slum clearance and better housing improved the situation, but people still could not afford to buy enough food. Children from the poorer classes were still undersized and suffered disease and handicap, caused primarily by malnutrition and their unhealthy environment. The difference in physique between the well-nourished upper

227

classes and half-starved lower classes was particularly noticeable in Army personnel during the First World War.

Improvement came slowly, but during the Second World War the health of the population showed a dramatic turn for the better. Although there were so many casualties, much destruction of housing by bombing attacks and all the emotional strain and suffering of war there was also full employment and food rations for everyone.

For the first time the general public was advised about health education and pregnant women received antenatal care; free milk, orange juice and cod-liver oil were issued to supplement diet, ensuring the nutritional health of mother and infant. There was talk of a free health service for everyone.

Free Health Care

In 1943 the Beveridge Report on social security was published to wide acclaim and later adopted almost in its entirety. A charter for the elimination of poverty and need, it represented radical innovation in the Western world and marked the most far-reaching development of those public services which had begun with the twentieth century.

A medical service became available to everyone free of all charge, by 1948. General taxation was to provide finance, supplemented by a weekly contributory insurance scheme.

Child Care and Immunisation

Following the Children Act of 1948, child care services were set up across the country, completely independent of other services – standards of care rose.

Scientific research had already produced vaccines and enabled immunisation programmes among children to take place. These had wiped out first diphtheria, which had taken the lives of more than fifty children a week in the UK and then polio, which had left so many youngsters paralysed.

Now vaccines were available which reduced the incidence of whooping cough, tetanus and tuberculosis.

Local Authority Care

Under the various Children Acts which followed local authorities were given responsibilities, particularly in supervising and caring for children and young persons below the age of eighteen years.

In particular these responsibilities cover four main groups of children. These include those who have to be cared for by the local authority because their parents or guardians are temporarily or permanently unable to care for them; those brought before a court for criminal proceedings; those placed by a court in the care of the Social Services Committee of the local authority in connection with marital proceedings; and children who have been placed in foster homes or who have been placed privately for adoption.

It became the aim of every single social services department to ensure that all children in care were brought up under conditions as similar as possible to those found in a happy and normal family. It was generally agreed that a warm and secure atmosphere is essential so that each child feels wanted, loved and respected.

Urban Deprivation

Difficult conditions found in inner city areas were regarded as a subject deserving of special consideration. The plight of such disadvantaged sections of the community, often including multi-ethnic minorities was seen as needing more resources. Community Relations Councils set up in 1968, and Community Health Councils in 1973, steadily developed into valuable advisory and watch-dog bodies. Services improved as a result of their vigilance, and the Government and local finance which was put into these councils was money well spent.

Social Service Provision

In 1970 the Chronically Sick and Disabled Persons Act gave the right to handicapped people to have their homes adapted, and also required that wheelchair access to public buildings should be improved. The unified Social Services Acts of 1971 meant an improved service for families with handicapped children. Following studies like the Court Report of 1976 and the Warnock Report of 1978 – and the implementation of their recommendations – significant improvements came about.

The current programme of integration of handicapped children in schools and the general level of provision for families without means or on low incomes has reduced acute poverty and suffering.

General health is better and preventive medicine is practised. It is accepted that patients are more likely to take advice from their doctors to give up habits like smoking, excessive or unwise eating or immoderate drinking – all of which can induce poor health.

Doctors have taken advantage of grants to update surgeries, have fewer patients on their lists and are encouraged to work in groups. They can each take on two ancillary staff and surgery nurses have the opportunity to be trained in preventive care. The emphasis now is on team-work and the patient benefits from shared expertise and knowledge available from the surgery.

Maternity Services

At the turn of the twentieth century untrained women attended childbirth, and there was considerable handicap and loss of life to babies. By 1948 the numbers of children who died during their first year of life had dropped to some thirty per thousand. By 1977 it had dropped to fourteen, and in the years since there has been annual improvement.

Trained midwives now attend childbirth, and doctors may only attend their own patients, unless they have passed the stringent requirements of local obstetric committees. They are then admitted to the obstetric list and may attend confinements for any mother.

A Review

Reviewing the years which bring us close to the twenty-first century we can feel satisfaction that so much has been achieved, but there is no room for complacency for things must be even better, in particular for our handicapped children.

Since 1979 there have been some forty new Acts, a number of which affect handicapped children and adults. Acts have been passed on Social Security, Education, Housing, Local Government Planning, Disabled Persons and Children's Homes. Community care has become an issue of fresh concern within social services, with emphasis on greater expenditure on care in the community so that carers, and those they care for, have an easier time.

Home is Best

It has been the consensus of opinion between local authorities and successive governments that the needs of handicapped children, as well as adults, can best be met within our own homes or communities – rather than in hospitals.

This can only happen successfully if local authorities are prepared and able to deliver the personal social services which people must have in order to manage either independently or with their families.

Furthermore, whilst families and communities are often prepared to take care of their own disabled members they need respite care in order to recover from the demanding regimes imposed by 24-hour care for the handicapped. And disabled people themselves need to be able to take breaks from those who care for them.

The NHS has for many years devoted its priorities to the

provision of hospital services. There is now a welcome swing away from hospitals and an increasing emphasis on domiciliary and primary health services. This must be accompanied by an adequate financial input to ensure that support services are provided. With the right planning and sufficient finance families can be prepared for necessary outlay and will be content to take care of their handicapped children.

Social Security Money

Financial support is available and for those in need there are grants, income supplements and benefits. The Welfare State employs a number of terms and there is often confusion in the minds of people about what they can and cannot claim. Numerous benefits cover every possible contingency that can temporarily or permanently reduce income, including sickness, loss of work or death of the wage earner.

Benefits should never be regarded as something for nothing. If a parent is taking care of a handicapped child then they are saving the state a great deal of money. It is worth calling into a Citizens Advice Bureau and finding out about what money is available, as of right. Attendance and mobility allowances are the entitlement of parents whose child is severely disabled.

Many families do not claim their entitlement. Cash is available for people who are in need, but millions of pounds is unclaimed every year. It is worrying that children may be without comforts that this money could bring. One-parent families are usually well-advised and know what they should get. Anyone who does not know should find out because the amount to be claimed can be quite considerable. Furthermore, receipts of income supplements may give automatic entitlement to a number of free benefits.

Medical care comes free in hospitals and from the general practitioner to everyone, but full or partial payments are required for dental treatment, prescriptions and articles like spectacles, wigs and elasticised stockings. These items so far remain the entitlement of the lower income groups. Families attending or visiting a child in hospital can apply for fares. One family spent over £800 in a year in travelling to and from a hospital with their baby who needed numerous operations before finally receiving partial reimbursement.

Enabling Independent Living

Much can be done to enable disabled children to be independent. The ideal is purpose-built housing, and some councils do make this sort of provision.

But additional ground floor accommodation or adaptations can be provided which give a measure of independence. Building bedrooms, bathrooms and toilets on the ground floor or providing lifts or stair-lifts, ramped entrances, wider doors – these are all ideas which can make life easier, and for which councils may give grants.

Fresh Legislation

In 1983 the Government began a review of the structure of the social security system. The Green Paper which resulted, *Reform of Social Security*, was published in four volumes in 1985.

Later in 1985 the White Paper was published entitled *Reform of Social Security: Programme for Action* and contained modified proposals.

The Social Security Act of 1986

After consultation and amendment *Programme for Action* was enacted in this Act.

Part of the Act's provisions is a simple system of income-related benefits.

The New Benefits

Income Support now provides for assessed payments to replace the familiar supplementary benefit allowances and supplementary pensions. Family credit will replace family income supplement and will provide benefit, in addition to child benefit, for families with an adult in work – but on low income.

This legislation has been heralded as 'the most comprehensive examination of social security since Beveridge.' It has been based upon the consideration of adequacy of benefit levels for the poorer families. There is always anxiety at times of change that legislation could operate to the detriment of vulnerable people, and there are serious implications for the disabled.

Whilst it is hoped that this section of the community will get increased benefits, care must be taken to monitor the way in which the new system works so that those in most need do not suffer.

A new Social Fund is now created to allow for appeals for single payments. Many of these Social Fund payments will be discretionary, some payments will be budget and crisis loans, and these are generally to be repayable. A number of disabled people who previously received supplementary benefit could be left worse off because some of the additional allowances previously available are directly related to ill-health and disability. The new income support already allows for this. However, the Government has promised that they will not suffer financially, and the value of their benefit will be protected until the income supplement rates catch up.

Those people who established a need before income supplement came into operation will receive additional allowances for heating, diet, laundry, special clothing, heavy wear and tear on clothing, attendance needs, bathing help, blindness and hospital fares. It does take some time to establish entitlement to additional allowances and there should be no delay in submitting claims where it is thought there is entitlement.

234

New explanatory leaflets are available and families in doubt as to their entitlement must seek advice promptly from voluntary or statutory offices.

Child Abuse and Rehabilitating Families

An important area of social service work is to prevent the break up of families. The early recognition of child abuse and rehabilitative work with the family can save much tragedy.

Recently, considerable publicity has been accorded to the problem of non-accidental injury to children. To deliberately hurt a child is outside normal behaviour and calls for investigation. Often, assault or neglect by parents may be associated with other antisocial and irresponsible behaviour. Alcoholic addiction accounts for some violence, but frequently trivial reasons can precipitate abuse. It may begin with poor living conditions, intolerance of excessive crying or sheer frustration which ends with parents ill-treating a child by slapping, punching and severely shaking them. Young children are vulnerable and can be badly injured in this way.

It is estimated that each year the deaths of some 400 children are caused by such treatment. Many more survive, some with permanent impairment.

Younger parents are generally less tolerant of crying children, losing their tempers and inflicting damage whilst losing self-control. Some are psychiatrically disturbed or emotionally inadequate and many may have been deprived of affection as children or were themselves treated brutally.

The Child's Safety Comes First

Whatever the reason, the child's safety may well depend upon those people around, neighbours, friends, relatives, who are sufficiently concerned to report to professional people. It is right in such cases to tell GPs, health visitors, social workers or a voluntary organisation such as the NSPCC, that they believe the child is subject to treatment likely to cause physical or emotional harm.

At school, teachers should be aware of a change in a child's behaviour or of any unusual injuries. Hospital departments, in particular, must be alert to the possibility that the injury sustained by a child is the result of deliberate abuse.

Sexual Abuse

The number of adults of both sexes who say that they were sexually used and abused in early childhood confirms that this form of assault must take place today on a wide scale. Both men and women are guilty, although it is a higher proportion of men that commit this form of abuse. Social service departments cannot alone discover and deal with such situations. Every adult who has contact with a child must be ready to recognise when there is a problem and be prepared to place information before the right people.

It is a sad reflection on society that some of our children are not safe from members of their own families. This must be accepted as a fact of life and dealt with in the best possible way.

Unjust Accusations

Inevitably mistakes will be made. Recent cases illustrate that symptoms attributed to sexual abuse in very young children were in fact due to natural causes. Other children with damage of broken legs and arms were removed from parents only to be found to suffer from a brittle bone disease. But thousands of children are suffering from abuse, some will become physically or mentally handicapped, some will die. Children need a vigilant public and effective social service departments.

Endangered children are flagged on confidential records

as being at risk. It is important that information remains
confidental, but also that a collaborative system between
Social Service Departments, Family Practitioner
Committees and District Health Authorities is set up so that
track is kept of every child in danger of or suffering from
abuse. The problem has to be tackled in a co-ordinated way.

26 Charitable and Voluntary Organisations

There are more than 160,000 agencies which have achieved charitable status as well as others which are exempt from registration under the Charities Act of 1960. Every year an updated edition of the Charities Digest appears giving guidance and information to those who, by reason of their circumstances, are in need of help. At the same time people who wish to choose organisations to which they may leave bequests find this and other similar publications useful for their descriptions of the objectives of these groups.

The strength of voluntary organisations lies in the commitment of individuals to give of their free time and energy without expectation of reward, and in this country people are extraordinarily generous in this regard.

Charitable Status

Before any group can be given the status of a charity which is registered under the 1960 Act of Parliament it must satisfy an expert committee drawn from legal and social work professions that its aims are bona fide and fall under four main heads. These are the relief of poverty, the advancement of education and religion, or any other activities beneficial to the community.

Legal advice is essential in either setting up a charity or making a will in favour of one, since the meaning of those apparently simple objectives has been the subject of much legislation and judicial interpretation. Charity commissioners are empowered to make enquiries into the work of any charities other than those exempt, so that there is a level of control upon them as well as certain benefits occurring, such as relief of certain rates and taxes.

A staff of over three hundred people assist the commissioners in administering and monitoring both the work and the distribution of funds, but it is recognised that bona fide charities themselves must exercise great caution before allowing anyone to raise or handle money on their behalf.

The organisation of charitable bodies is overall an important issue since very large sums of money are involved. In 1985 the aggregate value of stocks and investments held in trusts for charities was more than five hundred million pounds and this money must be dispensed strictly in accordance with the constitution of the charity and through its managing trustees.

Guarding Public Funds

The public must be guarded from fraudulent attempts to part it from its money for purposes other than those intended by the donors. Many charities receive offers from shady characters who are prepared to raise funds in the name of the charity, but who cannot be trusted to deal honestly. Such offers should be firmly resisted since one may end up by liberally lining the pockets of individuals, the charity benefiting by only a small percentage of the funds collected.

The aims of the charity must be clearly defined and unambiguous so that donors' wishes are observed. A charity set up to relieve blind children, for example, may not be allowed to spend its money on children otherwise disabled no matter how urgent the need.

Advisory Bodies

Legislation changes constantly and to be sure of offering up-to-date advice, organisations must regularly sift through the work of Parliament and local government. For example, organisations like neighbourhood Law Centres and Citizens Advice Bureaux prepare paperwork for their files on all changes in legislation. Every three months their files are changed, new information replacing any which is out of date. This keeps them current and ensures that clients receive correct information.

Most people know about Citizens Advice Bureaux and recognise the familiar blue and yellow logo. The bureaux offer an entirely free advisory service which is usually available on a walk-in basis, and many thousands of people benefit daily from the work of this organisation. The offices are run by professional personnel assisted by trained voluntary workers who give one or two days a week, totally free. Grant support from central and local government is essential, and is provided to enable this invaluable service to continue.

Numbers of public-spirited professional people ally themselves to Citizens Advice Bureaux. Organisers are then able to offer free advice relating to law, income tax, property or other areas by using the services of these lawyers, accountants, surveyors and others. In such cases appointments are made with clients so as to use the limited time that can be made available by these professionals, without charge.

The legitimate expenses of voluntary organisations have to be allowed for and these will include the cost of premises, rent, rates, lighting and heating as well as necessary office staff, if people cannot be found who are able and willing to work without charge.

A charity may have as its purpose the provision of all kinds of assistance which requires the employment of experts like social workers, therapists or counsellors. It is unlikely that many of these can be found who can afford to work full-time without pay since they are generally professional people in mid-career who depend upon earned income for their livelihood.

However, many well motivated persons make charitable work their hobby and give free services in their time off either to individual families in need, or to nationally known charities who have lists of cases on their books. These volunteers may either use their expertise or train to do the work they undertake.

The British Red Cross and St John's Ambulance Brigade are two organisations which train people in nursing and first-aid work. Their distinctive uniforms are to be seen at large gatherings where they are on duty in case members of the public fall ill or have accidents requiring treatment. It is often not recognised that these people give their services voluntarily.

The Government is well aware of the enormous value of these various groups and indeed is dependent upon them to support existing statutory organisations. Government grants are made to many voluntary bodies with charitable status to enable them to carry on their work. It is difficult for any charity to work in isolation, and close co-operation with central or local government agencies results in obvious benefits to all concerned.

The Objectives of Voluntary Groups

Following the Beveridge Report in the 1940s and the advent of the Welfare State the work of charities has become less vital but nevertheless remains important. Some charities determine to use a large proportion of their funds for research. The Muscular Dystrophy Group of Great Britain and Northern Ireland has, for example, 400 local branch organisations to help raise funding for research as well as to further their objectives of helping sufferers. Thus, they are a powerful group, able to lobby for their members and direct large sums to research at hospitals and universities throughout the United Kingdom.

They are a source of encouragement and assistance as well as providing friendly counselling and practical advice. They employ social workers, occupational and physio-therapists who can visit homes to see their members. This range of activities is typical of many charities which have achieved status and strength through affiliation, not only to small local groups but to government agencies. Working together they alleviate much of the suffering of handicapped children and adults.

The Charities Digest

It is vital to those working in the health field and who assist underprivileged or handicapped people that they know something about the various sources of help. For this reason the *Charities Digest* and similar publications have become the handbooks of welfare and social workers, as well as those hospital and general practice staff who seek aid for patients or clients.

Any parents can look into the pages of these reference books at a library and can write direct to the trustees of a charity for help, although they will usually be asked for back-up letters of support from their medical advisers or social workers.

The range of government and local authority welfare provision is wide. There should be an interchange of information between them and any of the charities which are concerned with matters relating to welfare, so that everyone is fully aware of provision or lack of it. There is room for national umbrella committees which could draw together all bodies with similar aims who may yet remain independent of each other. This should mean a more effective use of resources, less duplication and a better understanding of each other's aims and objectives.

Umbrella Organisations

There is a useful group called the National Council of Voluntary Organisations, NCVO, which undertakes the support of any local organisation in setting up and achieving its aims. It invites membership which entitles groups to a regular supply of information relevant to their objectives as well as a number of services, ongoing advice and assistance.

NCVO disseminates information through publications and conferences throughout the country. Local affiliated voluntary service councils help groups already in operation and assist new ones to set up. Once the need for an association is identified, whatever that need may be, they receive general advice at their initial meeting and practical help with typing, writing and printing of leaflets and appointments of staff.

They may require help with appeals for funding, finding premises, as well as attracting and appointing honorary officers like treasurers and secretaries. Getting the right advice at an early stage can save much effort and enable the group to begin its planned work sooner and to fulfil its agreed objectives.

Another such organisation is of growing importance and came into being as a federation of bodies which agreed to link to discover areas of common interest. Their declared aim is to devise a national policy for the under-fives.

The Voluntary Organisation Liaison Council for Under Fives, VOLCUF, provides for the exchange of ideas and information on provision for young children. It circulates information which increases understanding between central and local government as well as other groups with similar principles.

Users of these statutory or voluntary welfare resources know little about where the help comes from or exactly what a voluntary social worker does that is different from a paid social worker. A parent who reads about one or other charity may write to them on the chance of getting advisory or practical help or simply to express views. Getting the parent to make the right appeal to the right department or organisation may mean an extensive exchange of letters and certainly needs some experience on the part of the person at the charity who deals with correspondence.

Charity Workers

Charities have a responsibility to appoint people with

training and knowledge who can deal efficiently with their work, and if voluntary workers with the right expertise cannot be provided then funding should be found for paid workers.

Charities try to operate on a shoe-string, often hampering themselves and restricting the work they do, holding up the provision of assistance to the people they intend to help.

Using Funds Effectively

It is unlikely nowadays that families with handicapped children would go without the obvious forms of aid required. But more effective assistance could be found if the entire framework of resources, voluntary or otherwise, was monitored and expertly managed. There are vast resources tucked away between the pages of the grant-making directories or charity digests.

We ought to be directing this money much more effectively, perhaps to education, speech therapy, occupational and physiotherapy to give our children earlier independence and maximum use of residual abilities. They might then not need the equipment which charities are more ready to purchase than services.

The Family Fund

Most social workers are familiar with this York-based fund for families of severely handicapped children. Its aim is to help those who have the most serious forms of disability. Eligible families are those whose disabled member usually lives at home, although the absence of the child for hospital treatment or as a resident at school in term-time does not preclude them from receiving help.

The kind of help given varies from grants of money for specific purposes related to the child, washing-machines, help towards holidays, essential adaptations at home and bridging money to cover whilst awaiting other payments or for services to be arranged.

Any families in the United Kingdom may apply for help provided that the child is below sixteen – although this age limit may be extended at the discretion of the trustees.

The trust is administered independently by the Joseph Rowntree Memorial Trust, but funded by the Government.

Holidays

Special needs are catered for in a number of homes specially adapted and set up by various organisations. There are some charities whose specific objective is to provide holidays for stated classes of people, perhaps families with handicapped children who have not had a holiday in years, or indeed, ever. The Holiday Care Service in Horley, Surrey, provides information and advice on all aspects of holidays for disabled people and carers. It is a free service although welcoming donations. RADAR in London publishes a range of fact-sheets on holidays both in the UK and abroad.

The local authority social services departments have the power (under the Chronically Sick and Disabled Act, 1970) to give financial help towards the cost of taking a holiday. It is in their discretion to interpret this in a variety of ways, for example, if funds permit to offer holidays in places of their choice to people to enable them to go away. Some voluntary groups provide helpers to enable a disabled person to go away independent of family. The Red Cross provides assistance for international travel for severely disabled people who can get help in no other way.

Pressure groups are succeeding in getting more provision for wheelchair travel. As an example all buses operating services from Victoria and Euston to Heathrow will in future be wheelchair accessible. London Regional Transport are also hoping to restore an inter-station link, and to provide a service for people using wheelchairs.

This growing awareness of the needs of handicapped

people and provision of tangible help gives a sensation of relief to all of those who need assistance, as well as to anyone working in the field and aware of the frustration and disappointment of the disabled when plans to travel are balked by inaccessibility for wheelchairs.

Disabled Living Needs

One important need for the families of handicapped children is to see what kind of clothing, gadgets, equipment and wheelchairs have been designed, and perhaps to experiment with them. The Disabled Living Foundation is a professional organisation with charitable status, and here families can spend a comforting few hours trying out some of the many innovative and useful items.

It has a library of relevant material, numerous pamphlets relating to disability as well as large showrooms. In these are displays of equipment for use by the disabled. The kitchen which takes a wheelchair is thoughtfully planned, and many ideas can be adopted without great expense. Special beds are on view which enable the severely disabled child to lie down, to sit and to turn independently and without disturbing parents. These are expensive, but items should be considered for their practicality and fund raising considered later. Numerous wheelchairs and seating are available for trial, and expert advice can be given about these and many other items pertinent to disability.

Clothing is all important, for one's needs change when confined for a great deal of time to a wheelchair. Practical considerations rule and warm, light, easy to put on and take off clothes are necessary but these can still be attractive. The most up-to-date news and views may be recommended by this association on application, and enquiries are dealt with during office hours.

Sports Activities

All children enjoy sport and handicapped children are no

exception. The National Sports Day at Stoke Mandeville is good fun for children and teenagers who join in not to win but to take part, and everyone who makes the winning post is a winner. Lightweight sport wheelchairs are designed for use on tracks, wheelchair netball and games are enjoyed, and the swimming-pool is the scene of many competitive water sports.

Teams of children and adolescents from schools arrive with teachers and voluntary helpers, using the day not only as an occasion of sport but also to meet and exchange ideas. The British Sports Association for the Disabled in Aylesbury, Buckinghamshire, acts as the co-ordinating body of sport and physical recreation for all disabled children, depending upon volunteers to help with children's training and needs.

Disabled Children's Charities

The Invalid Children's Aid Society was established in the nineteenth century and now has special residential schools, social work centres and training schemes which aim to help youngsters in accepting and overcoming handicap. Their four boarding-schools take in girls and boys who are severely affected by asthma or eczema. Other schools take in children having severe speech and language disorders. This association also runs practical training courses for teachers and for students on social work as well as work projects for handicapped school-leavers.

Barnado's began in response to the plight of homeless children in the nineteenth century and now assists almost 14,000 children annually. In particular, handicapped and disadvantaged children are enabled to reach their maximum potential. Whilst previously the work was concentrated on residential care it is moving continually towards preventive work aimed at reducing handicap.

The Cystic Fibrosis Research Trust has a network of branches across the UK which provides income to spend on research. It publishes information packs, leaflets and lends home-made audio films which are used both to provide information and in fund raising.

The Lady Hoare Trust was begun in the sixties when thalidomide children were beginning to grow up and their many problems needed specialised advice. The trust later undertook to advise and to offer some support to all severely disabled youngsters from birth to eighteen years of age. They have built up a team of medical social workers who visit homes and undertake to find resources for special needs.

The Spastics Society was founded in 1952 by a group of concerned parents who wanted to improve the inadequate services available to their children, most of whom were at that time labelled ineducable. That tiny group has grown to be the world's leading organisation in the education, training, care and provision of other services for children and adults with cerebral palsy. They have created a network of establishments designed to further the quality of life for those with special needs.

The Sickle Cell Society was set up in response to the numbers of families appearing with members who had sickle cell disease. Its objectives are to give help and support to families in need. It publishes a practical handbook as well as information leaflets. It also has a Welfare Fund established to improve the quality of life for families and to help them cope with the illness.

The Handicapped Children's Aid Committee is a fund raising body committed to helping disadvantaged and disabled children regardless of race, colour or creed. It helps individual children with personal special needs, equipment and holidays. It also gives equipment to children's hospital wards, and assistance to special school units and residential homes. Especially interested in the provision of mobility for severely disabled children, it sponsors the Handicapped Children's Research Equipment Unit under the direction of the wheelchair designer, Eric Booth, and is now based at the Royal Hospital and Home, Putney. The members of the unit, design engineers occupational therapists, physiotherapists and members of the charity have collaborated to determine the needs of disabled children. This has resulted in the design and manufacture of special equipment and wheelchairs aimed at giving the children the ability to communicate and to enjoy independent outdoor freedom.

The Brittle Bone Society promotes research, provides practical help and advice for its members. It is a self-help group, run by Margaret Grant and her daughter Yvonne who themselves have brittle bone disease, and in 1978 gained TV's Magpie Appeal. This enabled it to provide mobility aids and home comforts for many children with osteogenesis (brittle bones).

The Variety Clubs are an international network raising millions of pounds annually for the benefit of children, providing all kinds of help ranging from buildings, equipment and vehicles to holidays and toys.

The National Toy Library Association has encouraged groups all over the country to build up collections of toys, educational and otherwise, which families can borrow. This has been immensely popular and useful, providing not only stimulus for children but a meeting place for parents.

These are but a few examples of the many charities which exist to provide help for children with special needs. A list of these and others, together with addresses, can be found at the back of this book.

Advice on Appealing to Charities

Applicants should bear in mind that Trustees have numbers of appeals to sift through, and applications should be clear and concise. Details should include the child's name, age and disability. It never hurts to include a brief personal description, details of family, siblings and background. It helps to know something of the work of the trust so that its time as well as the applicant's time is not wasted by appeals outside its terms of reference. Requests for particular needs or equipment should be described and estimates of costs included, as well as details of any funding already raised or available towards the project.

Supporting letters from medical advisers should be attached or there will be delay whilst these are sought. Any additional information should be concise and relevant to the specific request.

Charities do not generally make grants in retrospect and there is little use in asking for help towards something already purchased. There are always exceptions of course. Some grants are made subject to the balance being raised elsewhere within a given time. This can serve as a spur to all concerned to raise the money. A good and deserving project never fails to reach its target and the determination to succeed produces fruitful results.

Right to Receive Help

My belief is that handicapped children and their families should receive all possible support as well as the thanks and gratitude of those privileged to help them in their unending task of coping with disability.

The cost of equipment such as electric wheelchairs, special beds, bath hoists, computers and additional therapy is too great for all but the wealthiest families to afford. Needs that are recognised must be satisfied and no child should ever be denied that which will turn disability into ability.

The abundant goodwill within every community to help people less fortunate than themselves can be harnessed to provide invaluable support everywhere in the country. Volunteers with time to spare are trained and take up duties with the organisations they are interested in.

Retired people find new interests, saying cheerfully, 'I have never worked so hard in my life.' It is a privilege and immensely rewarding to know that one can relieve anxiety, pain and suffering and share the responsibilities of families less fortunate than one's own, and who carry heavier burdens than others.

Raising Funds

The popular concept of charity generally conveys little idea of the diversity of the work that goes on. Large sums are needed and are willingly raised by bodies like Round Tables, Inner Circles and the Townswomen's Guilds. These are made up of people who regularly meet and who define the areas of charity they wish to support during a particular year. Schools, businesses, clubs and families with handicapped members also raise funds to donate to one or another good cause.

The ways in which money can be raised are very diverse. They include sponsored activities, such as marathons, distance swimming, parachute jumps and so on. Coffee mornings are popular with fund raisers, as are bring-and-buy sales. Garage and boot sales have largely replaced temporary charity shops, but some major charities now have permanent sites in high streets.

Flag days and raffles may be organised but are subject to strict adherence to legislative control. Film and theatre preview performances are frequently given over to charities, and many restaurants are now prepared to donate an evening to local fund raisers. Well known personalities are often willing to attend these functions.

It is worthwhile offering to send a speaker to schools to encourage support for special projects. It is surprising how much money enthusiastic children can manage to raise, once their interest is engaged.

Major functions such as dinners and balls can be run in conjunction with advertising brochures, and are a source of considerable revenue.

New ideas are constantly developing to encourage a willing public to donate money to worthy causes.

A great deal of money is bequeathed each year and a welter of information is available through solicitors' journals, charity digests and handbooks. Prospective donors can make well-advised decisions about where to give their money or donate their possessions by reference to such publications.

A Valuable Partnership

The partnership between the statutory and voluntary sector has been a good one, but there is potential for producing even greater benefit. Local needs and opinions must continue to establish the priorities and to influence the decision making.

New ideas have emerged when the two sectors have realised how their individual systems work. One excellent example has been the establishment of hospices for children, which were pioneered by volunteers outside of the NHS and which have been immensely comforting to children and their families. No sector should remain ignorant of the work and potential benefit of other sectors. When the ability of the voluntary sector to identify needs, mobilise volunteers and raise money is added to the expert knowledge of statutory authorities then resources are harnessed most effectively.

My work and affiliation with both the voluntary and professional sectors has made me well aware of the value of the work done and the continuing need for it. Many families and many problems have come my way. I have made good friends among both the committees who raise money and the organisations responsible for helping families and children. I especially welcome the young people who follow us and continue to raise funds and to give service, helping those with special needs – giving them ability and a more equal opportunity to share our world.

The mutual aid groups provide the means of exchanging know-how and boosting the confidence of families with a handicapped child. They are enabled to benefit from all resources available rather than managing alone, unaware of help to which they are fully entitled.

Families having children with special needs are to be found in every locality. Health and community developments must take full account of those needs, and the channels of communication between statutory and voluntary sectors must be diverse enough to embrace them all.

27   The Law

Attention has been drawn in many reports to the special needs of children and the word 'special' defines those who are disadvantaged in some way. Those children who are victims of child abuse, from broken homes, in care and who are disabled are obvious examples. The care that parents give to their children has to be augmented by legislation which actively discourages the ill-treatment of children, but also assists in their well-being.

Every child, whether able-bodied or otherwise, has the right to social justice and to be protected by the law as well as to have equal opportunity to enjoy good family life and opportunity for education. Our Children Acts try to provide this protection and equality.

In Pursuit of Health, Security and Well-Being

Policies are debated in all sectors of public life resulting in legislation which attempts to promote healthier life-styles. There has been remarkable improvement in some areas, but still we fall far short of what some other countries are able to achieve. We bear burdens of premature death and disability which should be reduced in number. Responsibility lies with our MPs to take steps to secure our children from some of the hazards that face them and to provide resources that they need.

People should be encouraged and educated to take better care of themselves and of their children and should have the means to do so. For handicapped children resources must be available in sufficient quantity and quality to ensure that they have equality of opportunity to enjoy life. Families on low salaries or without means of support are guaranteed minimum income, and special provision is available to the parents of handicapped children to help with inescapable costs.

Provision Under the Law

Families with disabled members have special need to know what the law means to them, what they can gain from it and how it affects them in particular, as well as in general.

This chapter provides some of that knowledge as well as some general information and facts which may be of value.

Rights to Grants

A parent once remarked that since having a handicapped child she had fought her way through mountains of paperwork. She felt that she had been in a series of battles to get the rights she was entitled to.

The rights of individuals are expressed in legal terms in Acts of Parliament. The language used is often difficult and capable of misinterpretation by the layman, but people need to know what their rights are and in particular anyone who is disabled must be made aware of every entitlement.

Citizens Advice Bureaux and Law Centres are used to dealing with paperwork and can explain what legislation means. Many people need help in working out their entitlement of benefit and income and can find assistance in an advice bureau. Forms are not always easy to understand and many families do not claim their entitlement so that large sums set aside by the Treasury remain unclaimed.

Disabled Must Know their Rights

In order to defeat segregation and bring about a more natural and equal society for our handicapped children, their lawful rights and grants have to be made known to them and their families. They must be treated like anyone else, enabled to go to schools, colleges and universities along with their able-bodied friends; to travel without advance preparation so that they can use public transport more easily to get to school and recreation; pay visits to restaurants on the spur of the moment without having to book and explain 'I'm in a wheelchair.' They should be able to decide to see a film or hear a concert without worrying as to whether there is access.

They must be able to take part in sports activities, join clubs, share a social life, fall in love and experience the joys and pains of relationships. They should look forward to life without having to feel apologetic for existing. Equality must make more of ability and less of disability.

When society agrees that initiatives are necessary, legislation can be brought in to ensure that change takes place. Recent legislation has meant that there is more access for wheelchairs. It has meant the inclusion of all children in the mainstream of education wherever possible and already there has been an improvement in attitudes towards handicapped individuals.

Handicap and Finance

It is well documented that families who have a handicapped member experience a greater degree of poverty than those who are able-bodied. Well-heeled families are in a better position to buy the services and equipment which make ability out of disability. The law should require that financial benefits should accrue to anyone handicapped so that inescapable additional costs are met. To some degree, legislation has allowed for this in the provision of mobility and constant attendance allowance.

Even so, a middle-class family on comfortable income may have its standards considerably reduced because of the needs of a handicapped child. A bigger car may be essential, with special adaptations to take equipment and electric wheelchairs. Structural alterations at home such as building extensions or stair-lifts may be thought necessary. Additional speech therapy or physiotherapy is frequently recommended since there is never enough available from community service. There may possibly have been an interruption to the career of one parent in order to care for the child, all of which makes costly inroads on income and capital, representing sacrifice by the family for the child.

A single-parent family in full receipt of all the benefits with government support for home alterations and charitable support for a car and electric wheelchair might feel financially secure, but the unremitting care of a child can cause a breakdown in health and respite care must be provided. Being handicapped should carry the right to special provision to make for equal status with able-bodied people and less sacrifice for the carers.

Whatever the background the needs are great, and advantage should be taken of every provision – statutory or voluntary. An independent advice centre can give all the necessary information and will find out what the entitlements are. In addition, they can advise what extra resources are provided locally. Sometimes it is recognised that in another area of the country councils are more generous in their provision of services or special education. Pressure may be brought to bear on councillors to compare standards and persuade them to offer support equivalent to that of their counterparts.

Once councils recognise what parents are trying to do for their children and how much support they need, they usually respond with generosity. Families who cannot cope and have to put their children into care cost councils a very great deal more than is ever spent on families who look after their children themselves.

Mandatory and Discretionary Grants

Parents of handicapped children have rights to certain grants and allowances, others are at the discretion of local authorities. Local authorities are represented by councillors who should have cases of hardship or apparent injustice brought to their attention.

Some local authorities have higher incomes than others, some have different priorities and the financial outlay per handicapped person varies greatly from place to place.

Appeals to Tribunals

From 1988 supplementary income provision and benefit entitlement are to be known as Income Support and single payments will now be drawn from the Social Fund. This most not result in diminished income or benefits for any of the most needy people and anyone who is concerned about payments should go to the Citizens Advice Bureau, Law Centre or Disability Group for advice.

It may be suggested that there should be an appeal against a local decision to an independent body, the Social Security Appeal Tribunal. Appellants should always attend these hearings since the success rate is higher when there is personal attendance.

Tribunals have had their powers reduced in recent years, but can reverse decisions in favour of appellants. Appeals against tribunal decisions may go to a Social Security Commissioner on the grounds that the decision was erroneous on a point of law, but only by leave of the tribunal chairman. Appeals against commissioners' decisions go to the Court of Appeal.

Commissioners' Decisions

On 13 April 1987 the Appeal Court overruled a Social Security Commissioner's decision on attendance allowance. The case concerned a woman suffering unpredictable epileptic attacks. Her husband slept in the same room, waking to attend her if she had a fit. She had been refused higher attendance allowance as her husband's presence was not held to be supervisory through the night. The court held that supervision could be 'precautionary and anticipatory' and therefore the husband was providing supervision even whilst asleep. It was possible that she might need help and that was what mattered, not how often she actually received the help. It was therefore wrong in law to take the infrequency of her attacks into account.

People with handicapped children who could benefit

from this ruling should claim the higher rate of attendance allowance. If there is doubt it is best to seek advice. The needs of disabled people are defined in law, practically every word of which has been given a definition in the commissioners' decisions. Local disability groups are usually aware of legislation favourable to handicapped people and publicise such information.

Medical Injury or Accident

Parents' consent is necessary for operations on children under the age of sixteen (Scotland, boys under fifteen, girls under thirteen), and consent to any treatment does not imply consent to damage suffered through negligence in any form.

It is best to be quite clear in advance about risk through treatment and risk through non-intervention. Proving negligence is never easy since injury is not proof. It must be shown that the standard of care failed to reach that of a reasonably competent medical professional and that this reduced standard caused the child's injury.

Medical Negligence

When people suffer injury, damage or loss through medical negligence the law must be studied in order to decide what duty of care is owed by the medical staff involved. Patients who are aggrieved about their treatment and ask questions often feel irritated by the guarded responses they receive. But the medical profession is alert to the possibility of litigation. Many complaints turn out to be instances where patients really only want to be given to understand the reason something has happened. That is why informal hearings for complaints against GPs through Family Practitioner Committees, when time is given for detailed explanations on all sides, usually result in everyone going away satisfied and without needing or wanting recourse to expensive formal hearings or court procedures.

There are some complaints when further action, possibly litigation, is justified and where it is likely that the injury suffered through reduced standards of care will result in substantial compensation. Numbers of such cases occur annually.

Complaints are very few considering the number of consultations and treatments which take place daily. The quality of service is generally very high, but the public today is better informed and more inclined to query the decisions and actions of professional medical people which they would once have accepted without question.

Complaints to Family Practitioner Committees

In making claims against general practitioners for negligence, patients may write details to Family Practitioner Committees who can hear cases informally or formally. Formal hearings take place before subcommittees of the FPC which include professional and lay people. Informal cases against doctors can be heard if both parties agree.

A layperson presides, advised by an independent doctor and both the patient and his or her doctor are able to discuss any problem frankly. This very often results in conciliation but does not preclude formal complaints or litigation at a later stage, provided these are within specified time-limits.

Any complaints regarding chemists, dentists, opticians, ophthalmic general practitioners or general medical practitioners are limited to a breach of their terms of service under the NHS as independent contractors. They are not employees.

This means that there are limits to the kind of complaints an FPC may investigate. A general practitioner must exercise reasonable skill and care and the terms of contract for each of the professions are set out in schedules to the NHS regulations.

There are FPCs responsible for every area of the country (in Scotland and Northern Ireland there is a different system). It may be that a phone call to the FPC or relevant body will put the patient's mind at rest, but if they wish to take the matter further then details regarding complaints should be put in writing to the FPC as quickly as possible. The sooner they are dealt with, the better.

There are specified time-limits for complaints, but late ones may be considered if delay was occasioned through illness or other reasonable cause and if the consent of the practitioner or the Secretary of State is obtained.

Vaccine Damage Payments Act 1979

Under this Act anyone severely disabled as a result of a vaccine administered personally or to the mother before birth, or who has contracted the disease from someone to whom the vaccine was given, is entitled at the time of writing to a payment of £20,000.

This is a no-claim entitlement, whether or not there was negligence. Damages may still be claimed and if such a claim succeeds, the amount assessed would be reduced by the statutory sum. Claims can be made once the child reaches the age of two, but must be made within six years and, if the injured party is under eighteen, by a parent or guardian.

HIV Virus

Currently, haemophiliacs, including children, who have had the misfortune to develop the HIV virus as a result of NHS treatment are seeking an estimated thirty million pounds compensation from the Government.

The Haemophiliac Society has pressed for life insurance and mortgage protection so that families may not be evicted when their husbands or fathers die.

Injuries to Children

Under certain circumstances damages may be claimed

when children suffer injuries. It must be proved that th injury was caused by negligence, or that the person causing the injury did not exercise the reasonable care that could have been expected.

It may be considered worthwhile suing if a defendant is covered by insurance.

Injuries on the Road

All drivers must be insured against their liability to cause death or personal injuries to anyone, including their own passengers. The insurance companies will only pay if it can be proved that their party was at fault. A child cannot be held to be negligent therefore, even if the child was at fault with the driver the least negligent, damages can be claimed against the driver in full.

If a driver involved in an accident carries no insurance or cannot be traced, a valid claim would be met by the Motor Insurance Bureau.

Injury through Dangerous Premises

The Occupier's Act 1984 places the onus on the occupier to be responsible for any injuries caused by the state of the premises if they are aware of any danger and have reason to believe it exists; or have reasonable grounds to believe that a trespasser may come into the vicinity of the danger; or if the risk is one against which it is reasonable to take precautions and offer protection.

In the case of young children who wander off, an occupier might escape liability if it could be shown that a parent was negligent in looking after a child. Every case is different and numbers of different circumstances have been illustrated and fought over in the courts. People do not easily escape liability – everything depends on the facts in each case.

Contributory Negligence

It would be hard to find a very young child negligent at all, but older children could well be found to have contributed to their own injuries if they fail to take the care that children of their age might reasonably be expected to take. Parents' carelessness could contribute to negligence and reduce the amount of damages given.

The huge sums awarded in other countries for injuries suffered through medical treatment or surgical intervention which has not turned out as expected are not in the public interest, resulting as they do in increased cost to the health service and such back-breaking insurance premiums for doctors that those starting out in the profession cannot afford them but dare not practise without them.

Legal Action

If there are reasons to go to law careful consideration should be given to all relevant facts. I would never recommend legal action unless it was the last resort. It can be a worrying business, causing many sleepless nights and the results may not justify all the trouble.

In 1987 the Accident Legal Advisory Service (ALAS) was launched. A free initial interview is offered by a solicitor to people if they or any member of the family has suffered injury in an accident. This service is primarily designed to tackle a recognised but unmet social need. It is aimed at people who cannot afford solicitors and who may be ignorant about their rights and the legal remedies available to them. In the Government's Civil Justice Review, published recently, this need was highlighted and the Lord Chancellor's Advisory Committee has referred to the advisability to encourage more injured persons to seek advice and make claims. There are numbers of children whose families do not know their rights. Many are still ignorant of the fact that a claim can be made if the accident was someone else's fault.

A free initial session with a solicitor may also be possible at the local Citizens Advice Bureau. Action may be needed fast and a good solicitor can save much heartache and headache. Anyone who considers that their solicitor has been remiss can complain to the Law Society.

Legal Aid

Litigants may be entitled to legal aid. Eligibility for this is through a means test by the DHSS for the Law Society. A grant of legal aid depends upon the amount of income and any capital that an applicant has, but not including the value of their house.

Usually some contribution towards legal expenses has to be made, and if there is a successful outcome and the plaintiff receives damages the legal aid fund may claw back some of that money.

Wills

Parents with handicapped children worry about their child's future and about leaving property to them. It is not a straightforward matter to leave property, especially to a minor, and advice should be sought from solicitors conversant with all the details.

Rights to benefits and rights to a home may be involved, and there may be contestants to the will. It is essential that the interests of the handicapped person are protected and the wishes of parents, grandparents, or other relatives should be made clear, and there will be proof against attempts to overturn it.

Sexual and Other Abuse of Children

The law protects children – and there are times when the law must be invoked against the children's own parents.

Recent cases where little children have died as a result of multiple injuries, starvation and brutality, illustrate that parents can, and do, commit serious offences against their own young. It has been shown that handicapped children or those needing extra care and attention are more liable to suffer some form of abuse than able-bodied children.

Some parents feel both angry and guilty at the additional burden imposed upon them by having a disabled child and vent irritation upon the children. These are often young parents in poor circumstances, who are liable to lose patience quickly and need counselling as well as practical help and respite from unremitting care.

Recent publicity about sexually abused children has thrown up complex problems. Are we in Britain more guilty of this crime than people in other countries or are we merely exposing a world-wide problem? Dr Pithers of the National Children's Home is Director of the Centre for Study and Development of Child Care Practice. The centre plans to educate children about the dangers of sexual abuse and has launched a campaign and published a book, *We Can Say No* (co-authored by Dr Pithers & Sarah Greene).

Dr Pithers believes that the blame for much abuse lies in our social attitudes to men who are allowed to grow up immature, self-seeking and aggressive. When they meet problems, that aggression may be vented upon children. 'Our children,' says Dr Pithers, 'are treated as objects, something pathetic, whereas in France, Italy and Spain children are spoken to seriously and expected to converse with adults.'

Teaching children respect for each other and their elders is a matter not only of discipline, but also of example. According to the law, parents are expected to treat their children decently, to provide them with food, clothing and other necessities and to give them loving care. They have rights over their children, but they do not own them. Children who are regarded with respect and who are drawn into family consultations about problems or general matters, develop responsibility and family and personal pride.

Local authorities can remove children from the control of parents or guardians and take them into care if it is thought that they are in moral or physical danger. GPs, nurses or teachers who suspect that children are abused should consult each other and social workers so that agencies may consider whether any action should be taken and if so, in what form.

It is obviously far better to help the whole family and avoid the removal of the child rather than to allow matters to progress to the point where the child is irreversibly damaged either physically or emotionally. The signs are often clear enough, but ignored. On the other hand, it is possible to jump to conclusions based on insufficient investigations and hasty diagnosis. Breaking up families is a serious business not always justified by events.

Parents Rights at Risk

Parents who cause their children suffering through neglect or abuse must recognise that they jeopardise their parental rights. Following a case conference which concludes that it is necessary to take children from parents a Place of Safety Order may be applied for and the child involved is placed on the Non-Accidental Injury Register.

Unless it is resolved to return children to their parents, interim Care Orders can be made by the Juvenile Court and the child will be placed with foster parents. Depending upon the details, magistrates may recommend whether or not families should be reunited at a later stage. Access to children may be granted to parents, or it may be withheld.

Parents may contest these orders but, in the meantime, the law errs on the side of caution and Care Orders are carried out, the child remaining in the care of the local authority whilst decisions are made.

Meanwhile the person accused of abuse, parent or relative, may, if it is a serious charge, be prosecuted and if found guilty, will be liable to a term of imprisonment.

Case conferences about the child continue and it may be

decided that the family should be given a second chance and the child returned, although regular monitoring and visiting to the family will continue. If all goes well the child may continue to stay at home and eventually the name will be removed from the Child Abuse Register.

It is always hoped that children can be reunited with their families and any problems can be sorted out. Children love and need their natural parents, and the feeling of being unloved and unwanted by them remains a worry to many children long after they have grown up. Obviously if they are endangered then it is better that they be placed with foster parents who have love and patience to give and regard the care of a child as a grave responsibility, and a privilege.

Child abuse is not restricted to any social class or ethnic or religious group. Abusers are to be found among well-heeled professionals as well as long-term unemployed and among every known religious sect, as well as non-religious groups.

Child abuse implies that there has been a departure from the normal pattern of loving care by parents towards their children with a loss of natural respect and disregard for their happiness. It certainly seems alien to most people that this can happen. The mother of several children who is at her wits' end to deal with the endless round of washing, cooking and housework may reach the end of her tether and strike out in anger.

But when one child is constantly on the receiving end of physical ill-treatment, it is time for the situation to be dealt with outside the family. A mother who herself draws attention to such a situation will receive counselling and help.

Importance of Family Support

When families live in close proximity to each other and grandparents, sisters, brothers and other relatives are around to share problems, matters rarely reach ugly proportions. But the stress for a lonely parent is high and can cause problems.

The fact is that abused children may grow up to be abusers of their own infants and the pattern has to be broken. Improvements in housing, the alleviation of poverty, provision of employment – these will go some way to affording a solution.

Battered Child

The term 'battered child syndrome' has been used where abuse, other than sexual, occurs and this has drawn more attention to this particular problem. Parents recognising themselves as already guilty or potential child batterers, often seek help and have formed associations offering each other advice and counselling. These self-help groups are successful in bringing such matters to the fore and working out solutions.

Sometimes mothers bring children to surgeries with a sickness that gives rise to suspicion and needs investigation.

Roy Meadows, Professor of Paediatrics and Child Health, has written of the methods used to detect the real causes of these conditions. Mothers have suffocated their babies sufficiently to warrant apnoeic investigation (apnoea is a condition of failure to breathe whilst asleep), or have given their children drugs, producing symptoms which simulate illness. Videos have been covertly used to detect these attacks on children and there are arguments that such recordings are unacceptable as legal evidence. 'What of the child's rights?' says Professor Meadows. 'If that two-year-old who had periods when his air supply was cut off and he had to struggle to breathe had been asked if he wanted to be filmed so that the cause of these episodes could be found he would have answered "Yes".' (*British Medical Journal*, June 1987.)

Local authorities are vested with the power to remove endangered children into care while steps are taken to re-educate or otherwise treat their parents. There must be total confidence that episodes of cruelty will not be repeated so that children are not placed at risk again. It calls for everyone to be alert to the possible cause of unhappiness in children, to changes in their behaviour or an alteration in their school work and to find out with tact and sensitivity why these changes have happened.

Removing a Child from Hospital

Parents may decide that they do not wish a child to receive treatment which doctors argue is essential to the health, perhaps life, of the child. If, in an emergency, a child needs an operation or treatment then the doctor does not need the parents' or guardian's consent before going ahead. In cases of disagreement relating to treatment of non life-threatening conditions the doctor can refer the case to the local authority who can apply for a Care Order.

The best interests of the child must be the prime consideration. An authority which is in conflict with parents or guardians who wish to remove a child from hospital must apply to a magistrate for an order. Application for these orders is for a maximum of twenty-eight days only and this can be followed by a further Internal Care Order. Care Orders may also be made which give full control to the local authority until the child's eighteenth birthday.

Housing

Housing is a priority and the quality of life is so affected by environment that appeals to get the best available living accommodation are worthwhile.

A family living in a high-rise block with a growing child who is incapacitated by paralysis doesn't have an easy time and if people in like circumstances do not fuss they may never get help to move to suitable ground floor accommodation, preferably with access to a garden.

Purchase of Property

Legal advice should be sought before buying a property. It

may mean tying up too large a proportion of family income in a mortgage. Councils restrict the amount of grants for adaptations once they sell properties to tenants. Special arrangements for mortgages may, however, be possible and should be investigated, since there may be sympathy for the families with handicapped members on the part of some banks and building societies.

In considering purchasing property future needs should be anticipated. Storage space must be available for outdoor wheelchairs and expensive alterations to provide wheelchair access may be essential. It may be necessary either to provide lifts to get into bedrooms or consider a ground floor extension of bedroom, bathroom and toilet. All of these details should be given practical consideration by proposing purchasers and their advisers before going ahead and buying a property.

The expense involved in purchase as well as maintaining a property has to be considered apart from capital outlay. Ordinary repairs, decoration, surveyor's and solicitor's fees, insurance, heating, rates and water rates, electricity, gas – the cost of all these and more must be allowed for. Many families have undertaken house purchase only to find that it is too much of a commitment, they fall into debt and their homes are repossessed by mortgage societies.

But having bought a home, no one should give it up without having made every effort to keep it. Home ownership is best in the long run as properties increase in value and mortgages reduce, while rents go up and up and tenants own nothing.

Children's Liability in Law

A child under the age of ten is not criminally liable for any offence. Between ten and fourteen the child is liable if such a child knew the conduct to be wrongful. Above fourteen years children are liable for criminal acts.

As a general rule persons between fourteen and seventeen are tried by magistrates in Juvenile Court. If the case is serious then that child or young person may be committed for trial at a Crown Court. No one under seventeen can be sent to prison and other institutions are used for custodial treatment. Fines may be imposed for offences.

Where a minor commits a civil wrong and is without means then there may be no redress possible for the injured party since neither parent nor guardian may be held liable.

Land or housing may not legally be owned by a minor, but property may be left in trust until the minor comes of age. A minor cannot make a will although could under certain circumstances make an informal will.

Restrictions on Minors

Minors are restricted in certain activities usually for their own safety so that no one under sixteen can hold a driving licence to ride a motor cycle on a public road. No one under seventeen may hold a licence to drive a car on a public road. Marriages contracted between persons where one partner is under sixteen are not valid.

There are other limitations on children under age with regards to firearms and the purchase of cigarettes. Regrettably, this latter restriction is flagrantly disregarded and children are thereby encouraged to begin a lifelong addiction to smoking and will run a higher risk of early ill-health and death from cancers and heart-disease.

The Ill-Effect of Alcohol

There are restrictions on the sale of alcohol. Bars and public houses are not permitted to serve drinks to anyone under the age of eighteen. A new problem has arisen concerning children who help themselves to alcoholic drinks at home and may become addicted. This leads to antisocial and criminal behaviour, ill-effects on health and difficulties in the family.

It is horrifying to see the injuries suffered by some of the battered mothers and children who seek shelter and protection from their drunken husbands and fathers. Sometimes the damage is permanent and healthy children become impaired for life. Mothers, too, are not proof against addiction and alcoholic intake should be carefully controlled. It is not generally recognised that quite small amounts of regular drinking constitute addiction, and this can be responsible for unsocial behaviour.

One father who was normally a caring and pleasant man refused to recognise that even two drinks affected him adversely. So marked was the change in him following drinking alcohol that he was hardly recognisable. When his wife was in her seventh month of pregnancy with their second child he began a quarrel which ended with all the bedroom furniture being smashed irreparably.

The marriage ended a few years later despite all the wife's efforts to get him to recognise that he had a drinking problem and to accept help. She still loves the man that he was, but feels there is no hope that he will ever give up drinking and that she must find a new life with someone else.

Guardians

Guardians have the powers usually enjoyed by parents who have the duty to care for, protect and control their children.

Where parents have died or are unable or unwilling to provide for this duty, then someone must be appointed who becomes responsible and safeguards the interests of the child.

Divorce

Where a dispute arises as to who should be entitled to the care and custody of the child then a court must decide in the best interests of the child where and with whom that child should be placed.

The family home may have to be sold and the proceeds divided, but when the children are a prime consideration the marital home may be left with the parent who takes the child until the child is grown up.

Ward of Court

A child who is without parents may become a ward of court. Future decisions will only be made with the authority of the court so that any question of education, upbringing, disposals of property or investments would be heard before a judge, usually in the Family Court.

Under these circumstances the court will appoint a guardian who would act under the jurisdiction of the court. Wards of court may not leave the country or marry without the court's consent.

Illegitimacy

A child born during marriage or within nine months following divorce is presumed legitimate. Where the parents do not marry, the child is held to be illegitimate, but if, following the birth, they marry then the child can be re-registered as legitimate. A mother and new husband may jointly adopt the child.

In order to claim maintenance from a father unmarried to the mother, an affiliation order may be made against him and the father is then required to pay maintenance until the child reaches the age of sixteen or beyond if education is extended. Similarly, an order for maintenance may be made against a mother where the father has the care of the child.

Adoption

The relationship between a parent and child is not

necessarily one of blood. It may be by law through adoption. The same rights are given to adopted children as to those born to the parents, except that a titled family could not pass on the title to an adopted child.

There are certain provisos made before the courts can permit orders of adoption. The consent of parents must be given, although if parents have neglected their parental duties this may not be required. The child must be willing if of the age and discretion to understand. There must be no financial gain other than is thought necessary and agreed by the court.

Local Education Authorities

Parents are entitled to ask local education authorities (LEAs) to provide details of schools in the area, as well as information about the school's curricula, policies and teaching staff.

Whilst parents may express a preference for a particular school, the LEAs need only comply with such wishes if the provision of efficient education or efficient use of resources is not impaired and is compatible with arrangements between governors and LEAs in respect of admission of children (unless admissions are based wholly or partly on selection according to ability or aptitude and compliance with parents' reference would be compatible with the selection arrangements).

It is important for parents to feel that their children have as fair a chance at their school as is possible. There is an excellent publication called *Special Children* for anyone concerned with children having special education needs.

Ombudsman

The Parliamentary, Health and Local Ombudsman services have been set up to deal with complaints from individuals who believe they have suffered an injustice from the action or failure to act, of councils or authorities. Complaints are normally sent through a Member of Parliament or local councillor – and may be investigated by the relevant ombudsman.

Inquiries follow and the result may be that the grievance is remedied, although councils cannot be forced to act if they decide not to.

In Conclusion . . .

English law has been slowly built up over centuries, but much legislation concerning the rights and status of children is incomplete. There are working parties concerned with the need for reform and their recommendations will take care of some of the grey areas.

Hopefully, this will strengthen the rights of all children to develop as happy and fulfilled individuals. Children and adolescents with special needs of treatment and education, employment and housing must take priority over those who are able-bodied and healthy. In improving their conditions we raise standards of care for everyone and ensure that the highest aims of a caring society are met.

28 Education

Begins in the Cradle

When I saw my husband, our month-old daughter in the crook of his arm, walking around the garden and describing the leaves and trees to her I thought that her education had begun well.

Learning begins in the cradle. At no time in life is so much absorbed as in the first few months. Parents should not underestimate their own value and ability to instil in their children an interest and love of learning. As the five senses develop after birth, babies register and memorise impressions. They are startled by loud noises, a banging door, a clattered spoon. Identification of sounds begins.

During those first months, a baby focuses on familiar faces, remembering the warm scents of the mother, recognising parents, hearing loud or gentle voices; pleasant and unpleasant associations are made. The child smiles and gurgles, copies simple sounds, expresses pleasure or pain, learns and registers responses. The lessons go on daily, everything has a name, everyone has a name, vocabulary grows.

At a year, babies have learned a great deal; to identify the family, to prefer the mother's arms to those of a stranger, to understand the general meaning of many words, and to make known needs such as hunger or thirst or simply a desire for company. Language absorption becomes well established.

For handicapped children, things are not so easy. A child who cannot hear or does not see, who cannot crawl or clutch is disadvantaged. But whatever the degree or type of disability, every handicapped child is entitled to education, particularly if, as a people, we mean what we are saying about creating a more equal society.

In our recent history, handicapped children were

segregated and organised in disability categories. They had training first and education second, and only the highly motivated teacher and determined severely handicapped child could together aspire to higher qualifications and a useful and rewarding occupation.

If proof of the potential of some of our severely disabled children was needed, it is to be found today among the many mature but handicapped students who have studied part-time for degree courses in the Open University and have qualified in the minimum time. But, until recently, their capabilities were rarely considered and for reasons thought sound, special schools were either adapted or purpose-built so as to take wheelchairs and to house all the accoutrement thought necessary for the disabled child.

Education authorities provided teachers with the special training deemed necessary, and nurses or welfare care attendants were engaged to attend to the personal needs of the children. The segregation of adolescents and adults followed naturally from this pattern of divided schooling, continuing to widen the gap between disabled children and their able-bodied siblings and neighbourhood friends.

Parents have said what misery it caused them when they first sought schooling for their children, to find that they were to be labelled handicapped segregated and cut off from mainstream living.

This denial to handicapped children of equal opportunity for education and the chance to compete with their non-handicapped peers was at last seen as ill-judged. A system which is geared to able-bodied children might well, it was thought, be suitable for those who are handicapped, provided only that schools are accessible and can cater to special needs.

Special Needs Defined

Are there any children whose disabililties are so severe that they cannot be integrated and who have to attend special schools? It is rare for there to be no response to teaching, to environment or to other children.

The assessment of a child usually determines that capability for education exists, provided that certain essential priorities are met. Whether those priorities are, for example, speech therapy, physiotherapy, or hearing-aid or assistance at school with personal needs, they have to be satisfied before education can take place. This basic requisite was confirmed by studies commissioned by the Government.

The Warnock Report

The Warnock Report was commissioned in 1973 to consider special educational provision. Chaired by Mary Warnock, a committee studied the whole field of education for handicapped children and completed its report in 1978. A new concept was introduced, a new way of looking at children with special needs. No matter what any child's ability might be, said the committee, that child has a mandatory right to education. Children formerly filed under various categories of handicap were now to be regarded simply as having special educational needs.

The objectives of education were to be the same for every child, whatever school they might attend. Special need was defined as the provision of whatever might be necessary to allow disabled children to compete with the able-bodied. Whatever was needed to remove the obstacles between a child and education was to be furnished.

This meant that every child was to be entitled to go to a locally convenient school. The school would be of their choice, subject only to there being sufficient provision for them and their physical and educational needs, without detriment to other children.

Once it was established that education rather than physical conditions was to dictate the nature of the school system for children with special needs, it became sensible to try for improved pre-school learning opportunity.

Early assessment was immediately recognised as vital and equally important was the family background. It is beyond dispute that parents are able to teach their children a great deal. But when families are socially disadvantaged and have marital and financial problems with unsatisfactory home conditions, they are far less likely to be able to help their handicapped child in the way that a well-off and secure family can.

Through the social services, provision has been made to redress unequal conditions, at least to the extent of providing such structural alterations, equipment and finance as can provide agreed minimum standards.

Next came the concept of team-work, which was to include the parents. One of the objects of the team approach is to enlighten the parents about the reasons for their handicapped child's behaviour, which may be seen by them as naughty, wild or incomprehensible. Secondly, the team, doctors, nurses, therapists or social workers could gain insight from the parents about the child and also take advantage of meetings to observe the family relationship.

Preparing for Parenthood

Family relationships can develop naturally, following examples set in early life, but however good and secure a background may be, there is a real need for education in schools as a preparation for parenthood. It is such an important role, but many people take on the responsibilities of caring for a child without the least training. Is there a gap in secondary education?

Babies need loving care from the moment of birth and are responsive to parental warmth and affection. It is known that unloved children do not thrive, are sickly and liable to develop emotional difficulties which last into adolescence – and beyond.

Education should provide adolescents with a basic knowledge of caring for children and this might prevent some of the problems which later develop. In particular, it is possible that the open discussion of child abuse could be helpful to children who have themselves been abused.

When they come to understand why it has happened, they might escape the compulsion later in life to repeat the pattern and ill-treat their own children.

Early Education

Pre-school education is important to slow developers to enable them to reach average standards by the time they reach school age. Some areas provide a service whereby peripatetic teachers visit the home weekly to teach the child, supporting the parents who take the opportunity of watching the lessons in order to improve their own teaching skills.

The young handicapped child may derive benefit and pleasure from attending a pre-nursery group. The parents may wish to visit nursery schools in the area to find the one that is most suitable, and they will certainly want to feel comfortable about leaving their child in a new environment.

The Portage System

Researchers studying the value of early learning recommended a scheme which many parents have found to be of real importance. A partnership of teachers, parents and a professional forms and then the family is visited on a weekly basis with the purpose of teaching the handicapped child the valuable skills which have been delayed through slow development. These range from motor, language and behaviour to socialising.

A measure of monitoring is built-in to allow supervisors to receive details of completed work as well as to measure progress, and these are discussed regularly so that both problem areas and good results are highlighted. Finally, quarterly meetings are suggested when a team made up of all interested parties, education, health, social services, voluntary agencies as well as parents who work generally on the scheme, meet to evaluate the work done.

The strength that this support gives to parents is extremely valuable in two ways. The sense of despair and isolation that parents feel in attempting to teach their children by themselves is at once reduced. The dependable and regular nature of the support strengthens morale, replacing dejection with hope.

The tangible improvement in children is such that there is unanimous agreement in recommending the Portage scheme to anyone having a child with special educational needs.

Pressure Groups

Wherever children go to school, the provision of annual reports and discussion groups serves to highlight the gaps in provision. Teachers work on, endeavouring to do their best, making the most of what resources are available. But it must be recognised how much more can be done if the recommended minimum standards of various therapies and teaching, at the least, could be applied for all children at school.

Parents are best placed to press for action. Once they are made aware of the effects on their children of under-financing, they can form groups and press for changes through their councillors and MPs.

Teachers welcome the help they get in this way and the sharing of their responsibilities. They have enough to do in planning and carrying out teaching programmes without worrying about missed opportunities for their children though lack of specialist, therapeutic or other training.

Solving Problems

Children themselves, disabled or able-bodied, have a responsibility in helping to determine how problems may be solved. Encouraging every pupil in the school, with or without handicap, to come to grips with the practicalities of special needs, questioning how they may be satisfied, is important. Awakening interest in children is the one sure way to increase their capacity and enthusiasm for learning and, equally important, their sympathy and compassionate understanding.

Making provision for children with special needs in ordinary schools, and so ensuring that all of our children grow up together and with equal opportunity, is imperative. Parents agree wholeheartedly that it is wrong to separate disabled children from normal children. They are fearful, however, that their children may lose the benefit of the space, equipment, teaching and nursing provision which are to be found in separate special schools. However spiritedly one may endorse integration it is crucial to the successful education of children with special needs that there should be no skimping on any of the services they require.

The emphasis within special schools is for a concentrated level of therapy and a focus on structured and specialised education. If children from these schools are scattered throughout ordinary schools will it still be feasible for them to receive beneficial levels of education and physical therapy?

Integration

There has not been a rush towards integration, unquestionably desirable though it is, and no steps should be taken without positive assurance that the right back-up support exists. Appropriately trained teachers may be needed, in high staff to pupil ratios. More equipment is necessary when the users are no longer gathered together; and the transport of non-mobile children to and from school is another major consideration.

Finance bridging has to be allowed to give cover in the period before savings are made from special school closures. Will there finally be sufficient saving to pay for the right spread of resources? If not, then the intentions of the

Warnock Report would be overridden, perhaps lost, and the positive discrimination which is shown to children disadvantaged by handicap, to provide equality, would be eroded. We should never allow this to happen, so change must be advocated with caution and the practicalities examined meticulously.

Speech Therapy

Speech therapists play a crucial role in transforming children from silent and apathetic pupils to happy, communicative and bright ones. But it is not easy to get sufficient speech therapists to provide the hours of treatment which are recommended.

It is distressing to parents to know that their child's need is recognised and treatment advised which can effectively help, only to be told that they must wait because there are insufficient numbers of trained therapists.

The tragedy of children whose abilities are affected by speech defects and for whom help is denied is an indictment of our planners. There is a shortage of speech therapists in the country caused by an ever-increasing demand. Children benefit so much from remedial work on speech defects that this should be regarded as a major priority. The educational component is, of course, important but a therapy which teaches control of the tongue and mouth, and is therefore basic to eating and speaking, is essential.

No children should have to wait while their problems increase, becoming not only more difficult to cure but being affected by emotional and psychiatric disorders. For the sake of lost therapy, children lose valuable time and suffer effects which can alter their entire future.

Conductive Education

The success of conductive education is well established and parents claim that results warrant the expansion of this kind of teaching for their children. Conductive education calls for repetitive and patient training of muscles to perform exercises, one tiny movement at a time, over and over again. Discipline is strict and children work extremely hard. As the brain progressively learns and finds new ways of controlling the body, children accumulate sufficient skill to enable them to sit up, to talk and to walk.

The method is not entirely new. At the Bobath Clinic in London, a form of conductive education has been practised for many years. In America the Doman Institute introduced patterned crawling following which many children improved motor skills. Teams made up of family, neighbours and friends simulated crawling movements for the child, hour upon hour during many months, until in some cases the brain became accustomed to the patterning and the child was enabled to control body movements.

The Peto Method

In Hungary, doctors have achieved notable results with very disabled children using these techniques in concentrated form. This latest method of conductive education was begun at the Peto Clinic in Budapest where it is said that hundreds of chronically disabled East European children have been taught to walk. These encouraging results have given hope to many parents of children with disabilities like cerebral palsy, or to those youngsters who have suffered brain injury through accident.

Many families have sold their possessions in order to take their children to Budapest for initial assessment and training, and their local communities have raised funds to enable the education to continue.

The BBC have made a documentary called *Standing up for Joe* which examines the methods and success rate of this Hungarian project. Teams of doctors went to check it out and were sufficiently impressed to seek funding for trials in this country.

A Child's Experience

An eight-year-old child with cerebral palsy was sent to the Peto Clinic where in six months she learned to walk for the first time in her life. The cost was high and for her unemployed parents it would have been totally impossible to raise such a sum. A generous public rallied round and the money was raised. But further training is needed to maintain her hard-won mobility and hopefully to gain further improvement. For the child herself, a dream has come true.

In Birmingham, the local authority agreed to provide funding for doctors to set up a trial unit based on the Peto method. Voluntary organisations offered to supplement the fund and the necessary target was reached. Ten teachers are to be trained for the unit and a waiting-list of eager pupils awaits them.

In London, the Spastic Society has found support for a similar project and ministers have agreed to examine trial results before considering contributing funding. If those trials are successful then there should be unanimous agreement that these methods should be introduced.

Equality of Opportunity

It is acknowledged that equality of opportunity must be provided for our thousands of physically disabled youngsters. These children flourish when they are treated no differently than able-bodied children. Those with special needs are stimulated by their able-bodied school friends and make great strides both socially and educationally. So many have shown what they can achieve in the face of seemingly impossible odds, making successful careers and leading happy and fruitful lives, that no chance should be denied to them of making the most of themselves. They may take longer to get results but their value to the community is unquestionable.

But if all those children who might be taught to walk,

speak, read and write are to achieve these skills, then adequate financial provision has to be allowed. In terms of what it means to handicapped children, the acquisition of these abilities is beyond price. It may seem to some to be financially prohibitive to undertake costly teaching schemes, but if it gives greater independence and means children with special needs grow into adults better able to care for themselves, then it can never be termed expensive. There can never be true equality between handicapped children and normal children. But we must do our utmost to achieve near equality and enable determined and courageous children to reach their maximum potential levels of achievement.

Are Teachers' Fears Valid?

Teachers in normal schools are understandably apprehensive about mixing children who need special attention with non-handicapped. The chances are, it has been argued, that the rest of the class might be held back.

If it is of the opinion of those who know a child well that ordinary school will be of most benefit and if sufficient resources are provided so that other children will not be disadvantaged, then that child must be given the benefit of the doubt.

Formal single assessments may well be overrated and may not give a realistic reading of a child's potential. Continuous and ongoing assessments are needed. It is likely to be found to be better to modify provision in a school to suit a child than to force the child to fit into what is available.

Choosing a School

Local education authorities are required to give the fullest co-operation to parents seeking information about schools in their area. Parents feel great responsibility when they come to choose a school for their handicapped child and the choice may depend upon a number of factors such as area, facilities, reputation. Does the child have friends at school? Is it within reasonable distance? If they do not get the first choice, is there an acceptable compromise replacement?

These are important considerations and may outweigh other advantages, particularly where the younger child is concerned. Access to classrooms and toilets is important if there is a wheelchair or likely to be one in the future. Welfare care staff are essential and parents need to feel confident that a child's physical needs are catered for properly and competently. Interviews with teachers must leave both sides feeling assured that the child will progress and achieve maximum potential.

Consideration of the general environment is important, one school having space, trees and gardens, another having smaller classes, whilst others may have good outdoor play facilities. All of these factors play a part in the deliberations before a choice of school is made.

Parent-teacher associations can improve the range of equipment for their schools by raising funds and purchasing necessary amenities. Funds are finite and schools are limited in what they can have. Additional computers, soft play areas, outdoor slides and swings are expensive but greatly improve the potential for the progress and pleasure of the pupils.

Much depends upon the part of the country the family lives in, since the variations in provision vary widely from one local authority to another.

Staying in the Community

Children whose special needs can be catered for within their own localities are more likely to become accepted members of their communities. Their understanding friends protect and sustain them and any dissimilarities become less important. Going to school outside the home area gives the feeling of being an outsider and can cause emotional problems which only lengthen the list of disadvantages experienced by disabled children. Belonging to a community allows a flowering of personality and greatly increased achievement.

Consideration should be given to what children stand to lose if they are set apart in a group outside their own neighbourhoods. When they can become part of local friendly groups they develop a sense of their own worth. Specific educational skills may quite possibly seem less important to them than the stigmatising effect of separation. Children are bound to do better, learning alongside friends with whom they share neighbourhood experiences and leisure time in parks, playgrounds and each other's homes.

Planning for Special Needs

The future educational needs have to be planned in advance and professionals must now be paying serious regard to the views of parents. No outsider's knowledge can begin to compare with the depth of experience parents have about their children. It is crucial that the decision makers should take into account parental opinions. Trial periods in the schools of their choice ought to be possible, with everyone trying to make it work. They would be surprisingly successful, both parents and children putting in great efforts to ensure that any fears expressed are unfounded.

The regular meeting of a team attended by all those who are involved with the child must necessarily include the parents and they will consider both immediate and long term planning.

The concept of a chronologically based age limit for education may be totally irrelevant. As an example Paul, who is the subject of the prologue of this book, took his O levels at the age of twenty-two. So formidable were the obstacles to education for someone stricken severely with polio at the age of six, wheelchair-bound and with one arm paralysed, that despite his bright intellect he could not profit by education. He had to fit the system. The speech and physiotherapy he needed were not provided at school, whole days were occupied in queuing at hospitals for the brief sessions available. There was no access at ordinary school for his wheelchair or personal medical needs. He had to make do with whatever crumbs of learning he could pick up, but his determination enabled him to achieve at least some level of education.

Public attitudes change continually and any notion that someone with severe disability is not worth educating has been replaced by a realisation of everyone's worth and right to equality of opportunity. This approach is the correct one for any intelligent society and a return to uninformed attitudes should be resisted strongly. Whoever suffers through financial cut-backs, it should never be the most severely and multiply handicapped of our people.

The modern miracles of research have produced the means to prevent the birth of many handicapped children and have mitigated the worst effects of some diseases and defects. Those children who are survivors must assume a place in society, respected, cared for and with equal opportunity to enjoy life. Those opportunities must include education.

Wheelchairs need repair, hearing-aids need servicing, Optacon machines may suffer damage and require new parts. Computers are now an essential part of school life for children with communication problems, and it is frustrating for them to have to queue for time on a machine. Ideally they should each have their own. These are some of the causes of interruption which delay education for disabled children. Such factors stress the importance of providing high quality, trouble-free equipment and of a type likely to be used in future employment.

Despite all obstacles, they are closing the gap between themselves and their able-bodied peers. There are cautious grounds for optimism regarding employment of disabled school-leavers. Awareness is growing of their worth as employees; they have application, tend to move less from job to job and have very good work records. Being disabled does not mean being sick.

Education, the Key to a Future

What then, is available to parents who seek for their children an education not only suitable to their apparent capabilities, but one which will extend them and enable them to reach higher goals?

There are lessons to be learned from the comparison studies between curricula offered in other countries. There are examples of pupils remaining in education until their mid-twenties, in schools where facilities are superb and staffing ratios more generous than in the UK. A movement in this direction would be something to be proud of and to aim for.

Special Problems

It is the experience of some parents that the emotional difficulties of their deaf, blind or multiply disabled children are so severe that they respond better to education when they are based in specialist schools. There are some splendid residential and day colleges and application to relevant authorities will provide detailed information. It may be that once children's studies reach a certain stage, they cope better with integration and can return to mainstream at a later date.

Bernard is severely deaf but was diagnosed late, at nearly three years of age. He has always been a withdrawn child who was thought for years to be retarded. Except by his mother. It was eventually determined that he was a bright boy and he was accepted at a school for the deaf. At the age of fourteen, he was still somewhat withdrawn and did not mix well socially. His mother knew that he found adolescence difficult. It was decided that he would do better to continue his education at a college for the deaf.

This and other similar cases are the exceptions to the rule and illustrate that each case must be judged on its merit. Every child must be considered in the light of that child's problem. No one should automatically be isolated from the mainstream of life. They should be assisted to join it wherever and whenever it is appropriate to do so.

Who Provides Services?

Numbers of reports have attempted to establish where responsibilities for provision of different services lie, and views are based on historical or economic patterns.

There are still arguments about which authority, educational or health, has a duty to provide these services for children and adolescents with special needs. Parents find this confusing, being only concerned that the provision is made, never mind by which body.

Psychiatric Services

There is no argument about the value of counselling and psychiatric services for families with handicapped children. There is a need for sympathetic and informal advice as well as the more defined and serious needs of a disturbed child.

The Court Report recognised the need for a child and family psychiatric service in every area, to be provided by the NHS. This should not only respond to demand but also find new ways of helping families with problems.

Further Education

In order to fulfil the need for ongoing education for disabled students, colleges provide post-school provision to cover the transition from adolescence to young adulthood.

Three-year courses provide a curriculum which includes practical subjects, as well as discussions regarding sexual matters, financial independence and future housing needs. The Spastics Society is able to offer a few residential places annually for post-school education.

In the Future

Greater consideration must be given to the employment of disabled individuals and the resources needed to educate and equip students for better and more financially rewarding positions.

And it is disabled people themselves who must define future needs and make decisions about how to attain the best results for the children who will follow them into the schools, colleges and universities of tomorrow.

29   Equipment

The sharing of information and ideas between countries
has resulted in a wide variety of facilities for children with
special needs. Whether that need is for mobility, speech
training, feeding, visual or hearing-aids, computers, books
or simply toys to encourage development, there is usually a
choice wide enough to suit every requirement. If something
extra is needed, then either designers, companies or
biochemical engineering departments of hospitals will
produce suitable prototypes or, very often, technical
colleges will willingly help by offering the problem as a
project to classes of young students.

It is only possible to offer brief guidelines here on the
range and types of facilities available. Visiting Naidex
exhibitions or disability centres will give families a general
idea of the kind of equipment available.

Independent Mobility

It is the natural wish of all parents that their children should
walk at an early age and a baby's first steps are seen as
important. Independent mobility for the handicapped
child is no less an eagerly awaited stage. The change in the
development and personality of disabled children when
they can move unaided, away from parents, and explore
areas hitherto denied to them, is quite a dramatic one. They
find joy in escaping their reliance on others to help them
move around.

There is a wide variety of mobility aids already on the
market, many of which are available from the DHSS
wheelchair service. New chairs are constantly added to the
DHSS range and a recent welcome addition was a sports
wheelchair. The Government maintains approved chairs
and has also taken on responsibility for wheelchair seating,

which is an important item since custom-built seating can be added to commercial bases to make special chairs.

It is strongly recommended that professional advice is sought from appropriate medical and therapy staff before making any choice of chair. It must be ensured that optimum seating and control systems are provided with consideration for every use, outdoor, indoor, home and school.

The more severely disabled child may need a custom-built chair which makes use of residual ability. This special provision requires the expertise of design engineers and occupational or physiotherapy staff.

Specialist team-work of this kind must take into account the many relevant factors. It is essential to see the child's home and school, to consider doorways, surrounding terrain, to look at pavement levels, steps and ramps as well as to consider the child's physical capability.

The collaboration between therapists and engineers has resulted in new concepts for mobility aids to suit individual children. This type of work is being carried out by Eric Booth, the design engineer for the Development Trust for the Young Disabled, who explains, as an example, that the design of his chair *Super Sam* is aimed to allow better exploitation of remaining ability, whilst at the same time minimising contracture and deformity. He says that a significant amount of preparatory work is essential on each child before the radical change of posture dictated by specially designed chairs can be comfortably tolerated.

To cater for the correct working desk height, powered elevating seats have been incorporated in powered wheelchairs and various ranges of elevators are now available. These start with the smallest movement of seven inches and go to a maximum rise of twenty-four inches. In the latter case, the seat lowers to the floor level to enable lower limb deficient children to get into the seat, independently.

Powered outdoor Karts are not currently paid for by the DHSS, but can make a significant difference to children's outdoor play activities. It is interesting to note that often, when a wheelchair or Kart has been delivered, able-bodied children present have asked for a turn at driving. The handicapped child is thus enabled to confer favours on friends, so gaining, for once, some advantage.

Many activities previously thought far beyond the capabilities of youngsters confined to wheelchairs have been brought within their range. This gives them an increased quality of life, enabling them to join friends in play and helping to overcome the effects of disability.

Coping with Transition to Wheelchairs

The dilemma for both parents and child when wheelchairs become necessary is to appreciate realistically what standards of independence a child can expect to achieve. There are problems inherent in living in a wheelchair and experienced occupational therapists can anticipate the difficulties as well as the undoubted advantages.

There are some children who prefer to get about indoors without any kind of device or aid, but who could not hope to move about outdoors without a wheelchair. There are those who could manage short distances outdoors but who could not run or walk far. Children need to be able to join in play, games and sport and for this, sports wheelchairs are available which many children are able to use, perhaps at a stage prior to the use of electric wheelchairs.

Advice must be sought as to what the child should be encouraged to do and training can be given in the use of recommended devices or wheelchairs. Skill has to be acquired and using any wheelchair efficiently and safely takes time and practice. Coping with pavements, curb drill, and becoming used to self-propelling requires patience and training. It is important to find out which shops, libraries and buildings have wheelchair accessibility. Learning about this provision in a practical way, out in the streets, is best.

Providing sports wheelchairs when deterioration in physical condition begins, can often make the later transition to an electric wheelchair more acceptable. It is the quality of life the child will enjoy at every stage that is important. Children's confidence grows as they become used to the outdoor environment, mobile in wheelchairs and gain the courage to go into shops and speak to staff and the general public.

Seating

An important matter for the child with spinal defects is to have the support of tailor-made seating. This should help correct posture and allow more natural breathing as well as supporting the head so that vision is directed ahead rather than downwards. Children with spinal problems are sometimes able to have treatment and operations to correct posture and reduce the scoliosis and twisting backs which were once commonplace.

Matrix seating is composed of tiny nylon joints, each of which can be moved according to the child's shape and condition. Fibreglass seating can be modelled directly on to the child but must be discarded when a new shape is needed and corrections are made. Padded seating in wheelchairs provides ordinary support and most wheelchair manufacturers have a choice of size and shapes of cushions. Extras should be considered when estimating the price of wheelchairs since they add considerably to the cost. It should now be possible to have all medically advised types of seating paid for by the DHSS.

Maintenance

Insurance and maintenance costs are considerable items for families to take into account for items bought privately. Charities do not generally fund ongoing items like these and usually only make grants towards wheelchairs or pay for them outright.

Mobility allowance may be of assistance but this is usually absorbed by the cost of running a car.

Walking Aids

There are devices which enable some children to walk who have either never previously done so or who have lost the ability. A lightweight bracing system, originally designed at Guy's Hospital, was further developed in Louisiana State University, USA. This device has enabled many children to stand upright and walk short distances. The less obvious benefits claimed from the use of this orthosis by its developer, Roy Douglas, include significantly improved lung and general function. There is also, it is said, a demonstrable strengthening of long bones with a reversal of the decalcification that occurs with prolonged inactivity or paralysis.

Children suffering with spina bifida, cerebral palsy and accidental spinal injury are among those who have been accepted for the training in the use of this orthosis and found able to use it comfortably. It is thought to offer a new and desirable concept and the children can sit, kneel and lie down, soon becoming adept and independent and getting about with comparative ease.

Matthew is only three and has cerebral palsy. I saw him at St Vincent's Hospital, Northwood, where he had been accepted on the training programme. After a few months he is walking confidently in his orthosis and both he and his mother are delighted with the freedom from pushchairs. His smile on taking his first steps towards his mother was unforgettable.

When a young ballet dancer of seventeen woke up one morning unable to move, she couldn't imagine what had happened. The doctor questioned her closely, but other than a mild flu and tiring practice routine, she had been quite fit. She was finally told that a virus had attacked her spine and that she was unlikely ever to walk again. Two years later she heard of the WALK programme and after assessment was accepted for training. With the aid of the orthosis she is able to walk once again and looks forward to a career, teaching ballet to children.

It is as well to provide a cautious word. Whilst it is

beneficial to be able to walk, crutches or a walking frame must be used in conjunction with the orthosis and this means that hands are not free. Some people prefer the comfort and ease of a wheelchair from which they can write, do handwork and move about their kitchens to cook.

Rollator Walking Frames

These are available in a range of sizes and enable children to walk by using a rolling gait.

The frames may have a rest seat and shelf area for carrying items such as books.

Hearing-Aids

It is essential for the child suspected of hearing loss to have testing with the sophisticated equipment available today. Hearing-aids must be individually recommended and regularly serviced. Ring circuit systems in classrooms and radiophonic aids are available so that teachers at school and parents at home can stay in touch with children, even at a moderate distance.

Signing and cuing systems should be investigated and considered as useful teaching aids to deaf children, although these are not so much items as teaching methods.

Visual Aids

Enlarging screens make it possible for children with poor vision to read books. A number of braille printing devices make it possible for children to join in classes, for example with maps, using their own relevant material. Optacon machines are carried by many blind people, making it possible for them to read any kind of print or writing. A tiny camera is moved over the writing and translated via a small machine into letters which are 'read' by the forefinger. A girl who went suddenly blind at the age of twelve carries her Optacon everywhere and has learned again to read the books, papers and magazines she had previously read.

The disability of the child who cannot speak or write is greatly reduced by the use of a word processor. Operation of these machines is modified according to the ability of the user. Failing all else, they can be operated by breath control.

Sundry Equipment

Electronic pads to operate radios, TVs, and telephones; beds which make turning occupants easier; hoists which lift a child from bed to bath to wheelchair; shower trolleys which facilitate bathing; all these and many more can be tried and tested for suitability and value.

Research

Recently, a man was given the chance to walk again after the world's first push-button electronic 'brain' was implanted in his body. Surgeons had operated to insert mini-computers into his buttocks and he was enabled to walk by a form of muscle stimulation.

This sort of work, and other promising forms of research, must give hope to all our disabled children, and to their parents, that one day soon nothing will obstruct them from making full use of their capabilities.

30   A Philosophical View

An actress appeared in London's West End in the play, *Children of a Lesser God*. Her performance was acclaimed by critics and public alike. They found themselves impressed by her professionalism and her talent and moved by her performance. The fact that she is also severely deaf they considered last and they had things in the right order.

The true story told in the film, *The Elephant Man*, portrays a grossly deformed but gentle, refined and distinguished young man who lived in the nineteenth century. It tells of how he engaged the respect and affection of his doctor and of well-known personalities. The general public of the day saw him only as an object of derision and scorn, someone to be exhibited as a monstrosity and he was shamefully abused. Could that happen today? Are we yet ready to accept that outward appearances are not everything and that it is the character of a person that counts?

Public attitudes are changing slowly from ignorance to understanding and the open acceptance in all circles of those among us whose appearance is different or who are visibly affected by disability. But a percentage of people still shrink away from those who are handicapped or malformed.

Many of our restaurants, cinemas, theatres, shops and stores are inaccessible to wheelchairs. Hoteliers will often say that they don't cater for the handicapped and one misguided man confided to me that it would spoil the holiday for his guests if there were kids in wheelchairs around, didn't I agree? Didn't I agree!

Public transport for anyone handicapped and in a wheelchair is often impossible and in most trains, wheelchairs must go in the unheated guard van, sometimes with their hapless occupants. Some buses and a few taxis have been converted to take wheelchairs, but these are merely examples of the sort of provision that should be more commonplace.

Now that integration is becoming a reality in schools and children begin to understand about handicap and to want to help diminish the problems, much of the ignorance and misunderstanding should disappear and disability in the future will be seen as the secondary consideration.

First must come the person, the character and the capabilities. We are conditioned by newspapers, by television, by advertising hoardings to believe that appearance matters above all and that any imperfection is unacceptable and something of a social stigma. Journalists have a duty to reverse this image and make heroes and heroines out of some of the well deserving, successful and hard working disabled people among us.

Is it realised how much suffering is caused when the unusual becomes the unacceptable? Experiences confirm that the general public do not accept children and adults who happen to have disabilities. These attitudes dash the spirits of handicapped children, adolescents and their families. Their confidence seeps away as prejudices surface and they are treated as inferior beings.

Even adults who have become hardened to insensitive behaviour speak of their discomfort in restaurants when they have to be helped to their food and fellow diners gaze at them curiously or with disapproval. What is wanted is matter-of-fact acceptance, no more and no less. Disabled people who go out to public places can usually manage very well. They may need a little more time than able-bodied people, but if they do need any kind of assistance, then they will ask for it.

Perhaps this all means that if there is to be a radical change in attitude towards people with disabilities, handicap, special needs, whatever name we give, it may well have to come from the top.

The European Parliament has responsibilities which we should all be aware of, particularly in regard to available provision for people with disabilities or handicap. It has persuasive policy instruments in the form of directives, which it can issue when requiring member states to adopt its legislation.

In 1981, the International Year of the Disabled, a new programme was set up to promote the social and economic integration of disabled people. This initiative was called the *Bureau for Action in Favour of Disabled People* and had the support of the European Parliament. The bureau has a programme covering education, training, employment and many of the side-issues of independent living for disabled people. In the UK we do not appear to have grasped the importance of this initiative or of the necessity for conveying our hopes, our fears and the urgent need for additional provision.

A great effort is made to give quality to the lives of our handicapped children. Following birth, they are placed in intensive cot care units, often for months, with nurses to watch over them day and night. When necessary, the children undergo blood transfusions, open heart surgery and spare part transplants. As they grow, they are subject to continuing assessment, and speech and physiotherapy.

In due time, carefully considered and well-prepared programmes of special education take them through childhood. There are not yet sufficient resources for our doctors, therapists and teachers to achieve such results as are seen, for example, in the Peto Clinic in Hungary.

There, many children with profound handicap are successfully rehabilitated after intensive conductive education. But, a ward of warning – caution should be exercised before taking children abroad for assessments or treatment which could be carried out equally well in the UK.

But at sixteen, in some cases nineteen years of age, what special education and conditions are arranged? There seems to be a cut-off point. What happens to the quality of life for the older handicapped child, the adolescent, the young adult? These youngsters can rarely complete education in the chronological time limits usually set. They have to go at their own pace and it could mean that they take

O and A levels in their twenties. By then, they, and quite likely their parents too, may wish them to live independently, perhaps with a partner. But what provision is there for them in the way of accommodation? We need more advance planning so that sufficient housing of the right sort will be ready when required.

In some areas, there is thoughtful provision for the future of those of our youngsters who can look forward to many years of healthy, if handicapped life. Independent living schemes encourage personal fulfilment for severely disabled people and have been made possible through the shared concern of health and social services and the voluntary sector. But it is insufficient to satisfy existing and future need.

These are some of the matters which occupy the thoughts of adolescents who cannot achieve results in the time that their able-bodied friends can, but who would like to be able to look forward to a measure of independence from their twenties on.

Parents write despairing letters, wondering what the future will hold and what their children can do. Adolescents also write, looking forward with some eagerness to educational qualifications, employment and independent living in purpose-built or adapted housing. Is their optimism hollow, their ambition misplaced? These are young people who should, in time, be making a positive contribution to the community. Their hopes must not be allowed to wither.

Are these matters of sufficient interest and importance for the European Parliament to issue a few directives? We suffer, of course, from financial restraints. No one needs to be reminded of this or of how difficult it is for governments to decide priorities.

Whenever changes are made, it seems inconceivable that the old ways could ever have been acceptable or allowed. There is a core of belief and a growing acceptance that equal opportunity can only come about through positive discrimination. There is recognition that our disabled members of society should be given some priority in the share of the good things of life.

Ultimately, equality will come. Integrated education will allow disabled and able-bodied children to grow up together and the differences between them will decrease in importance. Moreover, disabled people will be treated as equals and will no longer be made to feel second class and inferior to other people.

Asking for a speedy change for the better in public attitudes in regard to disabled children and adults always seemed like asking for the moon. Yet surely the time for change is here and the reality of it will be felt from now on. We shall be seeing more of our public figures out and about with their disabled friends, we shall see more disabled people in a greater variety of jobs. They have proved themselves worthy of any position and capable of working as hard as anyone and their value has been appreciated.

The talents, the wisdom, the intelligence of handicapped people lie exactly where they lie with all of us. They may be slower to emerge and action may be needed to redress disability so that it is replaced by ability. But there are too many success stories illustrating their talent and courage for anyone to deny their worth.

There is really little that disabled people cannot accomplish. They constantly exhibit a variety of interests and skills in all sorts of fields. Who would have supposed that skiing would be possible for people unable to walk? Yet, recently, wheelchair-bound people have been taken on skiing holidays, where with special skis and sticks they can be balanced and held and experience the thrill and exhilaration of speeding downhill along with able-bodied skiers.

Does it take courage to welcome the handicapped into our homes, offices and sports centres? It is astonishing to hear people say that they are too tender-hearted and sensitive ever to be able to care for handicapped children or work alongside disabled adults. But it is those who accept disability in others without prejudice who are the tender-hearted, regarding it as the norm to accept every human being as a person and not as a disease or a disability.

Community care is infinitely preferable to care in

institutions where ordinary living would be regarded as a special treat. But there must be ample support from all the services and primarily from the GP whose interest and concern are so highly regarded. The family doctor's advice, whether it is about treatment or life-style is more likely to be followed than that of anyone else.

There have been sufficient reports about our health records and the damage we are self-inflicting to entitle us to change our habits. Other countries have seen the light, changed their habits and brought down the numbers of heart attacks, strokes and lung cancers and possibly reduced the numbers of births of malformed babies. Why are we in the UK so dilatory?

The meals generally eaten in Britain today are not good for us. They are heavy in hard, saturated fats, contain too much sugar and salt and are laden with chemical additives which are menacing to our health. The favourite food of many of our children and adolescents seems to be chips. If one could see the hard fat that can be squeezed from a packet of these fried potatoes they might not be so popular.

We may not have positive means of preventing disease but we have enough proof to understand how we risk adding to our numbers of handicapped people by unwise habits. Smoking is one of them and even a single cigarette a day smoked by the mother has been shown to be a potential danger to an unborn child.

This habit has been adopted by many of our young people and children are to be seen, out of school, standing in groups and earnestly puffing away, feeling, I suppose, that it is sophisticated and grown-up. I wish that they could come with me to visit a London ward. It is full of wheelchair-bound and sickly people of all ages, many only in their thirties. I asked why they were smoking. 'My dear', the charge nurse replied, 'the reason they are here is because they smoke. It is now their only remaining pleasure'.

One of the problems for disabled adolescents is far more freely discussed today than it ever was and that is the question of sex. An open and honest appraisal has to be made of what is sexually possible and it may be much more than was thought. The idea that physical disability means that one cannot develop normal sexual feelings is generally assumed, along with many other misconceptions such as whether one can speak when in a wheelchair or think when one has no power of speech.

Rigid attitudes and taboos about sex may have been relaxed for some but seemingly only for the physically able. Any young person growing into adulthood is naturally going to feel normal and natural inclinations. Denying that these feelings exist in handicapped people, or assuming that such feelings will die out if no one mentions them is insensitive, even cruel and quite unrealistic.

Preparation for adolescence for all children should be made and sexual education considered. Not whether it should take place, but when and how. One can comprehend that when parents feel that a child is unlikely ever to marry, then they will believe it best that sexual feelings should be buried. But to discourage the natural development of handicapped teenagers will only cause greater curiosity, some bewilderment and perhaps feelings of guilt. And these youngsters do not need more problems.

Normal children learn from a variety of sources, going independently to films, to bookshops and libraries and learning from friends. Television programmes are often only too explicit and handicapped youngsters are perforce at home more often than their able-bodied friends and so have more opportunity for viewing. They know that sex is a reality. They should not have to think that they can never be part of it and they must be given the opportunity to talk about how they feel. It is far better that they be well-informed and make independent judgements rather than feel puzzled, worried and repressed.

Special needs make youngsters reliant upon others and deny them privacy. We would all be inhibited if we were denied this precious quality. Limitations are irksome and restrict the opportunities for finding out about the physical change from child to adult. Identifying with peers, knowing that bodily changes and stirrings of sexual awareness are happening to everyone, discussing and learning from each other – these are the ways growing up should be taking place.

We all enjoy uninterrupted time with our contemporaries and if our young people indicate that they would like some privacy with their friends then they should be ensured whatever time they want. It does not follow that they are going to act in an irresponsible manner. A certain amount of trust is essential between parents and children.

Families everywhere like to go out together and families with handicapped members are no exception. But transport is always a problem when there are wheelchairs involved. If people have no private transport then they are very limited in the number of outings or shopping trips that can be taken. If there is no one to leave a child with, then someone has to stay at home and this often divides a family who should enjoy joint outings. Pushing a wheelchair is a tiring business, especially so over rough ground. Unless there is a specially designed electric wheelchair, it is often impossible to go to parks or grassy areas like commons. Going away for a day makes a welcome break, but carting wheelchairs on public transport, if they are acceptable, is a daunting business. Hiring transport is expensive and, despite mobility allowance, families on low incomes manage this rarely – if at all.

With no private transport, parents have to get shopping done during school hours. That means that children do not get to shops and miss the fun and experience that this could give them. Relatives with cars may help out with an occasional lift but it is always a great relief to families when they are enabled to be independent, with their own transport. They can look forward to picnics, drives to the country and the coast and rainy weather does not prevent welcome outings.

When cars get too old or run down and cannot be replaced it is very depressing to lose the amenity of transport. The feeling of independence, that one is able to get out with a child or children at will, is immeasurably uplifting. There are feelings of intense frustration when opportunities to go out must be refused, because transport is not there. It seems unfair and there is a sense of bitterness.

Most mothers feel that the daily grind of care needs to be relieved by an occasional evening out. Baby-sitters for handicapped children must be chosen with special care and it is hard to find someone prepared to undertake such responsibility. The anxiety of leaving a child who may have health problems like fits, asthmatic attacks or convulsions, or who is incontinent, is understandable. Parents may well resign themselves to staying in, sometimes feeling too proud to ask for help. Situations like this sometimes go on for years, until someone breaks down and becomes ill.

Families need our encouragement, our appreciation, our whole-hearted support but, above all, our understanding.

Changes in attitude are going to be, in part, the result of public opinion and demand. But the greatest persuasion will come in a lead from TV, films and newspapers. Journalists and writers must show disabled personalities enjoying good health despite handicap, living happy and fulfilled lives, as so many of them do.

It must be shown that disabled people do not detract from society. They add quality and an extra dimension to it.

Appendix

Genetic Counselling Centres

Infant Development Unit
Birmingham Maternity Hospital
Queen Elizabeth Medical Centre
Birmingham B15 2TH

Department of Genetic
  Counselling
Addenbrookes Hospital
Hills Road
Cambridge CB2 2QQ

Department of Paediatrics
Hammersmith Hospital
Du Cane Road
London W12

Paediatric Research Laboratories
The Prince Philip Research
  Laboratories
Guy's Tower
London SE1 9RT

Department of Clinical Genetics
Institute of Child Health
30 Guildford Street
London WC1

Department of Medical Genetics
St Mary's Road
Hathersage Road
Manchester M13 0JH

Muscle Clinic
Regional Neurological Centre
Newcastle General Hospital
Westgate Road
Newcastle upon Tyne NE4 6BE

Department of Medical Genetics
Old Road
Headington
Oxford OX3 7LE

Duncan Guthrie Institute of
  Medical Genetics
Yorkhill Hospital
Glasgow G3 8SJ

Medical Genetics Clinic
St Davids' Hospital
Bangor

Section of Medical Genetics
Department of Medicine
University Hospital of Wales
Heath Park
Cardiff CF4 4XW

Medical Genetics Clinic
Morrison Hospital
Swansea

Medical Genetics Clinic
Maelor General Hospital
Wrexham

Department of Neurology
Royal Victoria Hospital
Belfast

Consultant of Human Genetics
Department of Medical Genetics
Queen's University of Belfast
Institute of Clinical Science
Grosvenor Road
Belfast

Useful Addresses

Action Against Allergy
43 The Downs
London SW20 8HG
01 947 5082

Action Research for the Crippled
  Child
Vincent House
North Parade
Horsham
West Sussex RH12 2DA
0403 64101

Action on Smoking and Health
  (ASH)
5–11 Mortimer Street
London W1N 7RW
01 637 9843

Advisory Centre for Education
18 Victoria Park Square
London E2 9PB
01 980 4596

Arthritis Care
Grosvenor Crescent
London SW1
01 235 0902

Association for All Speech
  Impaired Children
347 Central Markets
Smithfield
London EC1A 9NH
01 236 3632/6487

Association of Blind and Partially-
  Sighted Teachers and Students
58 South Drive
Manchester M21 2FB
061 881 4147

Association of Carers
Medway Homes
Balfour Road
Rochester
Kent ME4 6QU
0634 813981

Association for Children with
  Artificial Arms
85 Newlands Road
Billericay
Essex CM12 OP11

Association of Parents of Vaccine-
  Damaged Children
2 Church Street
Shipston-on-Stour
Warwickshire CV36 4AP
0608 61595

Association for Spina Bifida and
  Hydrocephalus
22 Upper Woburn Place
London WC1H 0EP
01 388 1382/8

Association of Swimming Therapy
Treetops
Swan Hill
Ellesmere
Salop SY12 0LZ
069 171 3542

Asthma Society
St Thomas's Hospital
Lambeth Palace Road
London SE1 7EH
01 928 9292

Asthma Society and Friends of the
    Asthma Research Council
300 Upper Street
London N1 2XX
01 226 2260

Attendance Allowance Unit
DHSS
North Fylde Centre Office
Norcross
Blackpool FY5 3TA
0263 856123

Barnardo's
Tanners Lane
Barkingside
Essex IG6 1QG
01 550 8822

Braille Correspondence Club
Special Unit, Room 57
Social Services Department
Civic Centre, Barras Bridge
Newcastle upon Tyne
NE1 8PA
0632 32850

Breakthrough Trust – Deaf/
    Hearing Integration
Selly Oak College
Bristol Road
Birmingham B29 6LQ
021 471 1001

British Acupuncture Association
34 Alderney Street
London SW1V 4EU
01 834 1012/3353

British Amputee Sports
    Association
Harvey Road
Aylesbury
Bucks HP21 9PP
0296 27889

British Association of Cancer
    United Patients (BACUP)
121/123 Charterhouse Street
London EC1M 6AA
01 608 1785

British Deaf Association
38 Victoria Place
Carlisle CA1 1HU
0228 48844

British Herbal Medical
    Association
PO Box 304
Bournemouth BH7 6JZ
0202 433491

British Homeopathic Association
27a Devonshire Street
London W1 1RJ
01 935 2163

British Ski Club for the Disabled
Corton House
Corton
Near Warminster
Wiltshire BA12 0SZ
0985 50321

British Society for Music Therapy
69 Avondale Avenue
East Barnet
Hertfordshire EN4 8NB
01 368 8879

British Sports Association for the
    Disabled
Hayward House
Barnard Crescent
Aylesbury
Buckinghamshire
HP21 8PP
0296 27889

Brittle Bone Society
Unit 4, Block 20
112 City Road
Calunie Road
Dunsinane Industrial Estate
Dundee DD2 3QT
0382 817771

Calibre (Cassette Library for the
  Blind and Handicapped)
Aylesbury
Buckinghamshire
HP22 5XQ
0296 432339/81211

Calvert Trust Adventure Centre
  for Disabled People
Little Crosthwaite
Under Skiddaw
Keswick
Cumbria CA12 4QD
07687 72254

Camping for the Disabled
20 Burton Close
Dawley
Telford
Shropshire TF4 2BX
0952 507653

Cancer Help Centre
Grove House
Cornwallis Grove
Clifton
Bristol BS8 4PG
0272 743216

Centre for Advice on Natural
  Alternatives
26 Lighthouse Road
Solihull
West Midlands B91 2BD
021 705 9961

Centre for Learning to Learn
  More Effectively
636 Wilmslow Road
Didsbury
Manchester M20 0AH
061 445 2411

Child Accident Prevention Trust
76 Portland Place
London W1N 3AL
01 636 2545

Child Poverty Action Group
1–5 Bath Street
London EC1
01 253 3404

Children's Legal Centre
20 Compton Terrace
London N1 2UN
01 359 6251

Cleft Lip and Palate Association
(Cy Thirlaway, National
  Secretary)
1 Eastwood Gardens
Kenton
Newcastle upon Tyne
NE3 3DQ
091 285 9396

Coeliac Society
PO Box 220
High Wycombe
Buckinghamshire
HP11 2HY
0494 37278

College of Speech Therapists
Harold Poster House
Lechmere Road
London NW2
01 459 8521

Communication Link
Beverley School for the Deaf
Beverley Road
Saltersgill
Middlesborough
Cleveland TS4 3LQ

Contact a Family
16 Strutton Ground
Victoria
London SW1P 2HP
01 222 2695

Crohn's in Childhood Research
   Appeal
56a Uxbridge Road
Shepherds Bush
London W12 8LP
01 743 4940

Cystic Fibrosis Research Trust
Alexandra House
5 Blythe Road
Bromley
Kent BR1 3RS
01 464 7211

Development Trust for the Young
   Disabled
Royal Home and Hospital for
   Incurables
West Hill
Putney
London SW15

Disabled Income Group
Attlee House
Toynbee Hall
London E1
01 247 2128

Disabled Living Foundation
380–384 Harrow Road
London W9 2HU
01 289 6111

Down's Syndrome Association
12–13 Clapham Common
Southside
London SW4 7AA
01 720 0008

Equipment for the Disabled
Mary Marlborough Lodge
Nuffield Orthopaedic Centre
Headington
Oxford OX3 7LD

Family Fund
PO Box 50
York YO1 1UY
0904 21115

Friedrich's Ataxia Group
Burleigh Lodge
Knowle Lane
Cranleigh
Surrey
0483 272741

Friends for the Young Deaf (FYD)
Communication Centre
East Court Mansion
College Lane
East Grinstead
Sussex RH19 3LT

Haemophilia Society
123 Westminster Bridge Road
London SE1 7HR
01 928 2020

Handicapped Children's
   Adventure Playground
   Association
Fulham Palace Playground
Bishops Avenue
London SW6
01 731 2753

Handicapped Children's Aid
  Committee
(Investigating Chairman)
15 Phillimore Gardens
London NW10 3LL

Hyperactive Children's Support
  Group
Mayfield
Yapton Road
Barnham
West Sussex PO22 0BJ

IADIS
Roger Jeffcoat
Willowbrook
Swandbourne Road
Mursley
Buckinghamshire

Invalid Children's Aid Association
126 Buckingham Palace Road
London SW1
01 730 9891

John Groome's Association for the
  Disabled
10 Gloucester Drive
Finsbury Park
London N4 2LP
01 802 7272

Lady Hoare Trust for Physically
  Disabled Children
7 North Street
Midhurst
West Sussex GU29 9DJ
073 081 3696

Mencap
123 Golden Lane
London EC1Y 0RT
01 253 9433

Mobility Allowance Unit
DHSS
North Fylde Central Office
Normoss
Blackpool
Lancashire

Muscular Dystrophy Group of
  Great Britain
Nattrass House
35 Macauley Road
London SW4 0QP

National Association for the
  Welfare of Children in Hospital
Argyle House
29–31 Euston Road
London NW1
01 833 2041

National Council for Special
  Education
1 Wood Street
Stratford-upon-Avon
Warwickshire CV37 6JE

National Deaf, Blind and Rubella
  Association
311 Gray's Inn Road
London WC1X 8PT
01 278 1005

National Deaf Children's Society
45 Hereford Road
London W2 5AH

National Eczema Society
Tavistock House North
Tavistock Square
London WC1H 9SR

National Library for the
  Handicapped Child
Lynton House
7–12 Tavistock Square
London WC1H 9SR

National Physically Handicapped
and Able-Bodied
42 Devonshire Street
London W1
01 637 7475

Pre-School Playgroups
Association
61–63 Kings Cross Road
London WC1X 9LL
01 833 0991

Radar
25 Mortimer Street
London W1N 8AB
01 637 5400

Royal London Society for the
Blind
105 Salisbury Road
London NW6 6RH
01 624 8844

Spastics Society
12 Park Crescent
London W1N 4EQ
01 636 5020

Special Children (independent
magazine)
73 All Saints Road
Kings Heath
Birmingham B14 7LN

SPOD (Sexual and Personal
Relationships of the Disabled)
286 Camden Road
London N7
01 607 8861

Toy Libraries Association
Seabrook House
Wyllyotts Manor
Darkes Lane
Potters Bar
Hertfordshire
0707 44571

VOLCUF
Friend's House
Euston Road
London NW1 2BJ

Voluntary Council for
Handicapped Children
8 Wakeley Street
London EC1V 7QE
01 278 9441

Further Reading

Anderson, C. M. & Goodchild, M. C., *Cystic Fibrosis*, Blackwell (1976)

Anionwue, E. & Jibreil, H., *Sickle Cell Disease – A Guide for Families*, Collins (1986)

Blom-Cooper & panel, *A Child in Trust* (The report about Jasmine Beckford), The London Borough of Brent (1985)

Bobath, B. & K., *Motor Development in the Different Types of Cerebral Palsy*, William Heinemann Medical Books Ltd (1975)

Brenton, Maria, *The Voluntary Sector in British Social Services*, Longman (1985)

Brimblecombe, F. & Barltrop, D., *Children in Health and Disease*, Baillere & Tindall (1978)

Carr, J., *Young Children with Down's Syndrome*, Butterworth (1975)

Chanarin, I., Brozovic, M., Tidmarsh, E., & Waters, D. A. W., *Blood and Its Diseases*, (3rd Edition) Churchill Livingstone (1984)

Cohen, N., *Discovering Genetics*, Longman (1982)

Courtman Davies, M., *Your Deaf Child's Speech and Hearing*, The Bodley Head (1979)

Dubowitz, V., *Muscle Disorders in Childhood*, Saunders (1978)

Ford, E. B., *Understanding Genetics*, Faber & Faber Ltd, London & Boston (1981)

Fry, J., *Common Diseases*, MTP Press Ltd, Lancaster & Boston (1979)

Goldman, K. P., *The Chest in Health and Disease*, Health Horizon Ltd 1985)

Habel, A., *Aids to Paediatrics*, Churchill Livingstone (1982)

Holt, K. S., *Developmental Paediatrics: Perspectives and Practice*, Butterworth (1977)

Hood, J., *Problems in Paediatrics*, MTP Press Ltd (1982)

Illitch, I., *Limits to Medicine*, Marion Boyars Ltd (1976)

Jolly, H. *Diseases of Children*, Blackwell Scientific Publications (1976)

MacDonald, E. M., *Occupational Therapy in Rehabilitation*, Baillere & Tindall, London (1976)

Nathan Hill, A., *Against the Unsuspected Enemy*, New Horizon (1980)

Scott, R. B., *Cancer – The Facts*, Oxford University Press (1979)

Willmott, *Consumer's Guide to the Social Services*

Index

x